D0845740

Liturgy as Living Faith

Liturgy as Living Faith

A Liturgical Spirituality

Joyce Ann Zimmerman, C.PP.S.

Scranton: University of Scranton Press
London and Toronto: Associated University Presses

Associated University Presses
440 Forsgate Drive
Cranbury, NJ 08512

Associated University Presses
25 Sicilian Avenue
London WC1A 2QH

Associated University Presses
P.O. Box 338, Port Credit
Mississauga, Ontario
L5G 4L8 Canada

Quotations from *Early Christian Fathers,* translated and edited by Cyril C. Richardson, Volume 1: The Library of Christian Classics, published in the U.S.A. in MCMLIII by The Westminster Press are used by permission of Westminster/John Knox Press.

The paper used in this publication meets the requirements
of the American National Standard for Permanence of Paper
for Printed Library Materials Z39.48–1948.

Library of Congress Cataloging-in-Publication Data

Zimmerman, Joyce Ann, 1945–
    Liturgy as living faith : a liturgical spirituality / Joyce Ann
Zimmerman.
        p.   cm.
    Includes bibliographical references and index.
    ISBN 0–940866–25–0 (alk. paper)
    1. Liturgics.   2. Catholic Church—Liturgy.   I. Title.
BV176.Z56   1993
264'.001—dc20   92-85437
                                                        CIP

Contents

Introduction

The question of "meaning" looms large on the horizon today. To be sure, this question is more far-reaching than the adolescent search for identity, the middle-aged search for purpose, or the elderly search for significance. The quest for meaning seems to be a quest for life. In this age of liturgical renewal, then, it is not incongruous to put the question of meaning to liturgy as well.

One way to focus a liturgical quest for meaning is to ask a seminal question such as: What is the relationship between celebrating liturgy on Sunday and living as a Christian the rest of the week? Or, to phrase the same question in a more popular fashion: What is the relationship between liturgy and social justice? Much has been written recently on this fundamental relationship.[1] These works all share a conviction that liturgy and life are indeed related—even inextricably so. They also share a prevailing caveat: *demonstrating* the relationship between liturgy and life does not address *why* it is so. Often we have argued historically: it *has always been so*. We have even argued logically: it *must* be so. But can we argue ontologically: it *is* so?

The "why" of the relationship of liturgy and life invites us to walk hand-in-hand with an attentiveness to presuppositions and method when we cross into the domain of liturgical spirituality. This is the agenda of this volume. We are optimistic about it because new linguistic tools and methods permit different analyses that bring new data to light for our consideration of liturgical spirituality.

Until now available methodological tools have enabled us to recognize that the fruits of liturgy can be *applied* to everyday Christian living. We have used liturgical texts as a kind of "proof texting" where we take specific passages from the liturgy and show that they demand certain kinds of living or bring about an awareness of certain concerns. For example, theme Masses or particular ways of doing the Penitential Rite or a newspaper headlines approach to the General Intercessions can heighten awareness but too often at the expense of liturgy's integral dynamic and depth meaning. In this volume we draw on the gains of specific linguistically based methods to support our thesis that *the deep, dynamic structure of liturgy is identical to the deep, dynamic structure of Christian living.* Liturgy and life are essentially related because they share a generic dynamic structure that gives access to an ever-deepening experience of their common referent: the Paschal Mystery. Herein lies the key to our understanding of liturgical spirituality. What we celebrate in liturgy is none other than what we live as Christians committed to entering into the ongoing redemptive work of the Risen Christ. What we live is the content of what we celebrate.

The popular expression "we bring our lives to liturgy" is disconcerting in this line of thinking because it runs a high risk of positing a dualism where one, in fact, does not—or ought not—exist. We celebrate our (Christ's) life in liturgy—only *one* life. This is no small point. "Bring to" language injects a subtle dualism: liturgy and life are two separate identities that we must somehow struggle to reconcile. A truly liturgical spirituality shatters this dualism by rooting up its potentially disintegrating ground. Liturgical spirituality blossoms in the realization that everyday Christian living and liturgical celebration are but two expressions of the one gift of God's paschal Presence to us. This is the ultimate reason for our praise and thanksgiving, so definitive of worship.

The meaning of Christian liturgy is synonymous with the meaning of Christian living. We seek to elucidate this meaning by investigating the Paschal Mystery as concretized in the deep structure of its Christian ritual forms. Rituals have always been a means for people to "act out" their response to the mysteries of life, a way to live questions that can have no answers. To say liturgy "acts out" is not to reduce liturgy to drama that merely simulates; rather, ritual assimilates, that is, liturgy makes visible the Mystery we live as well as affords an opportunity to embrace ever deeper experiences of that Mystery.

The division of the book into two distinct parts points to very different tasks that beg our attention. The first task is to lay out a theological and methodological framework necessary for an equitable analysis; *Part 1: Methodological Perspectives* does just this. The second task rethinks familiar liturgical categories from this different orientation with an eye toward describing a liturgical spirituality; *Part 2: Pastoral Interpretations* does this. Our objective, then, is to integrate these tasks so that a pastorally oriented liturgical spirituality is solidly grounded by an articulated theology and supported by a consistent methodology.

At first glance, it seems improbable to bring together such unlikely tasks into a single volume, and, furthermore, that these tasks can even be appreciated in their own right. On the one hand, *Liturgy as Living Faith* demonstrates a carefully crafted methodology with accompanying data analysis. Much can be gained simply from a methodological study; this volume is one example of description and application of a postcritical methodology. Its use can profitably be limited to a methodological exercise. On the other hand, *Liturgy as Living Faith* proposes an approach to liturgical spirituality quite different from previous work in this area.[2] Much can be gained simply from reflection on this new illustration of liturgical spirituality. Its use can profitably be limited to pastoral application. Yet the real value of the volume lies in bringing these two areas—methodological perspectives and pastoral interpretations—together so that our understanding of liturgical spirituality is grounded in and consistent with a clearly articulated theology.

Chapters 1 and 2 bring into sharp relief the methodological question while pointing at the same time to the richness of the relationship of liturgy and life. As we stated above, this relationship between liturgy and life—or more contextually, between liturgy and ethics or liturgy and social justice—is a frequent theme of liturgical writings since Vatican II. Recall, too, that the 1976 Eucharistic Congress held in Philadelphia had as its theme "Eucharist and the Hunger of the World."[3] But however eager we might be to claim this relationship as a contemporary insight and concern, we need to be reminded at the outset that concern for others has always been part of liturgical tradition and that we can still learn something from the tradition.

Chapter 1 looks at the notion of "remembering" as it is used in the Old Testament book of Deuteronomy and how often this liturgical activity is associated with the phrase "the sojourner, the fatherless, and the widow," a symbolic expression referring to any and all of the downtrodden of society. This chapter begins with a liturgical complex (a Jewish liturgical formula) and demonstrates how authentic liturgical activity is necessarily connected to concerned human activity. By noting the number of times "remembering" is juxtaposed in Deuteronomy with the liturgical phrase "the sojourner, the fatherless, and the widow," chapter 1 establishes that liturgy cannot be relegated to a narrowly conceived sacred time and sacred space. Rather, liturgical remembering is a meaningful human activity permeating who we are and where we are.

We shift our focus in chapter 2 to the late New Testament period and there, again, discover a coincidence of liturgy and concern for the poor especially as it is evidenced by the Church Fathers. This second chapter looks at the same relationship of liturgy and life considered in chapter 1 but from another perspective: that of the consequences or effects of celebrating liturgy on daily living. In this early period of the church, concern for others was actually expressed as a liturgical act whereby members of the liturgical assembly directly linked charitable works and almsgiving to liturgical celebration. Doing for others is itself an extended liturgical activity. Concerned human activity is so basic to being Christian that it is an integral part of ritual expression.

In these first two chapters we are able to *assert* and *show* that where we find liturgical activity we find concern for justice or where we find concern for justice we find good celebration of liturgy. This hits home: Do we just "go to church" on Sunday or is there something more at stake? While we can establish a relationship that obviously arises between liturgy and right Christian living, nonetheless this is all we can do. Point, show, demonstrate, conclude: Chapters 1 and 2 are methodological examples well suited to *demonstrating* the relationship between liturgy and life but these chapters fall short of satisfying an analytical curiosity that asks, *why* is this so? They are important in the overall development of the work because they raise some of the intriguing questions that lead us to delve deeper into the relationship of liturgy and life.

These two chapters advance our inquiry for two reasons. First, they provide us with data indicating that liturgical activity has consequences beyond the cultic moment. Second, they provide us with information and conclusions from the respective studies that give us valuable insight into the meaning of liturgy and life. But they clearly stop short of exhausting the possibilities. These chapters raise questions that cannot be addressed by the critical methods that were applied to deliver the data.

Chapters 3 and 4 shift from the critical methods used in chapters 1 and 2 to a postcritical one that pays attention to the depth structure of texts.[4] The presupposition basic to this shift in method is that the text is held together by a certain underlying yet accessible dynamic. If we uncover that dynamic, we uncover the depth meaning of the text. In this next pair of chapters language philosophy, hermeneutics, and scriptural exegesis are our dialogue partners. With their help we construct heuristic tools that facilitate a new description of the Paschal Mystery, and we outline an interpretive hermeneutical frame that opens up the pastoral interpretation of Part 2. A comprehensive summary of these two chapters will ease the way for the reader who is not familiar with these analytic methods as well as point to some of the problems and questions we address.

Chapter 3 is concerned with two methodological considerations that expedite uncovering the depth meaning of a text.[5] The first consideration lays out French philosopher Paul Ricoeur's method of textual hermeneutics, which unfolds as three critical moments: participation, distanciation, and appropriation. The second sketches Ricoeur's concept of "meaningful human activity." We briefly explain these now.

The first moment of Ricoeur's textual hermeneutics, "participation," is just what the word suggests. Through participation we are connected to originary events that are communicated through time by means of a tradition.[6] Participation is an ontological moment that grounds meaningful human activity because it is a participation in being that identifies who we are. It is the starting point of the hermeneutical (interpretive) process.

But we must "distance" ourselves from participation in the tradition in order to bring an objective, analytical moment to bear on it. We wear "blinders" because we are always submersed in the tradition. Distanciation, the second interpretive moment of Ricoeur's textual hermeneutics, is a way to remove the blinders so we can see in a new way. We propose that liturgy itself is a moment of distanciation,[7] that is, liturgy itself is a reflective/critical moment vis-à-vis Christian living. We have tended to regard our Christian living as evidence of the effectiveness of liturgy. Liturgy produces fruits: right living. This suggests that *liturgy* has a primarily paranetic or ethical thrust; liturgy tells us how to live. In this volume we are taking exactly the opposite stance: liturgy is *a mirror of ideal Christian living*. That turnabout is an important one for what we want to say about liturgical spirituality. The liturgical act is a celebration of as well as a critique of our life. Rather than tell us how to live, liturgy challenges us to choose to enter more deeply into participation in Christian originary events, the Paschal Mystery. Therefore, right Christian living is a logically prior antecedent to the celebration of liturgy. Certainly liturgy affects our living, but if liturgical spirituality does not characterize Christian living then there is nothing to celebrate in liturgy. In other words, *Christian living is the content of liturgy.*

We do not *bring* our life to liturgy, although that is usually how we say it. As noted above, the problem with this kind of language is that it posits a dualism between liturgy and life that cannot be overcome. In such a dualistic approach liturgy and life will always remain two separate entities that are essentially foreign to each other. We can juxtapose them, but we cannot structurally identify them as sharing the same depth meaning. This is precisely the distance we wish to overcome. When we celebrate liturgy and experience emptiness or boredom, we might see this as a critique of our life. Pastorally, we generally assume there is a problem with the ritual itself or the way we celebrate liturgy (and often there is). But there is another possible explanation: If the thrust of our Christian living is not response to the Paschal Mystery, then no matter what we do to the ritual, its depth meaning will still escape us. We worship neither to be entertained nor to feel good but to be transformed into the Body of Christ. Liturgy is constantly a critique and a call to live Christian life as the Paschal Mystery.

Liturgy distances ourselves from participation in Christian tradition, proffers new perspective and insight, and thereby opens new possibilities for living. The other side of liturgy is that we choose new possibilities to be lived. This is what Ricoeur calls "appropriation," his third interpretive moment. Thus, not only a critique, liturgy is also very much bound up with fashioning the very shape of our ever-renewing Christian living.[8]

Chapter 3 also goes into Ricoeur's notion of meaningful human action, an important distinction necessary to enlarge our grasp of the interpretive act of liturgical appropriation.[9] We claim that Christian living is a meaningful living of the Paschal Mystery. But not all human action is meaningful action, so what makes some human actions meaningful? Four primary foci help us to grasp Ricoeur's notion of meaningful human action.

The first focus is an ethical-political sphere where persons interact in situations that have implications for right or wrong living.[10] Human action is always action within an ethical-political sphere (for our context this is the Christian milieu). The second focus is freedom, which Ricoeur describes as a dialectic between the arbitrary will and normative will, that is, between our own free choosing and the common principles and values that objectively shape that choosing. The arbitrary will must be mediated by a normative will precisely because we live together in an ethical-political sphere. We suggest liturgy functions as a "normative will" and guides our choices in the face of everyday challenges. The third focus, ideology, is the unique vision that forms and shapes the normative will, gives the blueprint of a society, and communicates the meaning of the originary events that gave rise to the society.[11] In a Christian milieu, the Gospel announces the Paschal Mystery and incarnates the ideology at the basis of Christian normative will. The fourth focus of meaningful human action, an imperative of praxis, is a necessary objectification of ideology. Action that makes a difference in society is meaningful; "making a difference" completes the hermeneutic process as, similarly, authentic Christian living completes liturgy.

This rather lengthy introductory narrative of Ricoeur's tripartite method of textual hermeneutics and his explication of meaningful human action equips us with heuristic tools for interpreting texts. In chapter 4 we do just that. We analyze the structure of Luke's Lord's Supper account, leading us to a description of the Paschal Mystery that shapes our pastoral interpretations of Part 2 and leads us to a description of liturgical spirituality.

Elements of the evangelical text suggest that Luke uses the structure of a Jewish festal meal to organize his narrative and divulge his meaning. The two cups mentioned in Luke's account[12] intimate that Luke may be using a festal meal structure, and so we may expect Luke's account to include embolisms (additions to the text) that would be proper to this particular meal, since embolisms help specify the meaning of festal meals.

Our question is, does Luke—in his Supper account—take liberties with whatever festal meal they were celebrating, and does he take liberties with the embolisms in order to help us understand its meaning? We think he does. Jewish festal meals begin with a cup of wine and an accompanying embolism. Perhaps Luke's "I will not eat or drink again until I do so in paradise" is this embolism; by its inclusion Luke is casting his narrative in an eschatological vein and thereby telling us something about the meaning of this meal.

Our main concern, though, is not with the text of this first cup or even the institution narrative. We are primarily interested in what the text says about the conclusion of the meal. Luke has conflated material into a literary subunit that the other synoptic Gospels exclude or place elsewhere. We presume that he has done so for a purpose. In chapter 4 we show, first of all, that the five dialogues Luke records are a literary subunit, and, given that fact, propose that Luke purposely constructed them in that peculiar way as part of his Supper narrative. Then we are left with the question, "Why?" We suggest those five dialogues were Luke's embolism, Luke's explanation of the meaning of this event. So to understand what Luke was conveying by the table talk is to understand what Luke was conveying about the meaning of the Supper. We analyze the five dialogues from the viewpoint of two different structural dynamics. These two dynamics are the key to the pastoral interpretations of Part 2.

The first analysis is shaped by a "linear" or thematic structure that asks, how does one conversation connect with the next and form a whole meaning? We conclude that in spite of the promise of reward in the Kingdom, we are still faced with our own misunderstanding, weakness, and alienation from the Master whom we are trying to serve when we come to the end of the table talk. The Messiah, the anointed One, is offering salvation, yet we still opt for our own way of doing things. From this initial analysis we suggest that there is a "soteriological" focus at work in the text that stresses the "not yet" of redemption. The second analysis is shaped by a concentric structure in which certain textual parallels converge on a central theme. This analysis shows how the concentric structure focuses on the central conversation with its theme of the Kingdom already present and is the promise of our full participation in it. We suggest that there is an "eschatological" focus at work in the text that stresses the "already" of redemption. The import of chapter 4 is to spell out the relationship of these two dynamics—a soteriological one and an eschatological one—as descriptive of the Paschal Mystery.

The last part of chapter 4 deals with the Paschal Mystery and liturgy. The meaning of the Paschal Mystery and therefore the meaning of Christian living is uncovered by a dynamic (or dialectic) between soteriology and eschatology.[13] Christian living is simply working out that dynamic in everyday human existence. During certain times of our daily existence, we come down more on the soteriological side when we are very aware of our own human weakness and our struggle to say YES to the Jesus event. At other times we come down more on the eschatological side when we are very much at one with the risen Christ and experience the fullness he promised. This chapter describes the meaning of the Paschal Mystery as a dialectic equipping us with a fresh approach for relating liturgy and life that is taken up in the second part of this volume.

Part 2: Pastoral Interpretations is an interpretation gained by applying Ricoeur's three methodic moments and his concept of meaningful human action to the liturgical domain. Part 2 uses the methodology and insights of Part 1 as an infrastructure to help us interpret the content of the Paschal Mystery for Christian living today. Even prior to interpreting the liturgical moments of our Christian living, however, we recognize ourselves as immersed in our own tradition. Since the first interpretive moment of Ricoeur's tripartite methodic approach acknowledges the interpreter's participation in a tradition of human activity, *mutatis mutandi* in chapter 5 we explore a common Christian self-understanding in which we all participate and which we articulate by means of the metaphor, Body of Christ. Chapter 5, then, lays out certain foundational notions or visages of Christian identity that together shape our Christian identity or self-understanding: Paschal Mystery, Baptism, Body of Christ, and Ministry of the Assembly. But this participative moment requires a critical reflection, and this is the task that shapes the next three chapters of our pastoral interpretation where we explore key moments of Christian living.

Chapter 6 interprets the Liturgy of the Hours as our daily expression of the Paschal Mystery dialectic. Chapter 7 shows how the celebration of our daily life finds its fulfillment in Sunday Eucharist. Chapter 8 explores the dialectical rhythm of the entire liturgical year as an integrating expression of the Paschal Mystery. Chapters 6, 7, and 8 are pastoral interpretations of our identity and function methodologically as moments of distanciation. Because these chapters have some of the more practical pastoral implications, a word of caution is in order: methodologically they cannot be cut off from chapters 5 and 9 without destroying the hermeneutical process, and, ultimately, obscuring their depth meaning. Interpretation is necessarily a holistic process.

Finally, chapter 9 brings the interpretive process to completion. It is the third hermeneutical moment that chooses a new way of being from among the possibilities uncovered during distanciation. The moment of appropriation constitutes a new self-understanding. For our purposes, the moment of appropriation climaxes in a liturgical spirituality, an integrating dynamic of all the facets of Christian living.[14]

Liturgy by its very nature is communal. It is fitting that a work dedicated to liturgical issues also reflects the cumulative wisdom of groups of Christians. This was certainly the case in the preparation of this volume, and, accordingly, a number of people deserve a note of gratitude. My students at St. Paul University, Ottawa, Ontario have been a constant source of challenge and inspiration. My colleagues on that Faculty of Theology have been most generous with suggestions and points of clarification requiring expertise outside of my own liturgical discipline. During the early spring of 1990, a study group met regularly with me to read and critique a preliminary text: Don Bolen, Barbara A. Bozak, Jennifer E. Cooper, Heather A. Reid, Dale M. Schlitt, and Joan Whittingham offered me incalculable and invaluable insight, corrections, and encouragement. Kenneth Russell read an initial draft and offered valuable suggestions early on in the project and Deborah McCann applied her competent editorial hand to the final manuscript and rendered it both more readable and consistent in style. More remote to the actual writing of this work but of inestimable value for its inception and completion are the Sisters of the Precious Blood who formed me in the spirituality of my Congregation and the monks of St. John's Abbey, Collegeville, Minnesota with whom I celebrated liturgy while a graduate student at St. John's University and who certainly opened me to even greater riches of a truly liturgical spirituality. To one and all, my heartfelt thanks.

Liturgy as Living Faith

Part 1
Methodological Perspectives

1
Concern for Others:
Remembering

A big part in the success of family gatherings is often reminiscing about the "good old days." Telling stories about ancestors and events that shaped family tradition is more than simply entertainment or filling in leisure time—it is a way to keep the tradition alive among the elders, the young, and new members alike. People long since absent often come alive, are truly present, and exercise real influence. Events long since past often retain their significance in casting values and ideals. Our sense of continuity with whom and with what have gone before provides us with many enjoyable hours during holidays, family reunions, and other similar occasions.

It is not surprising to discover that similar kinds of activities take place for similar reasons when a religious family gathers for worship. In fact, all liturgy is a "remembering" and celebrating of God's mighty deeds on our behalf. Liturgical remembering is a way for God to be known and divine events to cast our religious ideals and values. Telling our story keeps alive the religious tradition and perpetuates life and significance.

The Hebrew and Christian Scriptures contain numerous liturgical references and we may expect to find rich examples of worshipers who "remember." One Old Testament book in particular, the book of Deuteronomy, seems to emphasize "remembering." It would be difficult indeed to read this book and not be struck by the recurrence of the verb "to remember" (Hebrew root = *zkr*).[1] Further, *zkr* is not only traced to roots in Jewish liturgy.[2] The notion of remembrance plays an important role in Christian liturgy as well.[3]

A further observation about Deuteronomy frames our inquiry even more: Deuteronomy conveys that what is often remembered is the historical event of being a servant in Egypt. This is frequently

5

connected to the present circumstances of the downtrodden among
the Jews, at times by adopting the expression "the sojourner, the
fatherless, and the widow." The convergence of "to remember" with
"the sojourner, the fatherless, and the widow" suggests a relationship between the very act of remembering and a social concern to
relieve the suffering of others. In its broadest context, this convergence suggests a relationship between liturgy and life. Deuteronomy, therefore, is a telling starting point for our study of the meaning
of this relationship.

It is no accident that "to remember" occurs so frequently in
Deuteronomy. The liturgical activity of remembering serves as a
theological/liturgical infrastructure for interpreting Deuteronomy's
central message of the meaning of covenant and law—that is, how
Israel relates to God and each other—in seventh–sixth century B.C.E.
Israel. The point in Deuteronomy is not so much to keep the law per
se, but that the covenant is renewed (lived) by keeping the law.

Deuteronomy provides a blueprint for keeping the law that extends
beyond the necessity to obey specific commands. Fidelity to the
covenant is bound up with the liturgical remembering of how God acts
toward the people Israel. Obedience to the law is a *response* to circumstances that are recreated in the lives of the people not by an isolated, juridical exactitude, but by the cultic celebration of a past event.

Deuteronomy suggests that one purpose of cult is to remember the
originary events that formed the people so that they do as God does:
care for the downtrodden. *Zkr* links past event with present reality
in such a way that the living and renewing of the covenant is timeless; the worship of God is ongoing in the very living of the people.[4]
Hence, keeping the law and living the covenant are shaped by cultic
example: God does for you, therefore you do for others among you.
Only in this particular manner of relating to each other can Israel be
said to remember what God did for Israel and remain faithful to the
covenant because of the actions remembering brings to mind.

In this chapter we use time-proven critical methods to delve into
the meaning of the passages in question. The first and much longer
section carefully examines from several perspectives the verb forms
of *zkr* as they appear in Deuteronomy. This exegetical inquiry
locates Deuteronomy's *zkr* passages and their placement within that
book's general structure, identifies the specific *Sitz-im-Leben* [5] for
each *zkr* passage, discusses the levels of meaning for the *qal* form[6]
of *zkr*, and uncovers the level of meaning for each of these *zkr* passages. The second and shorter section of the chapter presents a similar analysis of the occurrences in Deuteronomy of the phrase "the
sojourner, the fatherless, and the widow," that is, identification of
the passages and their placement and meaning. More importantly,

however, we look at the relationship of "the sojourner, the fatherless, and the widow" passages with respect to the *zkr* passages. A final section of the chapter outlines some of the implications of the relationship of *zkr* to "the sojourner, the fatherless, and the widow" for the theology of Deuteronomy and emphasizes how concern for others, especially the downtrodden of society, is a predictable theme when a text has a compelling liturgical infrastructure. We also show the limits of a critical methodology that demonstrates relationships but can go no further to explicate them.

Our method for developing the content of this chapter is limited largely to vocabulary frequency and contexts and does not capitalize on the application of rigorous diachronic exegetical methodology. No textual criticism has been undertaken, nor has any comprehensive, systematic attempt been made to corroborate these findings in Deuteronomy with other books of the Old Testament.[7] We choose a more modest scope for this chapter: to expose select vocabulary frequency and to demonstrate a scriptural indication of the relationship between liturgy and concern for others. We use elements of source, form, and redaction criticism with some attention given to its literary and rhetorical features. These critical methods enable us to demonstrate a rather clear correspondence between a specific liturgical activity (remembering) and a specific ethical activity (concern for others).

The Use of *Zkr* in Deuteronomy

zkr Passages in Deuteronomy

The fifteen verb occurrences of *zkr* [8] in Deuteronomy appear in only four grammatical forms, all in the *qal*,[9] and these fifteen occurrences appear in only three different sections of Deuteronomy. They appear seven times in the paranetic section (4:45–11:32); seven times in the Book of the Law and Liturgical Texts (chapters 12–28); and once in the Final Recommendations and Conclusions (chapters 29–34).[10] The 7–7–1 division suggests, perhaps, a literary device on the part of the final redactor (a point we will take up later in the final section of this chapter).

Sitz-im-Leben

The specific context or *Sitz-im-Leben* for each of the fourteen *zkr* passages is important to establish. From our viewpoint, an easy way out would simply be to accept Von Rad's thesis that the main features of a cultic ceremony—that of a covenant renewal (see Dt 31:10ff)—can be recognized in Deuteronomy.[11] In his words, "*Deuteronomy* as a unity now reveals itself to us in a new light as a rather baroque agglomeration of cultic materials, which nevertheless reflects throughout one and the same cultic occasion."[12] It is not important here to argue for or against Von Rad's thesis, but only to be sensitive to the possibility that Deuteronomy "was intentionally composed as an attempt at reforming and reinterpreting the cult tradition of Jerusalem,"[13] implying a concomitant use of cultic material. The fact that Deuteronomy could stem from independent liturgical units[14] underscores the need to look there for different indications of cultic materials.

"Cult" is a broad term with a wide range of interpretations. To take only one: Mowinckel defines cult as "the socially established and regulated holy acts and words in which the encounter and communion of the Deity with the congregation is established, developed, and brought to its ultimate goal."[15] Capitalizing on this description, we look for and expect to find in Deuteronomy an abundance of "acts and words" that points to "encounter and communion" with God. Indeed, this is the case both in generally approaching Deuteronomy and for specifically considering the passages in question.

Dt 4:45–11:32. It is rather clear that covenant is one of Deuteronomy's major motifs. Moreover, "here is to be sought the *original cultic environment* into which all the Pentateuchal sources were compelled by the weight of a living tradition to fit their presentation of the history of salvation."[16] In Exodus we read "this day shall be a day of remembrance [*lᵉzikkārôn*] for you. You shall celebrate it as a festival to the Lord; throughout your generations you shall observe it as a perpetual ordinance" (NRSV, Ex 12:14; cf. Ex 13:9). Parallels abound between cultic passages in Exodus and Deuteronomy. For example, in Ex 13:3 we find "Moses said to the people, 'Remember [*zākôr*] this day.'" In Dt 16:3 Moses again instructs the people to "remember [*tizkôr*] the day." The *Kinderfrage* of Ex 12:26 is paralleled in Dt 6:20. Finally, the prescription to keep the three feasts of unleavened bread, of the harvest, and of ingathering at the end of the year (Ex 23:14–17) has its parallel in Dt 16:1–17.

Another general indication of liturgical material in Deuteronomy is the homiletic style that predominates. To this point, Childs remarks:

The homiletic style which belongs to the present shape of the book is an essential part of the explanation of the law. The new interpretation seeks to actualize the traditions of the past for the new generation in such a way as to evoke a response of the will in a fresh commitment to the covenant. The present form of the book of Deuteronomy reflects a dominant editorial concern to reshape the material for its use by future generations of Israel. The process can be termed canonical because it relates to the use of tradition as authoritative actualization or legitimating a process of continuous reinterpretation.[17]

Though Childs's point is in the context of canonicity, his insistence on the relationship of homiletic style and explanation of the law in terms of actualizing the tradition is quite relevant here. When Moses summons "all Israel" to hear the law proclaimed and begins with the words "Hear, O Israel" (Dt 5:1), we suspect cultic overtones.[18] This phrase "Hear, O Israel" is repeated in 6:3, 4 and 9:1[19] and sustains such cultic overtones.[20] We conclude, then, that the entire section 4:45–11:32 has a cultic *Sitz-im-Leben*.

These general indications carry additional weight because it is possible to establish other specific cultic ties for the *zkr* passages in 4:45–11:32. Liturgical occasions, postures, hymns, utterances, and a "timelessness" distinctive of cult suggest proximate liturgical reference points.

Liturgical evidence of the cultic event or occasion is perhaps the easiest evidence to establish.[21] Indeed, four of the six *zkr* passages occurring in 4:45–11:32 can be situated within a specific cultic event: Dt 5:15 within the Sabbath observance; Dt 7:18 within a liturgical law recital; chapter 8 continues this law recital with Moses outlining God's past favors to the people as fidelity to the covenant (Dt 8:2) and concluding with what will befall Israel if they forget the covenant. While it is not easy to divide the law into clear distinctions between moral and cultic responsibility, God's fidelity and favors do establish national restraints that remind the people of the source of their power and wealth (Dt 8:18).[22] Remembering the Lord's kindness and mercy establishes a cultic milieu for the paranetic prescription to keep the covenant.[23] Moreover, the use of the term "assembly" occurs in 5:22 and 9:10.[24] This term refers specifically to the assembling of the Israelites for a cultic occasion. Its proximity to 5:15 and 9:7 further supports a cultic *Sitz-im-Leben* for these *zkr* passages.

Posture is another liturgical indication that is easy to recognize. In Dt 9:25 Moses lies prostrate before the Lord.[25] This phrase establishes a liturgical tie more specific than the general context for the Dt 9:27 *zkr* passage.

Dt 12–28. The next seven passages appear in chapters 12–28. Again, our procedure will be to establish a general liturgical context for these chapters and then look for specific liturgical referents proximate to the seven passages.

It is supposed that the Decalogue and accompanying laws—the most ancient part of Deuteronomy—were preserved through cultic recitation. Dt 12–28, therefore, could be considered cultic material addressed liturgically to the Israelite community.[26] This generalization is supported by internal evidence of liturgical material. If we look for *zkr* passages attached to cultic occasions, there are three such passages in the Book of the Law: Dt 15:15 describes the cultic event that definitively attached the slave to the family;[27] Dt 16:3 refers to the Passover occasion; and Dt 16:12 is set within the Feast of Weeks. Four passages (Dt 24:9, 18, 22, and 25:17) have no proximate liturgical referent in terms of liturgical occasions, postures, hymns, or utterances. The fourteenth *zkr* passage in Deuteronomy (Dt 32:7) is incorporated in a liturgical hymn;[28] we may presume that this is cultic.

One more indication of a liturgical Sitz-im-Leben strengthens the above conclusions with respect to situating chapters 12–28 within a liturgical context. As we already mentioned, "timelessness" plays a significant role in cultic material. Von Rad points out that the use of "today" in Deuteronomy is a common denominator for homiletic material and has a direct tie with the cult for "this is a vivid reconstruction of the events of the redemption story such as only the cultus can furnish."[29] Hence, the use of "today" indicates not merely a recollection of a past event, but rather a cultic living of that event in the present. For example, Moses declares that "not with our fathers did the Lord make this covenant, but with us, who are all of us here alive this day" (*hayyôm*; Dt 5:3). "Today" (*hayyôm*) occurs no fewer than seventeen times in 4:45–11:32; in addition, the more definite "this day" (*hayyôm hezeh*) occurs five times. Even though scattered throughout Dt 4:45–11:32, some clustering is nonetheless apparent.[30] What is more, the final word of the section is *hayyôm*.

Chapters 12–28 have five fewer occurrences of "today" and "this day" though this section is about twice as long as 4:45–11:32. Five references are scattered in the main body of the law code.[31] The vast majority of the occurrences, twelve in all, are to be found in chapters 26 and 27 (the conclusion of the covenant) and chapter 28 (the concluding blessings and curses).[32] The number of occurrences and their clustering is significant enough to suggest further evidence for a liturgical *Sitz-im-Leben* for chapters 12–28.

We would expect the more lengthy chapters 12–28 to have proportionately more occurrences of "today" and "this day" than 4:45–11:32.[33] However, there is a pattern similar to that found with respect to the frequency of *zkr* verbs. Just as the number of *zkr* passages in 4:45–11:32 is identical to the number in chapters 12–28, so is there a similar number of "today" and "this day" passages in the two sections with the clustering of passages evident in both. Having established the liturgical referents proximate to all of the *zkr* passages in 4:45–11:32, the possibility arises to transfer that liturgical certainty to the parallel situation in chapters 12–28, suggesting further support for a liturgical context in this latter section.

Chapters 29–34. The final section of Deuteronomy (chapters 29–34) contains fifteen occurrences of *hayyôm* and one of *hayyôm hazeh.* Clustering is evident: there are seven occurrences in chapter 29[34] and seven in chapter 30.[35] The remaining two uses (vv. 2, 27) occur in chapter 31, the conclusion of the ceremony.

Today. Several explanations are possible for the repetition of "today" and "this day." It could simply be part of the repetitive pattern of deuteronomistic writing,[36] a position supported by the observation that these terms occur over 250 times in deuteronomistic writings (with almost one-third occurring in Deuteronomy alone), as opposed to only about twice that many occurrences in all the rest of the Old Testament. Or, with Weinfeld, we could simply see "today" and "this day" as the use of a rhetorical device for stressing the solemnity of the moment.[37] To this latter point, Muilenburg verifies the use of repetition as a major stylistic feature of Old Testament narrative.[38] Though he is speaking specifically about Hebrew poetry, his comments on the important role of repetition are pertinent:

> Repetition plays a diverse role in the Old Testament. It serves, for one thing, to center the thought, to rescue it from disparateness and diffusiveness, to focus the richness of varied prediction upon the poet's controlling concern. The synthetic character of biblical mentality, its sense for totality, is as apparent in Israel's rhetoric as in her psychology. Repetition serves, too, to give continuity to the writer's thought; the repeated word or phrase is often strategically located.[39]

In this case, the repetition of a specific term that relates to the cult serves to situate a cultic setting for the writing. Muilenburg later comments on repetition in the cult:

> In the cult, too, repetition rendered a special service. In the annual festivals commemorating the unique historical events of the sacred past, Israel

recited year after year her memorabilia: the theophanic accounts of the holy places, the stories of the fathers, the epic events associated with he Exodus and with the covenant at Sinai, and the *toroth* [laws] that were incumbent upon her. The various rituals and liturgies were themselves filled with numerous repetitions.[40]

This leads to a third possible explanation for the frequent use of the terms "today" and "this day" in Deuteronomy: it indicates a liturgical *Sitz-im-Leben*, which brings us back full circle to the same position with which we began. The liturgical context is further corroborated by the liturgical *Sitz-im-Leben* of a great deal of the material in Deuteronomy as established through the context of *zkr* passages.

Meanings of *zkr*. Having established the liturgical foundations for the pertinent sections in Deuteronomy under discussion, it is imperative now to turn to the various levels of meaning for the verb *zkr*. Since *zkr* appears only in the *qal* form in Deuteronomy, we will examine only the meanings in this verbal mood.

Three groups of meanings for *qal* forms of *zkr* are given in the *Theological Wordbook of the Old Testament:*[41] (1) Completely inward mental acts; remembering is contrasted with forgetting.[42] (2) Inward mental acts that are accompanied by appropriate external acts; remembering solicits accompanying action. This action may come from either of two directions—God delivers and preserves the people or the people repent and observe the commandments. (3) Various forms of utterances relate to recitals or invocations; this involves the public recitation of God's wonderful deeds.

The first meaning of *zkr*—to recall to mind in a completely inward act—is reflected in three passages (Dt 9:7; 24:9; 25:17) that simply recollect results of infidelity for the people. None of them involves any action on the part of God or of the people in the very act of remembering. Note that two of these passages (Dt 24:9 and 25:17) do not have a proximate liturgical referent.

We need to examine the passages in question for indications of a required action (response) in order to establish the second meaning (remembrance that leads to action). This action (response) can be detected in twelve passages, all but two of which have proximate liturgical referents.[43] There does not appear to be any example of the third level of meaning (liturgical recitation of God's mighty deeds) connected with the *zkr* passages in Deuteronomy.

Overall, this brief analysis seems to point in the direction that cultic remembering encompasses ensuing action. It seems that to understand the remembering as merely moral motivation[44] falls short of the reality. To this point Eising remarks that "observation of the context of zakhar reveals that the verbs used in parallel do not refer to the past only, so that the interpretation of zakhar as 'remember' in the sense of 'recall' can hardly represent its basic meaning."[45] Especially because remembering is a cultic event in Deuteronomy, it serves to actualize the tradition.[46] Covenant and law, then, are not external to the remembering of past events. Fidelity to the covenant through keeping the law is the action/response of liturgical remembering.

We have now established the liturgical context of the *zkr* passages in Deuteronomy in which most of them have proximate liturgical referents, and the level of meaning of *zkr* for each passage in which most of them involve action/response. The next part of the chapter specifies more clearly the shape of that action/response.

The Downtrodden in Deuteronomy

A liturgist could hardly ignore the references to remembering in Deuteronomy. Likewise, an ethicist could hardly ignore its references to the downtrodden. Particularly notable are passages that include "the sojourner," "the fatherless," and "the widow."[47] All but Dt 10:18 are found in the oldest stratum of Deuteronomy, the Book of Law. Some scholars[48] relate this to the humanitarian influence of Wisdom literature on Deuteronomy. Others[49] contend that its humanitarianism has prophetic origins. We see a third possibility, namely, that it derives from a common cultic tradition. A comment by Von Rad is to the point: "The cultic sphere always leaves a linguistic deposit in everyday speech."[50] Weinfeld observes that

> the humanistic vein of deuteronomic legislation is apparent not only in its socio-moral laws, but also in its distinctly cultic ordinances. The law of cult centralization, which opens the deuteronomic code (ch. 12), is punctuated with exhortations concerning the levite, the slave, and the maidservant (vv. 12, 18, 19). Indeed, one gains the impression that the primary purpose of the festal repasts at the "chosen place" is to provide nutriment for *personae miserabiles.*[51]

Further examination of the texts in question reveals that six of the eleven passages in Deuteronomy which include the phrase "the sojourner, the fatherless, and the widow" (Dt 16:11, 14; 24:17, 19, 20, 21), are in close proximity to *zkr* passages (Dt 16:12; 24:18, 22). In three of these *zkr* passages the *wāw* (and) consecutive is used, implying a connection between the passages. Moreover, a seventh passage (10:18), while not in direct proximity to a *zkr* passage, has the same content as the *zkr* passages cited above.[52] Three passages (Dt 14:29; 26:12, 13), while not proximate to a *zkr* passage, are set within a cultic occasion. The final passage (27:19) is also cultic material, relating one of the curses befalling those who are unfaithful to the covenant.

This cultic context for these passages suggests that doing for the downtrodden of Israel, as symbolized by the liturgical phrase "the sojourner, the fatherless, and the widow," is not motivated simply by humanitarianism, but also by a sense of what cultic life entails: "intention and motive are the same, viz. what may be called the *Godward view;* the doing of an act for the sake of God, and not only because it is a kindness to a fellowman."[53] At stake is an understanding of cult (giving to God[54]) that carries a conviction that we must do for others. Cult both motivates and directs. Since the cultus "forms a continual remembrance of God's act of love, and is meant to lead to the expression of grateful joy,"[55] the community cannot celebrate that joy unless all can participate. Dt 14:29 and 26:12,13 are especially significant in this context, for the offering of a tithe is directly related to providing for the downtrodden. The cultus makes relationships within the community very concrete; this lies at the very heart of covenant renewal.

The frequency with which the phrase "the sojourner, the fatherless, and the widow" occurs in Deuteronomy is neither a coincidence nor simply a part of the deuteronomistic repetitious style. Rather, it suggests an interconnectedness between covenant, law, and concern for the downtrodden in the community that captures the very theology of Deuteronomy. Remembering provides the key.

Implications

The *"šᵉma' yisrāēʾl"* is central to the theology of Deuteronomy. God is one and Israel shall love God with all its heart and soul and strength. Love of God is found not only in external cultic worship, but more particularly in living the covenant by keeping the commandments. Nor does Deuteronomy stop here. Keeping the commandments is given cultic significance through emulating those acts of God that are at the very heart of Israel's salvation history. As God had mercy (*ḥesed*) on the Hebrew people, led them out of their bondage in Egypt, provided for them in the desert, and led them to the Promised Land, so does Israel go and do likewise. In the cultic celebration of the deeds of God, the people live those events in the present life by leading their own people out of bondage, providing for them in their need, and granting them, too, joy in the "Promised Land." In other words, the covenant cannot be lived unless God's love (*hesed*) is expressed by the community's love. We can clearly see in Deuteronomy that which emerged later in Judaism and came to full light in Jesus: conflation of Dt 6:5 (love of God above all) with Lv 19:18 (love of neighbor as self). The unique twist in Deuteronomy is that the *liturgical context links this love with the very deeds of God.*

If the liturgical context had been absent from Deuteronomy, this link would not be clear. If concern for the sojourner, the fatherless, and the widow[56] had been absent, the concreteness of keeping the covenantal law would not have been explicitly linked with God's mighty deeds. Remembering creates a "timelessness" with respect to the covenant and the downtrodden create a concreteness with respect to the law. These are united in the liturgical celebration of God's love for the people. This love remains ever faithful.

It is evident that the frequency of *zkr* is limited within the book of Deuteronomy itself. This, coupled with our use of critical methods, raises some exegetical concerns. The evidence we presented earlier situates *zkr* as a liturgical term. These considerations suggest that further source criticism would be helpful. Since Deuteronomy contains several strata of material coming from different redactions, the question arises as to which redaction the *zkr* passages and the passages referring to the downtrodden of Israel belong. Limiting ourselves to Weinfeld's deuteronomic (=deuteronomistic) phraseology can be helpful in itself.[57] Virtually all of the passages we have examined would be classified as later material. This raises several questions: (1) To what extent is the *redactor* preoccupied with liturgy? (2) Is the relationship between *zkr* and the downtrodden a redactor's insight or does it indeed *derive from* the cultic tradition of Israel? (3) To what extent does the redactor's material reflect a later tradition in Israel, the one upon which our own interpretations are dependent?

Given the humanitarian motif, we would expect a frequent reference to "the poor" (*'anî*), but this adjective occurs only four times in Deuteronomy. Perhaps this points to a strictly liturgical context for the phrase "the sojourner, the fatherless, and the widow." "The poor" occurs most frequently in the Psalms which often have a distinctively cultic *Sitz-im-Leben.*[58] The major prophets (Isaiah, Jeremiah, and Ezekiel) have a high frequency of *zkr* verbs, "the poor," and "the sojourner, the fatherless and the widow."[59] This brief survey of vocabulary frequency points to three major sources for the terms under consideration: Deuteronomy (a deuteronomistic writing), the

Psalms (a postexilic collection of poetry from differing periods), and some prophetic writings. This raises the question of literary dependency. It also points to an alternative possibility that this is a cultic relationship that cuts across all the sources. Perhaps it serves to underscore Von Rad's thesis that cultic material formed the groundwork for the evolution of Deuteronomy. If we extend this to include the frequency of liturgical material in Psalms and the prophets, this may suggest that Israel was so embedded in cultic identity and so based in the Sinai covenant experience that this formed the most ancient strata of the religious tradition and self-understanding that was handed down from generation to generation.

Our study also raises another significant exegetical concern: whether *zkr* is always a cultic term in its second-level meaning, implying action (response). If it is, then examination of the extra-deuteronomic occurrences would indicate the pervasiveness of cultic requirements and point to the context and specific activities they demanded. The cult would, therefore, link the religious motivation (the covenantal relationship with God) to the ethical realization (emulation of God's mercy and justice) in such a way that the two become inseparable in the daily life of Israel. Moreover, worship and ethical behavior are inseparable. It is in this light that right living as a prerequisite for worship becomes apparent. When we take living the covenant seriously, love of God and love of neighbor are bound together.

Over and above the source question is a literary one: To what extent does the cult shape the rhetoric of the final redactor in all of the Old Testament writings? Or, how did this cultic rhetoric get implanted so deeply into the history of the nation? More to the point, we could again look at the frequency of distribution of the various elements that we have examined. The final form of Deuteronomy has *zkr* verbs evenly divided between 4:45–11:32 and chapters 12–28. This might serve to link these two sections of the book into one unit that reveals a unifying theology of covenant and law. The fairly equal use of "today" and "this day" could further support this conclusion. We also point out that these two terms do appear in 1:6–4:44, though with markedly fewer occurrences.[60] This equal use of the two terms is a departure from the other sections of Deuteronomy, in which "this day" is used fewer times than "today." Certainly 1:6–4:44, with its more historical narrative content, is quite different from the other sections in style and, we might also presume, purpose. This would handily support Noth's thesis that at least the first part of Deuteronomy is an introduction to the deuteronomistic writings and 4:45–11:32 is an introduction to chapters 12–28.

While it is true that no individual piece of exegetical evidence can serve to support our conjecture about the relationship of liturgy and life, a reasonable amount of evidence gleaned from Deuteronomy piles up in favor of accepting the relationship between liturgical remembering and ethical living when general liturgical indications are coupled with specific liturgical referents. Furthermore, the covenant is not only sealed in a liturgical celebration, but fidelity to the covenant is an expression of "liturgical living." This brief analysis of certain linguistic occurrences in Deuteronomy suggests that we might look for evidence of references to ethical living or ethical demands when we know we have a liturgical infrastructure.

Critical methods open up new ways for us to think about a text and its meaning. In our examination of Deuteronomy, we have demonstrated the relationship between cultic occasions and indications of how we ought to live in relation to others. We have raised a number of exegetical concerns and questions about the meaning of the text from several different methodological points of view. Indeed, a real value of critical methods is to bring us to the brink of asking key questions of the text. By demonstrating the relationship between liturgy and life, our study points to a dominant human problematic described variously by such polar opposites as being and action, spirit and matter, this world and the next. We are at the heart of a basic human drive toward wholeness, integrity, unity.

Demonstration, however, eludes logical necessity. The exegetical concerns and questions must be addressed because the rigorous demands of good critical method require as complete an analysis as possible. However, critical exegesis is not our primary interest in this chapter; we are concerned with another kind of inquiry. We still look for a way to conceptualize why the relationship between liturgy and life *must* be so. In other words, we are looking for a way to put dualism at rest. We are also looking for a way to gain access to the relationship between being and action. So far our inquiry has shown us that our hunch about an ontological/necessary relationship between liturgy and life can be borne out by textual evidence. Indeed, it is this textual evidence that spawned a nascent hunch that led to the ontological question and the realization that critical methods can only demonstrate; other methods are required to address the ontological question.

Before we turn to this different methodological task, we would like to consider the relationship of liturgy and life from the other direction: If a text exemplifies or exhorts ethical living, do we find evidence of a liturgical infrastructure? This is the task of chapter 2 and, again, we employ a time-proven critical approach.

2

Concern for Others:
Diakonia

The Greek word *diakonia* may be linguistically deceptive. Usually translated "service," *diakonia* could easily be compared with similar activities listed under "services" for various companies or public sector organizations. The system works something like this: We have a problem, we call a company or organization, they send someone who "fixes" the problem or we make an appointment to see one of their personnel, we pay the company or organization. There is a one-to-one correspondence in this scenario between two parties in the form of service rendered and some appropriate compensation received.

Our use of the term "service" in a Christian/liturgical context is different, and the recent tendency has been to use the term "ministry" in order to avoid linguistic misleadings. A key difference lies in compensatory expectations. Companies make profits from service; Christians give without expecting return. Service organizations solve problems; Christians open to Mystery. The public service sector accomplishes goals necessary for the good order of society; Christians strive for a fuller realization of their self-identity as the Body of Christ.

At a time when we find ourselves in the throes of a post-Vatican II ministry explosion[1] and liturgy renewal, it is enlightening to turn to Christianity's foundation documents that illustrate fervor over these same endeavors. Christian writings of the first two centuries provide today's Christian with rich and challenging material for reflection and study.

We began in chapter 1 with the liturgical infrastructure of Deuteronomy and learned to expect certain kinds of human activity (namely, concern for "the sojourner, the fatherless, and the widow")

18

to be affirmed. We continue our critical perusal of source material in this chapter, but we now begin with relational patterns that are established by early Christian manuscripts and see how this is mirrored in their liturgical celebrations. As in the last chapter, our interest is the perceived relationship of liturgy and life. We wish to generate questions from the data and to pinpoint what still eludes us in coming to a conceptual articulation of this relationship.

The organization of this chapter is simple enough: a first section on *"Diakonia* in Early Christianity," a second one on "Eucharist in Early Christian Writings," and a last section on "Implications." Thus, two themes and their convergence. The matrix of primary sources includes works of Clement of Rome, Ignatius of Antioch, Polycarp, Hermas, Justin, and Irenaeus as well as the *Martyrdom of Polycarp*, the *Didache*, the *Letter to Diognetus, Athenagoras' Plea*, and the *Letter of Barnabas*.

Diakonia in Early Christianity

The variety of ministries itemized in early Christian writings share a common concern for "service" (*diakonia*) to others. Many examples of *diakonia* can be found in Paul: as collection (Rm 15:31; 2 Cor 8:4, 9:1, 12:1f), as ministry (2 Cor 11:8), as hospitality (1 Cor 16:15) to mention but a few.[2] Within this context, *diakonia* "is best taken to mean a particular kind of service for which the same individual is regularly responsible, or regular acts of service of different kinds undertaken by the same person."[3] The key word here is "regular." *Diakonia* forms a pattern of life; indeed, it is a *way of life* for the Christian.[4] More than getting a job done, *diakonia* is human activity undertaken as an expression of Christian self-understanding.[5]

Principles

Early sources make clear two principles that are the bedrock of Christian service. First, *diakonia* is rooted in Christ. As such it receives its power from the Gospel. In the *Didache* we find "Say your prayers, give your charity, and do everything just as you find it in the gospel of our Lord."[6] Justin, in a conflation of several of Jesus' teachings, also offers a striking witness to the fact that *diakonia* is rooted in Christ and receives its power from the Gospel:

> That we should share with those in need and do nothing for [our] glory he said these things: "Give to everyone who asks and turn not away him who wishes to borrow. For if you lend to those from whom you hope to

receive, what new thing do you do? Even the publicans do this. But as for you, do not lay up treasures for yourselves on earth, where moth and rust corrupt and thieves break in, but lay up for yourselves treasures in heaven, where neither moth nor rust corrupts. For what will it profit a man, if he should gain the whole world, but lose his own soul? Or what will he give in exchange for it? Lay up treasures therefore in the heavens, where neither moth nor rust corrupts." And: "Be kind and merciful, as your Father is kind and merciful, and makes his sun to rise on sinners and righteous and wicked. Do not worry as to what you will eat or what you will wear. Are you not better than the birds and the beasts? and God feeds them. So do not worry as to what you will eat or what you will wear, for your Heavenly Father knows that you need these things. But seek the Kingdom of Heaven, and all these things will be added to you. For where his treasure is, there is the mind of man." And: "Do not do these things to be seen of men, for otherwise you have no reward with your Father who is in heaven."

About being long-suffering and servant of all and free from anger, this is what he said: "To him that smites you on one cheek turn the other also, and to him that takes away your cloak do not deny your tunic either. Whoever is angry is worthy of the fire. And whoever compels you to go one mile, follow him for two. Let your good works shine before men, that they as they see may wonder at your Father who is in heaven."[7]

Note here the motive for doing good works: that those who see them may be directed toward the Father in heaven. Christ-centered service both witnesses Good News of the Father and glorifies the Father. We already detect a link between doing good works and worship.

The early church's *diakonia* was none other than Christ's acting through his servants. *Diakonia* is but another face of evangelization, and perhaps the most explicit way to teach or introduce others to the Gospel message. Christian service is directed toward the Christ who abides in the very persons who are in need.[8] Hence, the second principle: the poor and needy are identified closely with Christ, who first identified himself with them.[9] Christians form one Body with Christ their Lord. The one Body must be preserved, and this by being attentive to the needs of others: "We must preserve our Christian body too in its entirety. Each must be subject to his neighbor, according to his special gifts. The strong must take care of the weak; the weak must look up to the strong. The rich must provide for the poor; the poor must thank God for giving him someone to meet his needs."[10] Or, to paraphrase Matthew: what you do to those in need, you do to Christ (Mt 25:45).

Diakonia was very much at the center of early Christian practice. Moreover, serving others was hardly an abstract ideal and words alone were inadequate. Serving meant *doing* for others. For example, in his *Plea Regarding Christians,* Athenagoras contrasts the non-Christian intellectuals who make skill in oratory their goal with Christians who are simple folk unlettered in the words that might be used to defend their faith but who abound in good works: "With us, on the contrary, you will find unlettered people, tradesmen and old women, who, though unable to express in words the advantages of our teaching, demonstrate by acts the value of their principles. For they do not rehearse speeches, but *evidence good deeds.* When struck, they do not strike back; when robbed, they do not sue; to those who ask, they give, and they love their neighbors as themselves."[11] Evangelical service is an ideal to be lived.

Diakonia as Fasting and Almsgiving

Early Christians realized service primarily in two related ways: fasting and almsgiving.[12] Numerous references in the Church Fathers offer insight into the breadth of these activities for early Christians and why they were so much at the heart of *diakonia.*

Fasting is more than a negative act of giving up food; it is a positive act that encompasses a whole program of Christian conduct: a petition to receive from the Lord what is needed;[13] keeping God's commandments;[14] a kind of "super" prayer.[15] Most important, however, fasting is a positive act related to fraternal charity. The *Didache* admonishes Christians to "fast for those who persecute you" (*Did* 1:3) and the whole community is invited to fast with the catechumen in final preparation for Baptism (*Did* 7:4). Thus, fasting has a missionary character in that it serves others in order to build up the community to a fullness of love.

There is also a material side to fasting; the *Shepherd* of Hermas suggests how fasting might strengthen the bonds of community in such a way that it effects joy and blessings:

"This fasting, which consists in the observance of the commandments of the Lord," he said, "is very beautiful. This is the way to keep the fast you intend to observe: Before anything else, abstain from every wicked word and every evil desire, and clear your heart of all the vanities of this world. If you observe this, your fast will be perfect. Act as follows: After having done what is prescribed, on the day of your fast do not taste anything except bread and water. Compute the total expense of the food you would have eaten on the day on which you intended to keep a fast and give it to a widow, an orphan, or someone in need. In this way you will become humble in soul, so that the beneficiary of your humility may fill his soul and pray to the Lord for you. If you perform your fast, then, in the way I have just commanded, your sacrifice will be acceptable in the sight of God and this fast will be entered in the account [in your favor]; a service so performed is beautiful, joyous, and acceptable in the sight of the Lord. . . ."[16]

Through keeping a fast and sharing the consequent material savings with others (that is, almsgiving), fasting is related to stewardship, wherein we recognize to whom all material things belong. All that we have is from God. The more we realize God's largess toward us the more we are drawn to share with others.

To this point, we read in the *Didache*: "Give to everybody who begs from you, and ask for no return: For the Father wants *his own gifts* to be universally shared" (*Did* 1:5; italics added). In a later chapter the *Didache* again picks up this theme of almsgiving, expressing it as giving to others:

> Do not be one who holds his hand out to take, but shuts it when it comes to giving. If your labor has brought you earnings, pay a ransom for your sins. Do not hesitate to give and do not give with a bad grace; for you will discover who He is that pays you back a reward with a good grace. Do not turn your back on the needy, but share everything with your brother [and sister] and call nothing your own. For if you have what is eternal in common, how much more should you have what is transient! (*Did* 4:5–8)

Sharing of goods is reasonable because the things of this world are of no consequence in comparison to the eternal gifts of God that Christians already enjoy.

There are numerous other instructions about almsgiving in early Christian writings[17] and, paradoxically enough, all hold a promise of benefit to those who are generous: "So, when a rich man goes up to a poor man and helps him in his needs, he has the assurance that what he does for the poor man can procure a reward from God (for the poor man is rich in his [power of] intercession with God and in his confession)."[18] The mutuality shared between giver and receiver cements a community bond that is the essential benefit of fasting and almsgiving.

Diakonia is incumbent on all Christians. Nevertheless, it cannot be denied that some Christians responded to a call of the community in a more formal and special way to exercise service as an officer of that community. To speak specifically to diaconal ministry: it did not differ *qualitatively* from that to which all Christians are called through the baptismal promise to live in Christ; the difference lay in a formal recognition of service as part of church order. As Torrance remarks, "the diaconal ministry is one in which the deacons act as representatives of the people and as examples of the way in which

Christ identified Himself with their need."[19] Initially, the deacons' role was a liturgical one, to distribute communion to the faithful and take care of the poor. To be sure, the deacons' role later encompassed more than this liturgical role.[20] But it is significant that their initial function was ministry (especially of the church funds) to the poor and needy;[21] in this they typify Christ.[22]

Diakonia is one of the foundations of the church, an expression of love and mutually shared self-understanding, not a mere performance of duty. In reaching out with the hand of Christ to those in need, the bonds binding the individual members in a community are so strengthened as to be the seed that forms the one Body. In the next section we discover that it is Eucharist that nurtures the seed into a visible unity, the Body of Christ.

Eucharist in Early Christianity

Early Christian sources will not provide us either with a treatise describing a comprehensive theology of Eucharist, or even a complete description of a eucharistic rite including the actual prayers. They are simply not there. Several explanations have been offered for the lack of development of a comprehensive eucharistic theology in the early Church Fathers.[23]

These early Christian writings recorded "professional" faith, that is, faith that was believed, lived, and celebrated in worship. At this early date they were not yet faced with the challenges that would lead to careful doctrinal statements.[24] Liturgy and prayer give evidence of the faith of the early Christian community.[25] The early writers provide a witness to their *belief.*

Lampe suggests that "one reason why references to the eucharist in the period of the Apostolic Fathers [are sketchy] is that Baptism was a sacrament of pre-eminence,"[26] and writers' attention was directed toward this sacrament. The baptismal writings of Cyril of Jerusalem and John Chrysostom would certainly bear out a baptismal preeminence, but these are third- and fourth-century writings, so they really do not explain eucharistic vagueness in the writings of the first and second centuries. Lampe offers a further reason:

> The chief reason for the paucity of theological expositions of the Eucharist in the early period, and the reasons why the Christian writers' occasional allusions are difficult to analyze systematically, is that the Eucharist stands at the heart of the early church's faith and life; it embodies, and proclaims in a single rite, the entire richness of the gospel; and for this very reason it

does not lend itself to precise definition or to clear-cut theories about presence, sacrifice, consecration, and the relation of the sacramental act and of the visible elements to the reality which they signify.[27]

Later he says it even more succinctly: "In fact, what might appear to be vagueness is an indication of a richness of understanding,"[28] an understanding that is lived and professed. Carpenter shares the same sentiments that such vagueness arises at least partially out of the very meaning of Eucharist: as an act of thanksgiving, commemoration, communion, and sacrifice, there is a richness inherent in Eucharist that can never be fully or satisfactorily expressed. It remains a mystery in the best sense of that word.[29] In spite of the lack of a comprehensive treatise on Eucharist in any of the early writings, a depth of understanding that comprehensively exhibits the professional, lived faith of the early church has emerged, at least when all the references are sifted out, organized, and analyzed. We cannot overlook these seeds for a eucharistic theology.

A particularly important theological/pastoral insight for our purposes is that faith is celebrated in Eucharist, and neither Gospel nor Eucharist can be delimited by theological explanations no matter how helpful they may be. Gospel and Eucharist are *lived*.

Unity. Ignatius of Antioch indicates in two letters that it is the bishop who presides over the Eucharist. In *Ephesians* (20:2) we read, "At these meetings you should heed the bishop and presbytery attentively," and in the letter to the Smyrnaeans (8:1) he writes, "You should regard that Eucharist as valid which is celebrated either by the bishop or by someone he authorizes." Ignatius further states that "where the bishop is present, there let the congregation gather, just as where Jesus Christ is, there is the Catholic church" (*Smyrnaeans* 8:2). He sees Jesus united with his Catholic church as a type for the bishop united with his local church. There are similar indications in chapter 4 of the letter to the Magnesians, where he recognizes the preeminence of the bishop and remarks that valid and authorized services depend on being in unity with him. Shortly after, in chapter 6, he speaks of the bishop as presiding in God's place. The bishop presides so Eucharist may be a sign of the church in union with the Lord Jesus.

Clement also attests to the important role of the bishop to symbolize the unity of the church. He advises the Corinthians to "gather together for worship in concord and mutual trust, and earnestly beseech him [the Lord] as it were with one mouth" (1 *Clement* 34:7). It would appear, in face of this prerequisite for unity before one can worship, that "strife, bad temper, dissension, schism, and quarreling" (1 *Clement* 46:5) have arisen among the Corinthians. Clement comments on the gravity of this situation: "For we shall be guilty of no slight sin if we eject from the episcopate men who have offered the sacrifices with innocence and holiness" (1 *Clement* 44:4, 5). Seemingly, revolt against the episcopate has already taken place. Some Corinthians "have removed a number of people, despite their good conduct, from a ministry they have fulfilled with honor and integrity" (1 *Clement* 44:6; also 47:6). Revolt against the episcopate effects a break in the unity of the church.

In his first letter to the Corinthians, Paul also warned against factions being formed by aligning (and thus dividing) the community with either himself or Apollos (1 Cor 3:4). Another kind of faction in the form of a lack of charity was apparently taking place at the Lord's Supper: "When you come together, it is not really to eat the Lord's supper. For when the time comes to eat, each of you goes ahead with your own supper, and one goes hungry and another becomes drunk" (1 Cor 11:20–21, NRSV). Disunity happens when there is no sharing among the community members. When there are factions, there is no sharing.

In the interest of unity, it is no surprise to read in *Clement* that "We must, then, put a speedy end to this [the revolt against the episcopate]. We must prostrate ourselves before the Master, and beseech him with tears to have mercy on us and be reconciled to us and bring us back to our honorable and holy practice of brotherly [and sisterly] love" (1 *Clement* 48:1). The community exists to practice love, not to engage in quarrels that lead to factions. As these early writings indicate, the episcopate at that time was a symbol of unity both in the measurable sense of no factions within a local community as well as in the intangible sense of the connection of the local community with the universal church. The community gathered around their bishop was visible evidence of the unity of the whole church with Christ.

The local community gathered around their bishop for liturgy. Liturgy and the love it celebrated is itself an expression of unity. In Ignatius's polemic against the Docetists, he contrasts the heretics with Christians on the basis of their lack of love and their staying away from Eucharist. We read in his letter to the Smyrnaeans:

> They [docetists] care nothing about love: they have no concern for widows or orphans, for the oppressed, for those in prison or released, for the hungry, or the thirsty. They hold aloof from the Eucharist and from services of prayer, because they refuse to admit that the Eucharist is the flesh of our Saviour Jesus Christ, which suffered for our sins and which, in his good-

ness, the Father raised [from the dead]. Consequently those who wrangle
and dispute God's gift face death. They would have done better to love
and so share in the resurrection. (*Smyrnaeans* 6:2–7:1)

Loving our neighbor, and therefore doing good works, parallels
Christ's love for us. Only this leads to resurrection, which is eternal life.

Elsewhere, Ignatius speaks of unity in similar terms of doing
good for those in need. Ignatius instructs the Bishop Polycarp to
"vindicate your position by giving your whole attention to its material and spiritual sides. Make unity your concern—there is nothing
better than that. Lend everybody a hand, as the Lord does you"
(*Polycarp* 1:2). Note that Ignatius precedes his comment on unity in
this passage by inviting Polycarp to give attention to the *material* as
well as the spiritual side of his position, then admonishes him to
"lend everybody a hand." The very structure here indicates that service to others is bound up with unity. Later in the letter Ignatius
spells out one way Polycarp is to aid those in need: "Widows must
not be neglected. After the Lord you must be their protector. . . .
Hold services more often. Seek out everybody by name" (*Polycarp*
4:1, 2). Here a reference to liturgy ("hold services more often") is
sandwiched between a statement that "widows must not be neglected" and "seek out everybody by name." The implication seems to be
that liturgy is bound up with a kind of community that helps those in
need and also one that knows its members well enough to call each
one by name. The community that makes Eucharist possible manifests a unity that evolves when community members know each
other well enough to determine those in need and respond to them in
loving service.

Loving service was the mark of the Christian community at
Rome,[30] one reason why the Roman church enjoyed a position of preeminence.[31] It is a spirit of loving, fraternal correction and a position of preeminence that prompts Clement to write the church at
Corinth, admonishing them for the lack of unity resulting from their
rebellion against the episcopate.[32] In part, loving service flowed
from the shape of the liturgy itself; as such it is an extension of the
liturgy, as Justin attests in his *First Apology*.

Presence. Our current colloquial use of "presence" is a much more
spatial denotation than they would have used in early Christianity
that affects, in turn, the observable symbol of unity. Unity was the
result of the charitative activity of the Body of Christ that was celebrated in Eucharist by the community gathered with the bishop.

Unity presumes a wholly committed faith that seeks expression. A member was absent (from spatial presence at liturgy) only for unavoidable reasons. Spatial absence did not preclude presence so long as one was united with the Body in mind and heart. Interestingly enough, the very structure of the eucharistic celebration enveloped a broad and varied perception of presence.

The outline of a eucharistic celebration in Justin's *First Apology* is the earliest that has survived.[33] Since this is not an actual eucharistic prayer but rather an outline of procedure, we might construe that it carries the same import as a set of directives for the eucharistic rite:

> And on the day called Sunday there is a meeting in one place of those who live in cities or the country, and the memoirs of the apostles or the writings of the prophets are read as long as time permits. When the reader has finished, the president in a discourse urges and invites [us] to the imitation of these noble things. Then we all stand up together and offer prayers. And, as said before, when we have finished the prayer, bread is brought, and wine and water, and the president similarly sends up prayers and thanksgivings to the best of his ability, and the congregation assents, saying the Amen; the distribution, and reception of the consecrated [elements] by each one, takes place and they are sent to the absent by the deacons. Those who prosper, and who so wish, contribute, each one as much as he chooses to. What is collected is deposited with the president, and he takes care of orphans and widows, and those who are in want on account of sickness or any other cause, and those who are in bonds, and the strangers who are sojourners among [us], and, briefly, he is the protector of all those in need. (1 *Apology* 67)

A parallel description of a Eucharist in chapter 65 describes a Eucharist concluding baptism. A comparison of these two descriptions helps us grasp the importance of presence with respect to unity.

There are some notable differences between these two rites: in the baptismal Eucharist there is no mention of readings or homily; presumably, the baptismal liturgy has supplanted and incorporated this. There is a kiss of peace in the baptismal Eucharist that is absent in the order of Sunday Eucharist. This holy kiss follows the intercessions; perhaps it was an opportunity for the community to personally welcome the new member(s), as well as a sign of unity and solidarity within the Body into which the new member(s) is being welcomed. A collection for the needy is mentioned in the Sunday Eucharist but omitted from the baptismal Eucharist. Perhaps this collection stands over and against the baptismal Eucharist's kiss of peace as the sign of unity and solidarity of the Christian community. At any rate, the collection was an integral part of the Sunday Eucharist. It was the deacons' liturgical role to distribute what was offered at the Sunday Eucharist to those in need. In his letter to the Trallians, Ignatius explains that "they [the deacons] do not serve mere food and drink, but minister to God's Church."[34] Polycarp ascribes this role to the presbyters who "must be compassionate, merciful to all, turning back those who have gone astray, looking after the sick, not neglecting widow or orphan or one that is poor" (*Philippians* 6:1). Both the Eucharists described in Justin's *First Apology* have intercessions, offering of bread, water and wine, eucharistic prayer, distribution and reception by the assembled community, and the note that the Eucharist is taken to the absent members. Those who could not attend were probably those who were sick, infirm, those who could not be present because they were of the poor working class who did not have time off from duties to share in the community celebration of the Eucharist on Sunday, those who were imprisoned, those who, in short, were not free to attend for whatever serious reason. The unity of the community was preserved, however, by the Eucharist being taken to them. Thus, all shared in the fruits of Eucharist, even if they could not be physically present at the actual ritual celebration.

Note how different the whole tenor of this discussion on presence is from what we might say today. Rather than focusing on the real presence in eucharistic species of bread and wine—which is not to suggest that this is unimportant—the *primary* emphasis with respect to presence is on the *community* and its love and concern for one another. The problem is transposed from "out there" to one that has implications for the way we live.

Eucharist is God's most gracious gift. Through it, the church celebrates Christ's resurrected presence as the center of the very life of the community that calls all to share in the one Body for the sake of all. Primary in its effects is the bond of unity it cements, a oneness intrinsic to itself: "for there is one flesh of our Lord, Jesus Christ, and one cup of his blood" (Ignatius, *Philadelphians* 4:1). It also effects a power to elicit oneness within the community.[35] There is a paradox here: We come to Eucharist in harmony, as community, yet it is Eucharist that kneads the community into one Body. Those coming to Eucharist must come together as a community of peace, or first be reconciled and then share Eucharist,[36] thereby effecting Jesus' presence and forming the one Body.

At this early date the hellenistic categories underlying our contemporary debate on real presence had not yet caught up with eucharistic theology.[37] Nonetheless, the real presence was not ignored. Hence, Justin is quite clear and unequivocal about Jesus' presence in the Eucharist: "For we do not receive these things as common bread or common drink, but . . . [it] is the flesh and blood of that incarnate Jesus" (1 *Apology* 66). Ignatius is equally explicit in his polemic against the Docetists: "They hold aloof from the Eucharist and from services of prayer, because they refuse to admit that the Eucharist is the flesh of our Savior Jesus Christ."[38] While it is true that neither Justin nor Ignatius offers any insight into *how* the bread and wine are the body and blood of Christ, there is no doubt that for them they *are* just that. This is equally true for Irenaeus; for example, he speaks of the "Cup of the Eucharist" as the "Communion of His Blood" and the "Bread which we break" as the "Communion of His Body."[39] But even this presence in bread and wine is connected to our earlier notion of presence to each other: We are "members of Him" (*Heresy* V, 2:2) and also of "that flesh which is nourished by the Body and Blood of the Lord, and is a member of Him: as blessed Paul saith in his Epistle to the Ephesians, *We are members of His Body, of His Flesh, and of His Bones.*"[40]

Sacrifice. Closely related to the presence of Christ in the community and Eucharist is the theme of Eucharist as sacrifice. Justin's *Dialogue with Trypho*[41] (chapter 41) portrays memorial and sacrifice as two sides of a Judaeo-Christian coin. It is precisely as sacrifice that Eucharist is a memorial indicating an affinity of second-century Christianity with second-century Judaism: "The conviction of Hellenistic Judaism that all sacrifice must ultimately be spiritual, and that it is primarily the grateful response of man to the Creator, is shared by the church."[42] We read in Justin of the "Eucharistic Bread, which our Lord Jesus Christ commanded us to offer in *remembrance* of the Passion He endured . . . and at the same time we should thank God for having *created* the world, and everything in it" (*Dialogue* 41:1; italics added). These two passages aptly refer to Eucharist as the spiritual sacrifice of the community that offers it in thanksgiving to the Creator.

In the context of sacrifice Justin quotes the prophet Malachi[43] and explains that God asks for a pure sacrifice not limited to Jewish types of sacrifice (but not extending to all nations). Justin equates this pure, universal sacrifice with Eucharist (*Dialogue* 41:3). The *Didache* also quotes Malachi 1:11 (*Did* 14:3), but focuses on the purity of sacrifice.[44] This follows 14:2 where the *Didache* calls for reconciliation among the members of the assembly, "lest your sacrifice be defiled."[45] Irenaeus also refers to this passage from Malachi (*Heresy* IV, 17:5) in a way analogous to that in the *Didache*, that is, that sacrifice must be pure in order that God's name may be glorified. Irenaeus explains that a pure sacrifice is one offered only when we are reconciled to our neighbor: "For if a man [or woman] according to that which is seen only, shall have tried to offer purely, and rightly, and lawfully, but in his own soul distributes not rightly his communion with his neighbor, neither hath fear of God."[46] Sacrifice, too, relates to the unity of the community, for sacrifice cannot be pure if the community is not reconciled.

The *Martyrdom of Polycarp* takes a different approach to Eucharist as sacrifice. Polycarp's personal sacrifice of his life for Christ is viewed in terms of images borrowed from the eucharistic sacrifice:

> So they did not nail him [Polycarp], but tied him. And with his hands put behind him and tied, like a noble ram out of a great flock ready for sacrifice, a burnt offering ready and acceptable to God, he looked up to heaven and said: "Lord God Almighty, Father of thy beloved and blessed Servant Jesus Christ, through whom we have received full knowledge of thee, 'the God of angels and powers and all creation' and of the whole race of the righteous who live in thy presence: I bless thee, because thou hast deemed me worthy of this day and hour, to take my part in the number of the martyrs, in the cup of thy Christ, for 'resurrection to eternal life' of soul and body in the immortality of the Holy Spirit; among whom may I be received in thy presence this day as a rich and acceptable sacrifice, just as thou has prepared and revealed beforehand and fulfilled, thou that art the true God without any falsehood. For this and for everything I praise thee, I bless thee, I glorify thee, through the eternal and heavenly High Priest, Jesus Christ, thy beloved Servant, through whom be glory to thee with him and Holy Spirit both now and unto the ages to come. Amen." And when he had concluded the Amen and finished his prayer, the men attending to the fire lighted it. And when the flame flashed forth, we saw a miracle, we to whom it was given to see. And we are preserved in order to relate to the rest what happened. For the fire made the shape of a vaulted chamber, like a ship's sail filled by the wind, and made a wall around the body of the martyr. And he was in the midst, not as burning flesh, but as bread baking or as gold and silver refined in a furnace. And we perceived such a sweet aroma as the breath of incense or some other precious spice. (*Polycarp* 14:1–15:2)

Martyrdom is viewed as a type of Eucharist because the sacrifice is pure and complete—one of total identity with Christ—even to sharing in his sacrificial death.

If we understand the eucharistic sacrifice as a memorial of Christ's sacrifice, then these two interpretations of sacrifice as universal or sacrifice as pure are not mutually exclusive. Christ's was a pure sacrifice that redeems all people of all ages. In this regard it is also universal.[47]

Eschatology. Finally, because Eucharist unites us with the Body of Christ it incarnates the eschatological assurance that we will also share in his everlasting life. Irenaeus promises that "our bodies which are nourished by it [Eucharist], and then fall into the earth and are dissolved therein, *shall rise* at the proper time" (*Heresy* V, 2:3; italics added). Irenaeus (*Heresy* V, 33:1) quotes Jesus' Last Supper promise that "I will not drink of the produce of this vine, until that day when I shall drink it with you new in the Kingdom of my Father" (Mt 26:29). Further, in v. 2 of this same chapter, Irenaeus quotes Lk 14:12–14, which relates the promise of the Kingdom to the poor. Earlier, Irenaeus speaks of professing a resurrection of the flesh and spirit because of "an Eucharist composed of two things, both an earthly and an heavenly one; so also our bodies, partaking of the Eucharist, are no longer corruptible, having the hope of Eternal Resurrection" (*Heresy* IV, 18:5). It is significant that Irenaeus in the next paragraph relates this eschatological assurance to service of the poor, for he quotes Proverbs 19:17: "He that hath pity upon the poor lendeth unto God," and then quotes Matthew 25:34–36, in which those who enter the Kingdom are the ones who feed the hungry, give drink to the thirsty, take in the stranger, clothe the naked, and visit the sick and imprisoned (*Heresy* IV, 18:6). Just as service to our neighbor is seen as an integral part of unity and sacrifice, it is also an integral part of eschatological assurance. In fact, without service to our neighbor, there can be no hope of sharing in the eucharistic, let alone the messianic, banquet. Finally, in chapter 36 Irenaeus returns to the Lord's Supper promise of Jesus he quoted in chapter 33: "The Lord also taught thus, promising that he would enjoy the new mixture of the chalice with [his] disciples in the Kingdom" (*Heresy* V, 33:3).

Ignatius, too, reflects an eschatological promise when he writes of the Eucharist as "the medicine of immortality, and the antidote which wards off death but yields continuous life in union with Jesus Christ" (*Ephesians* 20:2). Elsewhere, Ignatius uses another eschatological image by referring to Eucharist as "an immortal love feast."[48]

Unity, presence, sacrifice, eschatological assurance—the totality of the community's corporate act of thanksgiving is set against these themes.[49] Eucharist celebrates the community's recognition and acknowledgment that all it has comes from God. It is within the deepest meaning of these four themes that we are called to reach out to our neighbor. Eucharist is thanksgiving for the sacrifice of Jesus Christ, made present through memorial. It is thanksgiving for Jesus' presence in the community in his body and blood, real food for life eternal. More than thanksgiving for the community's giftedness from a gracious God, Eucharist is also thanksgiving for the power it effects within the community: a dynamic thrust that forms the one

Body through service that is also a thrust toward eternal life through actual participation in an immortal love feast. Lampe beautifully sums up thanksgiving:

> Thanksgiving implies offering, for thanksgiving and sacrifice are co-related; and the Eucharist is the church's offering of praise, blessing, self-dedication, and the expression of all this in practical service to the needy, for the "offering of gifts" was the source and the symbol of the church's provision for its poor and distressed members.[50]

Eucharist is a vertical movement of offering, praising, and blessing God. It is a horizontal movement of unity, sharing, and caring for others. Jesus is one with his community and at the same time he leads the community to the Father. We cannot reach the Father except through Jesus who is visible in his Body and shared in thanksgiving. There is a dynamic relationship between these movements that we consider in the next section.

Implications

Two general observations about the relationship of "Concern for Others" and "Eucharist" can be made at this point: 1) acts of charity were part of the everyday life of early Christians and 2) there was a decided sensitivity within the very shape of the eucharistic liturgy itself for the poor, the sick, the needy, and the oppressed. Justin's inclusion of instructions on how to regard the poor and to deal justly with all people in his outline of a eucharistic liturgy (1 *Apology* 67) is not pious admonition; rather, it is part of the liturgical action itself in the larger sense of "*leitourgia*" ("to render service"). This service is not something external to Eucharist;[51] it actually begins within the liturgy itself, then extends itself beyond the supper room to wherever Christ's presence, strength, healing, and reassurance are needed.

The intersection of the themes of Eucharist and concern for the poor in numerous references from the early Church Fathers also attest to their intimate connection.[52] Indeed, it almost seems as though to do Eucharist is to do for the poor.[53] Justin supplies the first key to deeper indications of why this is so.

After his description of the baptismal Eucharist in chapter 65 of the *First Apology*, chapter 66 provides an explanation of the meaning of Eucharist. Then a marvelously dynamic linking comment introduces chapter 67, which is a description of the Sunday Eucharist: "After these [services] we *constantly remind each other* of these things. Those who have more *come to the aid of those who lack*, and we are *constantly together*" (1 *Apology* 67:1; italics added). Three activities are described here: 1) to remind each other of the meaning of Eucharist, particularly in terms of how it is to be lived out, 2) to extend Eucharist beyond the Lord's table by coming to the aid of those who lack, and 3) to be together (because of the remembrance and the aid that result in the continued fellowship). Conzelmann describes this dynamic in terms of the collections. His remarks are pertinent to our context as well: "But of course the meaning of it [collections] is not exhausted in *caritas* as such. This collection is the visible demonstration that the church is a unity. . . . The collection demonstrates the historicality of the church and the universality of salvation: the two are a unity."[54] The unity of the church is the promise of salvation. Unless all members are drawn into this unity, the hope of salvation diminishes.

Another key to understanding the relationship between Eucharist and concern for the poor is to consider and compare the lists of those in need named in various early Church Fathers' writings.[55] The similarity of the lists suggests that this kind of naming was common in the early church,[56] perhaps at one time being a regular part of the intercessory prayers or other liturgical litanies. These texts imply that those in need were very much in the consciousness of the community. It does not seem improbable to conclude that those in need overtly challenged the Christian community on two levels. First, in a practical manner they were a challenge to the community to extend the Eucharist beyond the supper room into the very life of the community. Second, in a liturgical manner they were the occasion for a concrete expression of an action central to Eucharist: to bind together.

Two conclusions can be drawn. First, Eucharist is co-extensive with *ecclesia*. Unless church is people who have struggled for a common identity through mutual sharing, caring, and nurturing, Eucharist is necessarily as fragmented as the people. Christ's anamnetic, sacrificial presence cannot be fully realized in part because Christ's Body is whole. Thanksgiving and praise can only be offered to the Father when God's gracious giftedness is recognized in all. Thus, response to the needs of our neighbor is a prerequisite for coming to Eucharist, for it draws all together into a unity without prejudice toward position, means, or status. Response to needs flows from Eucharist because a thanksgiving celebration of Christ's Body compels us to strive for a wholeness of the Body that can only be experienced by taking care of the needs that keep others from sharing in the Body.

A second conclusion is that relationship to God is the source and inspiration for relationship to others. Lampe states this quite well:

> In the early Church the two great commandments were united at the focal point of Christian worship . . . *diakonia* and *leitourgia* were so indissolubly linked with one another as to be, in effect, two aspects of one and the same Godward act on the part of the Christian community; for service to man [and woman] was an expression of the worship of God and was itself in turn embodied in the divine service of the liturgy.[57]

It seems appropriate, then, to resist the temptation to express this relationship in the customary vertical/horizontal (to God/to community) relationship and instead to express it as convoluted co-privileges—praise of God builds up the community and building up the community praises God. Thanksgiving to God is recognition of gifts proffered to needy members, and sharing those gifts is thanksgiving to God. Supplication to God is expressed in the community by responding to needs, and responding to needs makes fruitful supplication to God. Community finds its communion with God because God deigns to share Godself with humanity in such a marvelously complete identity as to raise humanity to a share in divinity. This happens to people not as individual members of the community but within the very process of the members forming the one Body.

Two principles were discussed in the section above on *diakonia*: that *diakonia* is rooted in Christ and as such receives its power from the Gospel, and that in serving others we are serving Christ. We can observe these principles in operation. We receive the impetus to reach out to others within the shape of the liturgy from the Word spoken in the dynamic first moment of the eucharistic liturgy. Identity with Christ is realized in the second dynamic moment when we hear the story and seal it by receiving Communion. It is even more fully realized when we extend Eucharist beyond the supper room by human actions so much directed toward concern for others that they actually characterize our daily life. *Diakonia* and Eucharist are inseparable.

No doubt this brief survey of some early Christian writings on concern for others and Eucharist leaves us with a genuine and somewhat urgent challenge. The challenge is this: to make the kind of eucharistic living that was evident in the early church imperative in today's world, that kind of eucharistic living that effects unity because it draws members into solidarity by means of concrete expression in real, daily contact with each other. The challenge is genuine in that the early Church Fathers have shown that it can be done. When today's Christians gather the strength and mutual support necessary to once again localize *ecclesia* into a ministering community, forming the one Body will not be an empty promise but a reality. As Torrance comments: "The church needs today a massive recovery of authentic diakonia if it is to hold forth the image of Christ before mankind and to minister the mercy of God to the needs of men [and women] in the deep root of their evil and the real sting of their misery."[58] The challenge is urgent in that the church has already waited too long to recover the deepest sense of who she is: a people in communion with their Lord who is kind and compassionate.

We discover in the early church writings that it is relatively easy to demonstrate the relationship between life and liturgy. These Christian writers, perhaps out of their own lived experience, help us advance our knowledge insofar as they clearly indicate a basis for this inextricable relationship: our self-understanding as Body of Christ that we both live and celebrate. Both ministry and celebration express our very self-identity. Conversely, we might suggest that when ministry is less than adequate and celebration is less than authentic praise and thanksgiving, we may need to examine our self-understanding and its concretization in human activity. Having come thus far, we are now ready to shift methodology in order to better address why the relationship between liturgy and life is so.

3

The Paschal Mystery:
Methodological Openings

The Paschal Mystery is the very heart of Christian liturgy and as such it deserves the continued attention of liturgical scholars. The pioneers of the liturgical movement—including Beauduin, Guardini, Casel, Bouyer, and Michel—who brought us to the threshold of *Sacrosanctum Concilium* equipped us with a solid foundation upon which to build continued research into the meaning of the Paschal Mystery. Recent liturgical literature, however, has hardly kept pace with earlier enthusiastic research into this foundational area. This is not to say that liturgists today ignore the centrality of the Paschal Mystery. It does suggest that they have been more absorbed with various aspects of the *implications* of the Paschal Mystery for contemporary church life than with probing deeper into the meaning *for us* of the Mystery itself.

It is hardly possible that research has been exhausted apropos the Paschal Mystery. With the continued growth in liturgical theology, and especially with the advancement of new methods for doing liturgical research, it seems that investigation into the meaning of the Paschal Mystery could take off in new directions. The pastoral stimulus and objectives of the early liturgical movement are well known. A marriage of methodological advancements with pastoral issues could prove beneficial as well as interesting.

From the purview of the limited writings we examined in the previous two chapters, we are confident to say that when we find liturgy truly being celebrated we find a community whose lives witness to God's way of relating; they are lives marked by love and justice, kindness and mercy. Conversely, a community concerned for others is one drawn to celebration, and various expressions of that concern can be found within the shape of the rite itself.

Our critical reflection on sources is limited, however, in that we have only been able to *demonstrate* that where we find liturgy we find right living. This would be true even if we were to undertake the formidable task of examining virtually all of the extant sources. The limitation we point out is one of methodology. Therefore, we proceed to another stage of our inquiry and will focus on more technical pursuits for the time being. Just as the first two chapters worked in tandem to help shift our attention to a new set of questions concerning the relationship of liturgy and life, these next two chapters work in tandem to help situate the questions in a new methodological framework.

Our thesis is that if we capitalize on the advances made possible in text interpretation by postcritical methods of textual analysis, we have new tools that will allow us to move beyond affirming the relationship of liturgy and life and expose the ontological underpinnings that constitute this relationship. The present chapter lays out a workable textual method in broad brushstrokes; chapter 4 applies the method to a select text—Luke's account of the Lord's Supper—in order to paint a new picture of the Paschal Mystery.

Two methodological considerations must be in place before we can interpret anew the meaning of the Paschal Mystery. Our starting point must be a solid theory of interpretation because our approach to liturgical spirituality is based on a specific interpretation of a Lucan text. We must also look to a theory of meaningful human action since our aim is to show the essential link between liturgy and life. These two methodological axes are the focus of this chapter. We sketch out the three moments of French philosopher Paul Ricoeur's method of interpretation and his requirements for meaningful human action. With these two heuristic tools in place we will be in a position to carry out a structural interpretation of Luke's Supper account and propose an interpretation of the Paschal Mystery derived from this analysis.

Ricoeur's Methodic Hermeneutics

Hermes was the Greek messenger god, the interpreter, the herald, of the other gods. His name is the etymological source of the Greek word "to interpret" from which the word "hermeneutics" is derived. Hermeneutics is the art of making known meanings heretofore hidden or unavailable. It is a discourse on things unknown that allows us to imagine the unimaginable. It is an activity of creation. It is a process of self coming into new being. To the extent that liturgy

manifests mystery, hermeneutics promises good results for interpreting liturgical texts.

Paul Ricoeur has assisted us to be better interpreters of texts. For
Ricoeur, "text" has a broad extension, including any enduring sign of
human existence, not only written texts. Works of art are texts and
can be subjects of interpretation. So are music and dance. So are
ritual and liturgy. In fact, Ricoeur deems any manifestation of
human action to be a text that functions analogously to written texts.
Therefore human action itself can be the subject of interpretation.

The implications of Ricoeur's theory for liturgy are immediately
obvious since the value of liturgy lies in its actual celebration (a specific kind of human action) and not in a written text (for example, the
Roman Missal or *The Book of Common Prayer*). Some methods of
interpreting written texts have the same objective as the field study
of behavioral scientists because they are both directed toward understanding human action. Ricoeur offers liturgical analysts an alternative to such field study. Instead of studying his method of textual
hermeneutics in a purely theoretical way,[1] we will think it through
from the viewpoint of a very specific kind of text, liturgy.[2] This will
help prepare us for the pastoral interpretations that make up Part 2
of this volume.

Ricoeur's method unfolds as a process that moves through three
methodic moments. He calls these "participation," "distanciation,"
and "appropriation." These moments do not unfold in a recognizable,
chronological sequence as stages through which we pass. They are
interpretive activities that lend credence to a dynamic relationship
between "reader" and text that leads to understanding[3] the text.
They unfold as polar opposites, as dialectics that inform one another
and propel the interpreter ever deeper into the textual moment.

Participation

A fundamental principle of Aristotelian epistemology is that all
knowledge comes through the senses. *Mutatis mutandi*, we might
say that all interpretation is possible because we participate in a
common reality that already provides us with a preliminary "pre-
understanding" of what we are to interpret. This is not to say that
there is a single, given meaning such that interpretation is merely a
discovery of that meaning. On the contrary, although we have an
"inkling"—Ricoeur suggests we "guess"—about possible meanings
of a text, interpretation is necessarily a creative process involving the
construction of meaning.

Participation is a fundamental "belonging" to a particular tradition; interpretation is always undertaken within certain parameters of that tradition. An interpreting community resides within a common tradition in such a way that interpretation can never take place outside that tradition. Interpretation is a radical acknowledgment of a certain identity. We do not interpret from within a vacuum. We can never stand outside our tradition. In addition, participation also enables a communication of the originary events that gave rise to the tradition. We are a community who finds its roots in some common originary event(s). Those events and the culture, society, institutions, and experience—the tradition—that shape them make us who we are.

We Christians live within a shared tradition and our originary events are the Paschal Mystery. Christian identity is a baptismal identity through which we recognize ourselves as the presence of the risen Christ.[4] Whether we use John's metaphor of vine and branches or Paul's metaphor of the Body, the reality we are trying to grasp and express is that we are one in Christ. This Christian identity shapes all our interpretation, unless we overtly reject it. Our "guess" about the meaning of Christian existence, then, is conditioned by our own self-understanding as Body of Christ. And because we are all the same Body, our interpretations are based on the same shared self-understanding. There is a common bond, a common pre-understanding, that places each Christian community within the tradition that authentically interprets what it means to be the Body of Christ.

Liturgy is the fundamental "at hand" interpretation of Christian existence. Shaped by the wisdom of a tradition of celebrating communities, liturgy makes mysteries that are timeless and nonspatial present in time and space. We participate in the very object we are trying to interpret, which is itself already an interpretation.[5]

Participation in a common identity assures certain parameters for authentic interpretation but it never *gives* an interpretation. The methodic moment of belonging stands in dialectical relationship to another interpretive moment, distanciation, which opens new and creative possibilities for Christian living.

Distanciation

As the word itself intimates, distanciation is a "distancing" ourselves from the moment of belonging in order to reflect on the meaning of human existence and to be challenged to new possibilities. It is an analytic moment during text analysis that utilizes postcritical analytic methods—for example, structural or narrative analysis—to bring a certain objectivity to bear on the interpretive process. We usually do not sit down and consciously reflect on our participation in being through tradition; we just live it. Distanciation, on the contrary, is a conscious, deliberate interpretive activity. It does not just happen; we make it happen.

Distanciation is a distinct moment of interpretation directed toward the internal structure of a work in itself without any regard to the subject who produced the text or the one who interprets it.[6] A text has its own "world" of possibilities that opens up alternative ways for human living. A horizon or a world is available through textual interpretation and is intelligible on its own terms apart from both "author" or "reader" of a text. Texts develop a kind of life of their own. The purpose of the analysis proper to distanciation is to bring to light alternative ways of participating in human existence; in other words, alternative ways to live out who we are. Interpretation, then, is a creative process that capitalizes on this proffering of new possibilities for living. Participation moves us along the path of tradition; distanciation opens forks along the way.

Textual analysis cannot be cut off from the moment of participation (nor, as we see later, from the moment of appropriation) since a text is the objectification of signs of human existence. The object of interpretation is a ready-at-hand sign of our lived tradition. A text, then, brings our participation in human existence to language[7] and makes it readily available for interpretation. As such, text is the objectification of the relation of belonging. It is precisely this relationship to the ontological moment of belonging that makes text interpretation so fruitful. Rather than being simply a remote academic exercise, text interpretation has to do with human *living*.

Because it is an objectification of belonging, the depth structure of a text discloses the human existence that gave rise to its objectification. Thus, *an analysis of the depth structure of a text is really an analysis of human existence*. This is ultimately what is at stake in interpretation as well as in our present liturgical enterprise. If we can authentically interpret what is readily at hand—liturgical texts—then we have a new way to grasp the meaning *for us* of what is not readily at hand: the Paschal Mystery. This is no small point; it is the basic presupposition upon which any ontological rewards of liturgical interpretation rest. It rescues the interpreting of liturgical texts from the realm of intellectual activity and casts it into the normative unfolding of Christian living.

Ricoeur uses his notion of text as a paradigm and applies it by analogy to human action itself; in other words, the recovery of action is analogous to the recovery of discourse in texts.[8] He justifies this on the basis that, just as discourse has a meaning that endures beyond the event—and it is that meaning that can be recovered by interpreting the text—so does human action endure beyond the instance in which it occurs. Each human action, like discourse, is fleeting or passing as an event. Nonetheless, it leaves traces or marks that can be recovered and interpreted as a document of human action.[9] Since human action endures and is objectified through such recoverable documents of life as records or statistics (for example, birth certificates or voting lists are traces of someone having contacted the health or polling offices), human action itself can be treated as a text whose meaning is recovered through interpretation. Distanciation from human action and an analytic moment of interpretation are possible because these traces of human action are fixed in textlike documents of life. Just as the meaning of a story unfolds through the plot, so does the meaning of human action unfold in its emplotment. History is a paradigm example.

These generic remarks on text and human action have their extension into the liturgical realm. As ritual, liturgy is a fixed concretization (i.e., text) of those meaningful events we Christians refer to as Paschal Mystery. The Jesus event certainly occurred in chronological time and physical space, but is not limited to that era and locale. *Liturgy is the trace of the Paschal Mystery that endures through tradition.* Liturgical texts objectify the meaning of the Jesus event and make it available for all time to all people. Liturgy is a document of Christian living available for interpretation. It is the privileged access to the meaning of the Jesus event.

All texts require interpretation if their enduring meaning is to make a difference in human existence. Since liturgy is a text it, too, requires interpretation. One obvious hermeneutic activity is undertaken by the professional liturgist; numerous studies have resulted from the impetus of the liturgical movement and much knowledge and insight have been gained. Important as this scholarly activity is, another not-so-obvious hermeneutic activity is the one undertaken by the Christian community during liturgical celebrations; this is directly concerned with shaping and continuing Christian tradition. The *celebration* of liturgy is analogously a kind of moment of distanciation during which our participation in the Christian tradition is "bracketed"—set aside—in order to recognize new possibilities for Christian living. The liturgical assembly, by its very celebrating, is interpreting the tradition. We ever create liturgy anew: not in the sense of constructing a new ritual but in the sense that liturgy always opens up—presents to us—new possibilities for living Christian tradition. The seemingly rigid structure of liturgy is never just a body of preconceived deductions. The celebrating community enters into the Jesus event through meaningful ritual action that objectifies the Paschal Mystery and opens up new possibilities.

Although liturgy celebrates the depth structure of the Paschal Mystery, it is always a fresh recreation so that each celebration of liturgy is a new event. This is why the celebration of liturgy can make a difference. One way to get at the meaning of Christian life is to analyze liturgy. Not just communicating the meaning of liturgy is at stake, but also communicating the meaning of Christian living *for us*.

If we begin with the fact that a Christian's self-understanding is revealed in the Paschal Mystery (which is the full expression of Christ's self-understanding), then any analysis of the Paschal Mystery is an analysis of our own self-understanding. The analysis that is proper to the interpretive moment of distanciation can be realized by every Christian whenever s/he opens self to new possibilities for Christian living during liturgical celebration. The meaning of the Paschal Mystery is available to everyone. It is a life to be lived to its fullest.

Liturgy is a paradigmatic moment of distanciation for Christians because liturgy is a privileged expression of the Paschal Mystery. To celebrate liturgy is to bracket participation in Christian existence, to distance self from self in order to reflect on new possibilities for self-understanding. Liturgy is a moment "out of time"[10] that enables us to critique and realize different possibilities for living our Christian existence. The celebration of liturgy presents the meaning of our whole Christian living to us in a concrete and manageable ritual moment. To discover the inner dynamic—the deep structure— of Christian liturgy is to discover the inner dynamic—the deep structure—of Christian living. We see ourselves in the liturgy both as we are and as we can become. To celebrate liturgy is to assimilate to ourselves an ever-deepening realization of ourselves as a manifestation of the Paschal Mystery.

Participation in Christian existence is dialectically related to the liturgical moment of distanciation that opens up new possibilities for Christian living. But this is still only part of an integral act of interpretation. A third interpretive moment is needed—one dialectically related to the other side of distanciation, which, in turn, becomes a new moment of participation. Ricoeur calls this third interpretive moment "appropriation."

Appropriation

The process of interpretation is completed by this third methodic moment. Appropriation is a choosing from among the possibilities—the various forks and crossroads along the path of tradition—

offered by the world of the text in the moment of distanciation and thereby making the text's meaning our own. Meaning has less to do with an objective reality "out there" and much more to do with a subject's (interpreter's) *response* to a text. Analogously, the meaning of liturgy has less to do with rubrics or ceremony and much more to do with the worshipers' *response* to liturgy as measured by the quality of their Christian living.

Appropriation leads to a new self-understanding that is actually a new way of existing. The ultimate goal of interpretation is a new self who lives a new human existence with new situations and new possibilities. The interpretive process proceeds from a participation in human existence (objectified as a "text") to a distanciation from existence in order to recognize new possibilities for appropriation.

Appropriation is an essential aspect of liturgical celebration.[11] In liturgical celebrations we are constantly confronted with new possibilities for living the Paschal Mystery. Liturgy is incomplete until we have chosen new expressions in our daily living of that Paschal Mystery from among the proffered possibilities. Liturgical appropriation has finally to do with building up the Body of Christ, because in choosing new possibilities that enable a new self-understanding we are ever groping toward a fuller expression of the presence of the risen Christ in today's world.

This brief sketch of Ricoeur's methodic hermeneutics already affords us a glimpse of our perceived essential relationship between liturgy and life. Liturgy and Christian living both derive their depth meaning from the Paschal Mystery. To put it another way: liturgy, an objectification of the Paschal Mystery, has a depth structure parallel to the depth meaning of Christian living. Authentic celebration of liturgy makes a difference in our lives not because liturgy is essentially paranetic (the purpose of liturgy is never to *tell* us what to do) but because liturgy invites appropriation of new possibilities for living the Paschal Mystery. Our pre-understanding of self is challenged by liturgy is such a way that new self-understanding is embraced. These three moments of the interpretive process might be diagrammed along with their counterpart Christian realities in the following way:

Interpretive Process and Christian Realities

Participation	Distanciation	Appropriation
Christian Tradition	Celebration of Liturgy	Living Faith
Self-understanding	Liturgy of Hours Eucharist Liturgical Year[12]	Liturgical Spirituality

We spell out this preliminary overview of method and content in the pastoral interpretations of the second part of this volume. For now, we shift to a different methodological concern: If appropriation involves new ways of living the Paschal Mystery, what is meant by the notion of meaningful human action? Again, we turn to Ricoeur for help in our analysis.

Meaningful Human Action

The pre-understanding of participation through a reflective process unfolding as the moment of distanciation culminates in the self-understanding of appropriation. The whole point to Ricoeur's interpretive process—and, indeed, its real value to liturgists—is that true interpretation always leads to a change in self. This suggests that interpretation has something to do with ourselves and the way we live. But not just *any* human action is an appropriate consequence of interpretation. Appropriation leads to *meaningful* human action. The emphasis on "meaningful" separates this action from mere motion or random action. Meaningful human action makes a difference in the world. This is why its interpretation is a worthwhile enterprise.

The actions of Jesus have certainly endured beyond the first-century event and have given us examples of meaningful human action. Followers of Jesus from eyewitnesses onward have lived the meaning of the Paschal Mystery and have left traces of their belief and commitment. Without those traces there would be no Christian tradition. Furthermore, meaning can be recovered through interpretation of those traces that are documents of human action (liturgy and Christian living).

Four considerations or foci help us grasp the complexity of meaningful human action: it is prompted by circumstances in a particular *ethical-political sphere*, it is expressed in *freedom*, it involves a *critique of ideology*, and it culminates in an *imperative of praxis*. These same considerations can help us grasp the complexity of the Paschal Mystery.

Ethical-Political Sphere

Meaningful human action is never solitary.[13] It requires an interaction between/among human subjects that unfolds in a community or society. Whenever there is society, there are organizational structures and mores that condition relational patterns. Because we are social beings, we contend with an ethical-political sphere. Meaningful human action unfolds within this shared ambience.

Meaningful human action, as inter-subjective, begins with a confrontation of individual and collective wills. For Ricoeur, the will is more concerned with doing than with intention. Thus the will (action) cannot be considered in itself in terms of an interior ordering that is no more than a simple legislated will. We are not concerned here with "obedience" or conformity to law or even with right and wrong. The will we describe is an arbitrary will (i.e., belonging to the subject) that must be considered in terms of choices and their effects in the world.[14] Meaningful human action operates on a larger scale in terms of the world, culture, history: "Briefly, it wants to 'change the world.'"[15]

A reminder: the arbitrary will is not solitary. An extended notion of human action as meaningful recognizes self not only in another's will but also in the will of the entire community.[16] Our choices for action not only affect our own possibilities but those of others. Human action implies a responsibility to others because it is situated within a common tradition in which we participate.

Decision is fundamental to the exercise of will; only one who can choose can enter into a relation of wills. Meaningful human action includes reflection, a critical stance in face of possibilities. We make our own—are responsible for—a critique of the stamp of human action on society. By means of reflection, meaningful action engenders new works, institutions, and monuments belonging to the responsible subject and also to the "edification of the sphere of coexistence in the community of thinking and willing subjects."[17]

The reflective aspect of meaningful human action transposes the accent "from what is arbitrary in choice to its *norm* within the framework of a theory of the will."[18] Never isolated, the arbitrary will (that of the subject) makes decisions from within a tradition of norms. Isolation is overcome in a discourse of action in terms of the reflection that assures taking responsibility for our own actions, but only when we are situated within historical communities where we recognize the meaning of our own existence.[19]

We are speaking of a subject, of another, and of a community of subjects who bear a responsibility for each other because of the confrontation of wills. In past Christian milieus we have tended to emphasize "the other" ("the Church says . . ."), and this has served to skew the whole question of responsibility and community. The years of renewal since Vatican II have attempted to bring individual Christian, authoritative church, and community into a better balance of mutual support and cooperation. We are at least assuming responsibility for a critique of our institutions and discovering that our very actions are important if the church is to engender a new ethical-political order.

Even by embracing ethical-political (liturgical) norms, the arbitrary will is never totally eclipsed. Ricoeur resolves a dialectic of arbitrary and normative wills by considering the alliance of nature (existence) and freedom.

Freedom

Ricoeur begins the process of subsuming and recovering nature (which mediates the normative will) within freedom (which mediates the arbitrary will) by a fundamental affirmation of the act of existing.[20] In this affirmation, nature mediates freedom.[21] In other words, (logically prior) existence makes the exercise of freedom possible. How is this so? By first seeing the act of existing as *actions*.[22] Human existence is dynamic; it is human actions. An understanding of freedom begins in an inquiry about the activity (works) of humanity (i.e., texts) that concretize that freedom.[23] Human freedom documents an explication of the world[24] that is discovered in the experience of action. Freedom is not manifested by the act *of* experiencing, but freedom is manifested by acting *in* experience.[25] The ground of freedom, then, is the concretization of action in works[26] because "this *ergon* [work] is the veritable emergence of being as *energeia* [action]."[27]

The concretization of freedom in works is a concretization of the actions and works that are linked to actual history. This history is really a history of "modes of being, the history of the manifestation of being."[28] It is this "depth history," as Ricoeur calls it, that unifies human action by means of human works and gives history a human meaning.[29] This brings us to the position that subjectivity (acting as subject) is the predominant mode of being.[30] When we speak of freedom, then, we are concerned with *acting* rather than *being acted upon* (without denying that our actions implicate others).

To rephrase this in terms with which we Christians are more familiar, freedom is never license. Responsible freedom acts within the norms of tradition because participation disallows our standing totally outside of our mode of existence. In this sense, freedom is itself an expression of the tradition (or being). Christian freedom is most surely manifested by our *response* to liturgical celebration, which is a fundamental affirmation of participation in the Paschal Mystery. Appropriating new possibilities for living the Paschal Mystery pertains to far more than specific behaviors (this is why moral exhortation falls short of liturgical import). Appropriation is *choosing a new self-expression* from among possibilities. Appropriation is nothing less than an expression of self-understanding. Liturgy mediates Christian freedom, and its truth is spelled out by the works that are linked to a concretization of the Paschal Mystery in time and space.

We can ask what kind of discourse is necessary to articulate that truth that manifests the will itself. Ricoeur's answer to this question is *interpretive* discourse because, as Aristotle maintained, being can be said in many ways: "This ontological polysemy is recognized in a philosophy which characterizes itself as a philosophy of interpretation."[31] The subject is restored to a central position in terms of interpreting the depth history that is the embodiment of freedom. Freedom conquers nature when freedom is no longer a question of cosmology but of subjectivity. A critique of ideology goes hand-in-hand with the recovery of subjectivity with respect to freedom.

Critique of Ideology

For many people, the word "ideology" conjures up negative emotions rooted in its contemporary Marxist exposition in terms of class struggle.[32] Ricoeur rejects this unfavorable view of ideology and chooses to approach it from the broader perspective of ideology as social integration.[33] We begin with social actions as having a double direction (meaningful for individuals and oriented toward others), and social relations as providing stability and predictability of a system of meanings within a society. Here, ideology is a symbolic constitution of the society in general and of authority relationships in particular.[34] Ideology plays a mediating role in society; an ideology in this favorable light is necessary for any viable society.

Since the church, too, is a differentiated society, an ideology underlies its tradition. The Paschal Mystery defines the Christian ideology that constitutes church and mediates the network of relationships that function within it. Ricoeur explicates four stages of ideology: social integration, legitimation, illusion, and critique. One challenge to the contemporary church is to recognize the implications for renewal that these stages of ideology pose.

Social Integration. An ideology is a necessity because it gives a social group a self-image.[35] In what way does it confer a self-image, and from where does that image come? Ricoeur addresses these questions by noting five features of social integration, any one of which may be distorted in such a way as to lead to dissimulation of the ideology.

First, "ideology is a function of the distance that separates the social memory from an inaugural event which must nevertheless be repeated."[36] In other words, ideology links the originary events (e.g., the Paschal Mystery) that marked the beginning of a social group to its present realization. An important implication of social integration is that a society can never stand outside of itself. It is both shaped by and shapes the ongoing effects of the originary events. Societies are, inherently, participatory.[37] This leads to the second feature: dynamism.[38] Ideology has a generative character about it that has a power with respect to enterprises and institutions (e.g., church). Ideologies are more than conceptual constructs; they always lead toward meaningful action. A third feature of ideology is that it is simplifying and schematic,[39] that is, it has a code character (for example, ritual) that can be inscribed.[40] The code allows an overview, "not only of the group, but also of history and, ultimately, of the world."[41] A society schematizes (ritualizes) the ideology as a system of belief from the very moment of the originary events. Hence, the fourth feature: ideologies are operative rather than thematic.[42] This feature results in a certain opacity whereby the ideology is nonreflective and nontransparent, an uncritical instance from within the society. Herein lies the greatest possibility of illusion and distortion. This is closely linked to the fifth and final feature: ideologies are inert. Ideologies necessarily operate within certain orthodox stances. When something new confronts a society, the new is either accommodated to what is typical in the society or, if accommodation is not forthcoming, the novelty will be rendered intolerable to the extent that it "threatens the possibility for the group to recognize and re-discover itself."[43] Ideologies perpetuate a resistance to change that positively serves the socially integrating character of that ideology.

Legitimation. A second stage of ideology is legitimation. This stage is linked to the hierarchical organization of societies and is concretized in authority and domination.[44] Authority exercises its power because it lays claim to legitimacy. For example, Paul claimed to be an apostle on the basis of a personal encounter with Jesus Christ. The church hierarchy claims authoritative magisterium because of an unbroken apostolic succession. However, legitimation is never fully transparent, so the exercise of authority always calls for an interpretation (or should). Ricoeur posits what he calls a "surplus-value": the exercise of all authority demands more than the belief of the subject can bear. The third and necessarily negative stage of ideology enters at the point where ideology encounters domination.[45]

Illusion. The third stage of ideology is an illusion or distortion that leads to dissimulation. Ideology is both function and content. When ideology degenerates to illusion, the function and content are split and the latter undergoes an inversion. In a positive stage of ideology, social integration is the result of a common embodiment of re-actualized originary events that were grounded in real life. When that content is inverted, those real life originary events are replaced by what the dominant authorities may "say, imagine and represent."[46] Judaeo-Christian history is filled with examples of the confrontation of ideology and domination, from prophets and kings to Jesus and Pharisees to conscience and magisterium. The Reformation and Counterreformation is another good example of the struggle of ideology and domination, as is Vatican II and those who still resist its vision of *aggiornamento*. Only a critique of ideology can allow for the positive stage of ideology to be preserved and continue to be formative of a society. A courageous critique of ideology is fundamental to any renewal of a society.

Critique. A critique of ideology is directed toward reversing the inversion of content so that the ideology given birth by the originary events, rather than what the dominant authorities determine, is once more normative for the society. Ricoeur proposes four propositions that must be kept in mind for a critique to restore an authentic ideology. First, absolute knowledge is impossible for anyone in the society because no one in the society can be both in and out of it. Second, a relative autonomy is possible through the objectification of historical conditioning. Third, there can be no totalization of the vision. Fourth and finally, the critique can never be complete.[47] These four propositions are good reminders for Christian churches engaged in the work of renewal. Liturgy is a paradigm critique of Christian ideology at the same time that it celebrates it. Christian tradition is the objectification of Christian ideology but at no one period of church history is there a totalization of its originary events *except during authentic liturgical celebration*. Christian ideology may suffer illusion at certain times in the history of the church, but liturgy guarantees that the ideology will never be totally lost and can always be restored to authentic expression.[48]

Action continually leads to other action. A hermeneutics of action, then, is completed only at the third interpretive moment of appropriation as an imperative of praxis.

Imperative of Praxis

Human reality has both a private observation and a public description that prescribes a dialectic between the historical situation of the "this-here" and of the enduring "essential structure" that is uncovered in the saying. Both subject and "other" are taken up in human reality. Praxis—reflective action—begins with the subject because all action is reducible to a specific agent who acts. Yet, praxis is "the entire sphere of human reality, considered under the aspect of its historical predicates."[49] An (initial) problematic of praxis is set up between a dialectic of the limits of individual and society. The resolution of this dialectic is an explosion of the limits that is concretized by the mediating role of society. Rather than restrict possibilities, societal norms open us to a wider experience, that which we hold so dear.

Value proceeds from subjectivity and actualizes freedom. There is a movement from verb to substance, from valuing to what is valued. Values are incarnated in praxis. We have values but we also know that the values are not of our making; on the contrary, we discover values in the larger sphere of the confrontation of wills and freedoms.[50] Values do not originate from the subjective pole, though they proceed from there. Values reside in society—a community of the one and the many—and it is society that gives the norms that are received as constraining elements. A norm is a universal prescription that "demands" that what is preferable take precedence over what is desirable. This "demand" is not yet an imperative because an imperative is always directed to a single action. First there is a dialectic of value and norm (of individual and society; of arbitrary and normative wills; of nature and freedom). Then there is responsible, meaningful human action.

The imperative of praxis is to preserve freedom as the origin of human action linked to the actual history of modes of being. This can only be achieved in a society founded on an ideology as a positive social integration rather than as domination or illusion. Human action (works), then, can be interpreted vis-à-vis the originary events that ground the society rather than in terms of duty or obligation or binding norms and laws.[51] The imperative of praxis is the ultimate culmination of a hermeneutic of action and, indeed, of the whole historical sphere of human "be-ing."

The imperative of praxis proper to an authentic interpretation of liturgy has far more at stake than specific choices regarding individual actions (though individual action always has its place). First there is a dialectic of limited pre-understanding with the Paschal Mystery. Then there is a new self-understanding concretized in good works.

If we limit the response to liturgy to writing a check to our favorite charity and then resuming life as usual, we have sadly missed the point. An imperative of praxis means human action that makes a difference for the tradition because it has first made a difference with the Christian subject. An imperative of praxis means no less than a change in self-understanding that ever more closely aligns us with Jesus Christ. The demand for specific action is a consequence of, but not identical with, a new self-understanding.

The Paschal Mystery is originary to the Christian tradition with its own ethical-political sphere and demands that necessarily interact with the larger society. Liturgy is a critique of Christian ideology that sets parameters for Christian freedom and critiques society at large. The reality lying in front of the celebration of liturgy is brought to the fore by the imperative of praxis inherent in the completion of the ritual action in Christian living. This is at least a partial explanation for why Judaeo-Christian liturgical material will always have allusions to ethical conduct, and why ethical material that respects human freedom and contains a critique of ideology will also have liturgical underpinnings. Ethical-political sphere, freedom, critique of ideology, and imperative of praxis are *sine qua non* features of meaningful human action. Our conclusions from chapters 1 and 2 are good examples.

We have traveled two lengthy paths, Ricoeur's methodic textual hermeneutics and his theory of meaningful human action. Certainly these two descriptions shed light on each other. Texts are an apt object of analytical inquiry because they evidence traces of human action that we can recover. Traces of human action draw our attention because they evidence the meaning of the originary events that give rise to the tradition in which the interpreting community participates. Textual hermeneutics begins with a common tradition and leads to appropriative action. Meaningful human action begins with social integration and a confrontation of wills and leads to an imperative of praxis. Both textual hermeneutics and meaningful human action incorporate an analytic moment that guards against the dissolution or fragmentation of the tradition. The fusion of these two considerations takes text analysis out of the academic arena and assures us that our interpretive work has something to do with life. Meaningful action helps us understand what happens to self-understanding during appropriation. This opens the ontological door, for text analysis is a window onto human existence.

When we combine the complexity and richness of a theory of meaningful human action with Ricoeur's methodic textual hermeneutics, our methodological tools are in place. Armed with a solid interpretation theory and with an eye to what constitutes meaningful human action, we now turn to a consideration of the Paschal Mystery in terms of its depth structure.

4

The Paschal Mystery:
A Lucan Structure

Christian liturgy celebrates the Paschal Mystery. We could hardly disagree with that simple but profound statement, yet it does have built-in difficulties. The word "celebration" itself suggests a linguistic dilemma. Too often this word conjures up great times we have had with family and friends, good food and drink, laughter and "cutting loose." Birthdays and anniversaries, graduations and promotions, births and retirements are all occasions for celebrations. We know how to "party" at such gatherings. And this is the crux: "celebration" means "party." We can easily confuse priorities if we bring this set of expectations to liturgy.[1]

In its deepest sense "celebration" carries the capacity to affirm the slice of life that occasions the gathering.[2] There is far more to it than the externals of having a good time. Celebration is a joyous and wonder-filled occasion that brings home to us the deeper meaning of who we are and what we are about.

Liturgical celebration assimilates to us the ongoing fruitfulness of Jesus' life, suffering, death, Resurrection, Ascension, sending of the Spirit, and promise to come again—in short, the whole Jesus event. That event is originary to Christian tradition, is constitutive of it, and is at the heart of the identity of Jesus' followers. It is reasonable, then, to look to the Paschal Mystery to find a clue for discovering our own self-understanding as well as grasping the essential relationship between liturgy and life in such a way as to put dualism at rest.

How do we understand that what Jesus meant and did "then" is what we mean and do "now"? What more can we say about the Paschal Mystery than simply describe the Jesus event? These new questions are crucial because they address a post-Enlightenment historical concern. These questions disclose more than curiosity about what a text means; they seek to bridge the gap between past events and the meaning of those events for a different historical context— their meaning *for us*. As we have said, critical methods are limited in that they cannot search beyond the context in which a text was produced. Postcritical methods bracket (set aside) original contexts to focus on meaning in a new context.

Delving deeply into the Paschal Mystery involves more than a mere bridging of a time gap. It involves even more than affirming our own implication in the Paschal Mystery. Jesus' relationship to his Father, his utter fidelity to God's loving plan (*mysterion*) for us, and the manifestation of that relationship and fidelity in the work of salvation—all of these describe our own relationship to the Father and our own work of salvation. We are looking for a way to understand this. We will see that Jesus' relationship and fidelity can be accounted for by a dynamic polarity or dialectic that so informed his way of living as to be itself one door onto living that Mystery. If we concretely grasp the dynamic that enspirited Jesus' life, we can identify a means to engender that same dynamic in our own lives. We, too, can live the Paschal Mystery.

The authoritative record of the Good News—Jesus' unfolding the Paschal Mystery—is given in the Gospel accounts. Many commentaries and analytical studies on the four Gospels are available. It is not our intention here to duplicate these nor even to take on this massive task from a different methodological perspective. Rather, we choose to concentrate on a brief time in Jesus' life when his mission was coming to a climax and he was trying to convey this to his disciples. All four Gospel accounts record that Jesus shared a Supper with his disciples just prior to the actual events of death and Resurrection. It would certainly be reasonable to conjecture that at that meal Jesus shared something of the meaning of what he was about. We turn our attention to this small portion of the Gospel accounts.

At first glance the Lord's Supper accounts in the synoptics generally focus on the Institution Narrative and the ensuing Passion. But there is a substantial difference between Luke's account and those of the other two synoptics. Two striking variant features of Luke's account of the Lord's Supper prompt us to broach a study of the Paschal Mystery from another point of view. Distinctively, Luke mentions two cups (Lk 22:17 and 20) during the course of the meal. This is reminiscent of the three (and possibly four) cups of wine shared during Jewish festal meals. Also distinctively, Luke conflates five seemingly disjointed dialogues and places them after the Institution Narrative, we suggest as "table talk" (Lk 22:21–23; 24–27; 28–30; 31–34; 35–38). This is consistent with Luke's pen-

chant for meal situations and the table talk accompanying them
recorded elsewhere in his Gospel.

A number of exegetical problems and questions besiege an analysis
of Lk 22:14–38,[3] but since our present concern is not primarily
exegetical, we do not intend to address all of them. Our intention
instead is to put *liturgical* questions to the text that may help us to see
the Paschal Mystery in a fresh perspective. The strategic leading
questions are these: Why did Luke mention two cups? What is the
meaning of his Supper account? Why did he transpose material to
compose the table talk? Why those five particular dialogues? What is
the overall effect of Luke's compositional hand on the meaning of the
text? From a structural perspective, does the Passion Narrative context have any bearing on our understanding of the Paschal Mystery?

We propose that Luke purposefully constructed his account of the
Lord's Supper, and especially the table talk, as a window through
which we might clearly see how the Lucan community understood the
meaning of that Supper as well as the approaching events. The
hypothesis that guides our analysis is this: *the five disjointed dialogues following the Institution Narrative are Luke's explanatory
"embolism" (insertion, intrusion into a text) on both the meaning of the
actions over the bread and cups and the post-Supper events.* Thus, to
understand the structure of those five dialogues taken as a skillfully
crafted literary unit helps us not only to grasp Luke's intended meaning of the dominical actions, but also—and, we believe, ultimately—
to understand the whole Jesus event, that is, the Paschal Mystery.

This chapter is divided into three major sections. First, in a section designated "Meals," we discuss preliminary data important for
our interpretation of Luke 22:14–38 in two subsections: the *seder* of
Jewish festal meals, and the six meal pericopes in Luke that precede
Lk 22:14–38 and provide a guiding hand to interpret Luke's meals
and table talk. In the second section, "Luke's Account of the Lord's
Supper," we examine the Lucan Supper account. In two subsections
we redress pivotal exegetical problematics: establishing the table
talk as a literary unit, and assessing the structure of the Lord's Supper as paralleling the structure of the first six Lucan meals.[4] In the
final section we lay out a structural interpretation of a meaning of
the Paschal Mystery.

Meals

Two different investigations command our attention in this section.
On the one hand, structural elements of a Jewish festal meal provide

a framework for situating the meaning of the table conversation in Luke's Supper account and suggest three subunits at work: the Institution Narrative, the table talk, and the Passion events. On the other hand, a structure common to the first six meal pericopes recorded in Luke's Gospel cues us into looking for a similar structure at work in his account of the Lord's Supper and ensuing Passion events and suggests certain parameters for addressing the question of the meaning of these texts *for us.*

Jewish Festal Meals

Meals were significant events for devout Jews. Even simple meals were liturgies,[5] a recognizable ritual form in the case of festal meals. These meals were distinguished by their *berakoth,* their blessings, those actions that transform an ordinary meal into a religious meal. At the heart of this transformation are the blessing over the cups and bread and especially the great thanksgiving over the cup that concludes the meal.

A first cup of wine with accompanying blessing begins the meal on Sabbaths and feasts; this is followed by the *haggadah* (an explanation of the feast) and a second cup of wine. We are familiar, for example, with the *Kinderfrage* of the Passover *haggadah* in which the youngest asks the father of the household why they are doing these things *this night.*[6] The blessing over the bread and the eating of the meal come next. The meal is drawn to a close with a third cup of wine, the thanksgiving cup.

There were three *berakoth* accompanying the thanksgiving cup,[7] each with its own particular theme: *birkat ha-zon* (thanksgiving for creation and God's abundant blessings), *birkat ha-arez* (thanksgiving for the land, covenant, and Torah), and *birkat ha-Yerushalayim* (thanksgiving for Jerusalem, the house of David, and for the promise of redemption). The third blessing, with its theme of redemption, is especially significant for our study. Since this blessing focused on messianic expectation, it was a future reckoning. Moreover, on certain feasts the third blessing for redemption included an embolism pertinent to the feast—a further comment, if you will, on its meaning.[8] The embolism would specify an opening toward redemption differentiated by and interpreted within the meaning and celebration of the particular feast.

The structure of a simple festal meal can be diagrammed, along with the parallel verses from the Lucan Lord's Supper account, as follows:

Jewish Festal Meal Structure

1. First cup of wine and blessing	Lk 22:15–18(?)
2. Second cup of wine and *haggadah*	Lk 22:15–18(?)
3. Breaking of bread and blessing	Lk 22:15–19
4. Eating	———
5. Thanksgiving Cup and *birkat ha-mazon*	Lk 22:15–20.[9]

"Blessed be thou, YHWH, our God, King of the universe, who bringest forth bread from the earth"[10] is the blessing accompanying the bread. This is familiar to some Christians because of the eucharistic liturgy. The blessing over the cups of wine is similar. We do not know if Luke's cup of v. 17 was the first cup of a festal meal or the second, *haggadah* cup.[11] If the latter, then v. 18 could be interpreted as Jesus' *haggadah* reinterpretation of the Supper where he speaks of not drinking from the fruit of the vine until God's kingdom is established. At any rate, Luke moved rather quickly from the blessing over the first (or second) cup to the blessing over the bread, and then to the blessing over the thanksgiving cup. It is as though Luke did not wish to dwell on the preambles or even the meal itself, but was more interested in the actions at its conclusion. It is the postmeal thanksgiving cup mentioned in Luke that is of particular interest to us.

We propose that Luke's five disjointed dialogues coming on the heels of v. 20b, "This cup that is poured out for you is the new covenant in my blood," may be Luke's own embolism, *his* editorial expansion on and explanation of the third, redemptive blessing of the *birkat ha-mazon*. It is Luke's way of specifying the meaning of "new covenant" and "for you." Evidence for this suggestion may be found in verse 21, which begins with *plēn* (but), a Greek conjunctive adverb possibly indicating a break with the preceding material and introducing a new subject, and also serving to emphasize what is important. If we accept the festal meal context as affecting Luke's redactive purposes, then we suggest that the new subject introduced by *plēn* is that future redemption, a theme proper to the *birkat ha-mazon*, is now upon those sharing in the meal.[12] For Luke, these five particular dialogues clarify what redemption as announced by Jesus' actions is really about. Thus, the focus of the meaning of Luke's Supper account is located not in the *verbum* of the Institution Narrative, as has been customarily accepted with respect to the synoptic accounts, but rather in the embolism to the *berakoth* over the thanksgiving cup which, we suggest, is given in the five dialogues following the Institution Narrative. Luke provided this embolism in order to elucidate the meaning *for us* of Jesus' actions.

Before we look to the structure of the five dialogues, we turn to one more preliminary consideration, namely, the significance of the meal context in Luke.

Luke's Jesus and Meals

In most families holiday celebrations center around a special meal. Business luncheons are a popular means for breaking down defenses. Testimonial dinners are a fitting way to honor special persons or occasions. In spite of a society where more and more people opt for "eating out" and where more and more restaurants are characterized as "fast food" stops, meals still hold a favored place in the average person's life. The social context and accompanying conversation particular to meals invite an interpretive stance quite different from the same social situation or conversation unfolding under different circumstances. The meal offers a forum for profound personal sharing and for experiencing equality in community.

Sharing, equality, unity, choice, meaning—these are the hallmarks of a meal in its deepest sense. If "meal" contains the symbolic power to mean so much, we suspect that we need not look too far into the New Testament to see meals as part of the story Jesus unfolds. And, indeed, this is exactly the case.

One evangelical sign of the Kingdom is the bestowal of dignity on all as they share in Jesus' table fellowship. The Lord's table is inclusive; it offers a universal invitation to share: "God invites all men [and women] to it; he will save places for them at the table, if one dare put it that way."[13] Thus Jesus transforms this earthly sharing into the promise of an eschatological sharing (Lk 14:15–24; Mt 9:14–15; Mt 22:1–14). The end times are already being realized through a reversal of the plight of sinners, the poor, and outcasts. The final events of Jesus' earthly life are set in the context of eschatological glory revealed at meals (Lk 24:30–31; 24:41–43; Mk 16:14; Jn 21:9–12). These general remarks on the relationship of Jesus' meals and the eschatological Kingdom take on flesh when we consider more particularly the meals recorded in Luke's Gospel in which Jesus shares.

Luke has many parallel passages with the other two synoptics and John with respect to table fellowship, especially those passages that include food images Jesus used in his teaching. However, the number of meal pericopes and material unique to Luke leads us to conclude that Luke's Gospel has a special message with respect to table fellowship.

Jesus shares food nine times in Luke's Gospel.[14] The following diagram lists these nine meal pericopes with their respective synoptic parallels:

Luke's Meal Pericopes

1. Lk 5:27–39 (Mk 2:13–22; Mt 9:9–17)
2. Lk 7:36–50 (Mk 14:3–9; Mt 26:6–13)
3. Lk 10:38–42
4. Lk 11:37–41 (Mk 7:1–23 [no meal]; Mt 15:1–20 [no meal])
5. Lk 14:1–14 (Mk 3:1–6 [no meal]; Mt 12:9–14 [no meal])
6. Lk 19:1–27 (cf. Mk 4:25; Mt 25:14–30)
7. Lk 22:14–38 (Mk 14:17–25; Mt 26:20–29)
8. Lk 24:13–35
9. Lk 24:36–49.

The first six meals from the above list all occur during Jesus' teaching ministry, and, as we shall see shortly, they both confront us with the human situation as it is and announce unprecedented criteria for recognizing a new presence of the Kingdom. Luke's seventh meal scene has Jesus at a supper with his apostles just prior to his suffering and death. This serves to connect the previous meals and their criteria for realizing the Kingdom with the eighth and ninth meals recorded in Luke—meals of the Risen Lord—thus bringing together the whole of Jesus' table fellowship. The last two meals reveal the presence of the Risen Lord and closely associate this recognition with an opening of the disciples' minds to the meaning of the Scriptures being fulfilled this day (cf. 24:32 and 45) and with the realization of the Kingdom.

The common structure of the first six meals is our starting point in uncovering the meaning of the Lord's Supper. Two meals (5:27–39 and 7:36–50) have a parallel in the synoptics,[15] but it is enlightening to note the Lucan material after and before the pericopes under discussion: the accusation that John's disciples fast but Jesus' disciples eat and drink appears in both instances. This serves to highlight the power of meals to reveal an order other than that which is juridically or customarily prescribed. Therefore, even though there are synoptic parallels, Luke seems to be making a strong case for a deeper referent for the meal.

Two meals (11:37–41 and 14:1–14) have a synoptic parallel for the teaching, but in Matthew and Mark the instruction is not given as part of table talk. Luke, however, uses the meal context as a vehicle for the imagery of his teaching in the case of 11:37–41 and, in the case of 14:1–14, as a means for introducing the parable on humility using the imagery of a banquet.[16] This meal context allows for a more pointed interpretation and a contextual ambience for elaborating the instruction that also points to a deeper referent.

Two meals have no parallel in the synoptics. Both shed light on the material immediately following them. The story of Martha and Mary (10:38–42) contrasts two opposing kinds of "meal" preparation with two opposing kinds of banquets. The "Our Father" that follows (11:1–4) reinforces Jesus' support of Mary's preparation for the Kingdom. The Father will provide for those who are attentive to God. Preparation for the messianic banquet is preferred over concern for earthly food. In the other meal with no synoptic parallel (19:1–27), Zacchaeus makes restitution to those he has wronged and shares his goods with the poor. Jesus assures him of salvation. The parable that follows is a commentary on right use of earthly goods (19:11–27). Those who use this world's goods rightly—even though they gain in the process—are assured of God's favor. Those who fail to use this world's goods properly—even though they gain nothing or even though they may not have much at their disposal—will lose everything. Again, the referent for the meals goes beyond literal meaning.

These six meals in various ways critique the status quo and challenge us to reinterpret our reading of what is necessary to establish God's Kingdom anew for ourselves. The structure recurring in each pericope already gives us a glimpse of how a new order will be brought about. The six Lucan meals recorded before the Lord's Supper share three common structural elements:[17] (1) the meal situation that establishes the identity of the host or hostess and includes a description of an initial encounter; (2) an instruction by Jesus that draws a parallel between the distractions of this life and the wisdom of life with God;[18] and (3) a parable contrasting this world's banquet with the messianic banquet (this latter is missing from the 10:38–42 and 11:37–41 meals). A breakdown by verses of the six meal pericopes into these three structural elements may be diagrammed as follows:

Lucan Meal Structure

Meal Pericope	Structural Elements		
	1. Situation	**2. Instruction**	**3. Parable**
1. Lk 5:27–39	vv. 27–30	vv. 31–33	vv. 34–39
2. Lk 7:36–50	vv. 36–39	vv. 40; 42b–50	vv. 41–42a
3. Lk 10:38–42	vv. 38–40	vv. 41–42	———
4. Lk 11:37–41	vv. 37–38	vv. 39–41	———
5. Lk 14:1–14	vv. 1–2	vv. 3–6; 12–14	vv. 7–11
6. Lk 19:1–27	vv. 1–8	vv. 9–10	vv. 11–27

Luke's meals refer to a new order at the level of priority of what is possible with God over what is actually happening with humankind.

Meals were a very important part of Jewish culture and scores of dietary and purity laws governed them. Jesus rejects this juridical approach, placing emphasis instead on an alternative referent. By welcoming sinners, the poor, and other societal outcasts, Jesus' proclamation of the Good News becomes a lived reality, instructing the elite, the wealthy, and oppressors about the new order of the eschatological Kingdom.

We cannot help but conclude that table fellowship is an important structural pattern in Luke. Could his message have been conveyed just as well without the meal context? We think not.

Luke's "table fellowship as interpreted by the table talk constituted the Gospel."[19] In the meal scenes, Luke shows Jesus as much at home with Pharisees and tax collectors as he is with the poor. He uses this very hospitable situation (in which the fellowship has presumably fostered a relaxed and congenial camaraderie) to further his Good News message. Minear remarks that "nothing revealed more clearly than behavior at table the divine reversal of social norms and men's [and women's] reaction to that reversal."[20] In table fellowship the presence of the Kingdom as messianic banquet is contrasted with hindrances to the realization of the Kingdom as symbolized by the exclusion of some from the table.

Perhaps Luke was merely reflecting the importance of meals for early Christian communities[21] by using this familiar gathering as a simple device for shaping his message. But the importance of the relationship of meals to an understanding of the messianic banquet pushes us to delve deeper.

Luke's Account of the Lord's Supper

We suggest a parallel exists between the threefold structure of Luke's meals and the structure of Luke's Passion Narrative taken as a single literary unit.[22] First, the situation is a supper where Jesus is the host and the apostles are the guests. The Institution Narrative is so revolutionary—the food to be shared is the Master's Body and Blood—that the scene is set for the two subsequent structural elements. Second, the meal concludes with disjointed dialogues that are a teaching opportunity during which Jesus explains what he has just done and prepares his apostles for what is to unfold. The third structural element of Lucan meals, a parable, is not so explicit (at least in the usual parabolic form).[23]

The parallel between the threefold structure of Luke's meal pericopes and Luke's Passion Narrative makes the same contrast between future and present or between the Kingdom and its hindrances apparent in both. This contrast is made even clearer by the table talk which is the middle element that connects the Supper with the Passion proper. Two tasks are now before us. First, we need to account for our position that the table talk, vv. 21–38, is a literary unit. Second, we need to consider the implications of this table talk when considered as the middle element between the Supper and the Passion.

Vv. 21–38 as a Literary Unit

The first step in determining vv. 21–38 as a literary unit is to settle exactly how many disjointed dialogues Luke records. We take the position that there are five: Judas's betrayal (22:21–23), the dispute over who is the greatest (vv. 24–27), the prediction of the apostles' glory (vv. 28–30), the prediction of Peter's denial (vv. 31–34), and a mission statement (vv. 35–38). Though some exegetes list only four dialogues, taking all of vv. 24–30 as one,[24] two arguments support a fivefold division. The first draws on obvious thematic differences between vv. 24–27 and vv. 28–30: a shift from disputation to a prediction of glory. Another looks to the various sources for these verses. The following diagram lays this out, where "M" signifies that Luke follows Mark (though usually with his own reworking), "L" signifies Luke's own composition or his drawing on a source unknown to Mark and Matthew, and "Q" signifies a source known to Matthew but not to Mark.

Vv. 21–38: Source Analysis

1. M - vv. 21–22 (cf. Mk 14:20–21; Mt 26:23–24)
   L - v. 23
2. L - v. 24
   M - vv. 25–26 (cf. Mk 10:42–43; Mt 20:25–26)
   L - v. 27
3. Q - vv. 28–30 (cf. Mt 19:28)
4. L - vv. 31–32
   M - vv. 33–34 (cf. Mk 14:29–30; Mt 26:33–34)
5. L - vv. 35–38[25]

It is striking that vv. 28–30 are the only verses from the "Q" source. All the other verses are either dependent on Mark or else show Luke's unique editorial hand. This source evidence lends support to our position that there are five, rather than four, dialogues.

The next step is to show evidence that the five dialogues themselves form a single unit. The tendency by exegetes has been to avoid referring to vv. 21–38 as a single unit, simply regarding these verses as part of the larger unit, the Lord's Supper. A first hint that the dialogues form a unit comes from the fact that these verses so clearly show Luke's compositional hand. Four of the conversations have parallels in Matthew and Mark but are located elsewhere in those Gospels.[26] The fifth dialogue—the mission statement—has no parallel in the other two synoptics. Since Matthew follows Mark so closely we might ask whether Luke had a particular purpose in mind for this permutation. Did Luke follow his own source[27] and have his own purpose[28] for arranging his material as he did? We think so.

One justification for Luke's intentionally arranging this material is his penchant for parallelisms, for example, the parallel between Jesus at a supper (Lk 22:19), and Paul at a meal (*Acts* 27:35).[29] In the *Acts* account, however, the fourfold action over the bread—take, bless, break, give—is not followed by table talk, as in the Lucan account. This suggests that Luke had something very specific in mind for the table talk in the Gospel account. Another parallel may be noted between sections of Lk 9 and Lk 22: 9:3 || 22:36; 9:14–17 || 22:14–20; 9:20 || 22:33; 9:27 || 22:16, 29; 9:46 || 22:24. This parallel is dependent more on a similarity or contrast in content and language than on sequence.[30] The fact that Luke scatters the dialogues about chapter 9 but gathers them together in chapter 22 supports our argument for an intentional composition for 22:21–38 and our position that these verses be taken as a single unit.

Another argument for accepting the dialogues as a unit rests on whether or not Luke's Supper is a farewell speech.[31] If "yes" is the only possible choice, then the structure of a farewell speech precludes thinking that the table talk comprises a unit since the various dialogues would fit under different elements of a farewell speech.[32] If "no" is a possible choice—and there is support for this position[33]—then the dialogues could stand as a unit.

A third argument for Lk 22:21–34 being a literary unit derives from our conclusion above that there are five distinct dialogues. Luke often seems to group things in fives.[34] Consider these examples: the Infancy Narrative (annunciation of birth of John, annunciation of birth of Jesus, Magnificat, birth of John, birth of Jesus), Passion predictions (9:22, 9:44, 13:33, 17:25, 18:31–33), and the two praises and three petitions of the Our Father (Lk 11:2b-4).[35]

We have given evidence for a position that the table talk is composed of *five* dialogues forming a *single* literary unit. We now analyze these dialogues with an eye toward uncovering a different dimension of the meaning of the larger unit, the Passion Narrative.

Table Talk

Ideally, "after Peter's confession [of Jesus as Messiah] every act of eating and drinking with the master is table fellowship of the redeemed community with the redeemer, a wedding feast, a pledge of a share in the meal of the consummation; so also the meal on Maundy Thursday."[36] Yet the five snippets of conversation at the Lord's Supper testify that the ideal is far from realized even when the Master is still present. Each of the five individual dialogues is recorded by Luke in order to make a distinct impression on the reader:

1. Neither table fellowship nor Eucharist is a guarantee of the community's unity.[37] At a most solemn moment, the closest moment of unity between Master and apostles, one among them chooses to destroy the unity by betrayal.

2. A dispute at table is not something new in Luke (cf. 5:30; 10:40; 11:38; 19:7). Even the Lord's Supper is not exempt. Again, the community's unity is incomplete and the Master's message about the Kingdom has not become a lived reality.

3. The apostles' dispute is a continuation of Jesus' trials.[38] His ministry has been to bring those who share table into a fellowship that includes all. In spite of not achieving this, the apostles still share privileged places at the messianic table of the New Jerusalem.

4. Unlike Matthew and Mark, Luke places the painful announcement of Peter's denial at table (but after the meal) where "the intimacy of the dinner table casts deeper shadows of shame and guilt about Peter's denials; Jesus' anticipated forgiveness lays down a basic condition for how Christians are to approach the table."[39]

5. Luke's redaction of a mission statement at the Lord's Supper is a direct contradiction of Jesus' earlier instructions (Lk 9:1–11). Although there is little agreement among Scripture scholars as to the meaning of this puzzling statement,[40] it does seem apparent that Jesus hints at difficult times to come for his disciples. They cannot expect to be openly and warmly received as they formerly were in their missionary ventures, hence the need to be prepared.[41]

Could these five instructions have been taught outside of a meal context and still convey the same message? Or to put the question another way, what does the meal context bring to the message that Luke felt it imperative to include the statements as part of the post-Institution Narrative table talk?

One answer is that the meal context heightens and shapes the message. Meal means fellowship, so any departure from unity at a meal is doubly reprehensible. Another possible answer lies in the fact that so many of Jesus' important teachings about outcasts take place at meals. The dialogues at the Lord's Supper point to the apostles' continued misunderstanding about the Kingdom in spite of their being present with Jesus. The Lord's Supper table talk also points to the chasm that yet remained between the Master and his apostles. In spite of sharing in his greatest gift—his own Body and Blood—understanding and acceptance of who he is and what being his disciple entails would not be fully realized until the outpouring of the Risen Lord's Spirit.

The table talk at the Lord's Supper parallels the table talk in Luke's earlier accounts of Jesus and meals. Jesus' message is still about the poor and outcasts, though it now includes the wider sense of the apostles' lack of comprehension of who he is and what his act means and their identity with his destiny. Rather than a teaching or a parable of contrasts to help clarify what is needed for the coming of the Kingdom, the Lord's Supper table talk concludes by initiating the dominical action that is the paradox of paradoxes and the parable of parables: the Passion, death, and Resurrection of one man who finally and for all times makes the messianic era eminently visible and possible. The meaning of the Paschal Mystery is deepened by interpreting the dominical actions—both the sharing of bread and cup and the death and Resurrection—by means of the table talk. We are now in a position to examine Luke's account of the Lord's Supper table talk more closely to see what it says to us about the Paschal Mystery. The diagram on page 65 outlines our analysis. We examine the structure of the five dialogues from two analytical points of view.[42] One we call a "Linear Structure" and lay it out in the middle column. The other we call a "Concentric Structure" and represent it in the right column. We believe that through an interpretation of those dialogues, considered as a purposeful whole whereby the dynamics of the two structures interact to point to a single compelling referent, a meaning of the five dialogues is uncovered.

By "linear structure" we mean a sequential progression through the five dialogues exposed in terms of how one or more of the apostles is/are spotlighted. The apostles might symbolize the poor and outcasts, paralleling the focus of Luke's earlier meal pericopes. However, here the exclusion is not because the host failed to invite them to the meal but because the invitees' actions separate them from the host. Essentially, then, the focus is on the relationship of the apostles to the Master. The apostles' actions are the determining factor in that relationship.

Lord's Supper Table Talk

Text	Linear Structure	Concentric Structure
vv. 21–23 Judas' betrayal	Traitor ⇒ who is the worst? "it has been determined"	A Betrayal
vv. 24–27 Dispute over who is the greatest	Who is the greatest? How leadership is exercised: table service	B Boastful "which is regarded as the greatest"
vv. 28–30 Prediction of apostles' glory	Sequel to service: sit at table in Kingdom Table overcomes weakness ⇒ Promise: hope	C Kingdom realized "I appoint for you"
vv. 31–34 Prediction of Peter's denial	Because of promise, able to *turn* and strengthen others Consequences of table service	B' Boastful "Lord, I am ready"
vv. 35–38 Mission statement	Yet, transgression: possession of swords Consequences of lack of table service	A' Betrayal "this Scripture must be fulfilled in me"

In the first dialogue, announcing Judas' betrayal (vv. 21–23), the response of the apostles suggests that they are uncertain of their relationship for "*none* of the disciples knows who would be the traitor."[43] The dispute that breaks out (v. 23) conveys an answer to the question, Who is the traitor? The real question is, Who is the worst? (In reverse parallelism to the question in the next dialogue, Who is the greatest?) One answer points to the worst being the one who is uncertain of her/his relationship with the Lord. Another answer is given in the next dialogue (vv. 24–27), not by conclusive evidence of who is the worst but by discovering who is the greatest. Jesus' reply is a description of actions appropriate to discipleship: table service. Proper leadership is exercised in activity other than that which is expected. The greatest is the one who serves. So far, the linear progression is from uncertainty on the part of the apostles about their relationship to the Master to a revelation of the kind of actions that bring about the desired relationship.

The third dialogue,[44] a prediction of the apostles' glory (vv.

28–30), gives us a glimpse of the rewards of faithful relationship. The use of "appoint" in the present tense "indicates that the promise is fulfilled in a more proximate time."[45] To eat and drink at the Lord's table is already a fulfillment of the promise intrinsic to right relationships. Although the attention has thus far been on the apostles, we are reminded at this point in the linear progression that the relationship is nonetheless reciprocal. In fact, our fidelity to the relationship is finally advanced by the realized promise of future glory. The fourth dialogue (vv. 31–34) contrasts the apostles' infidelity (the second person pronouns in v. 31 are both plural in the Greek) with Peter's fidelity of leadership. Jesus pronounces that Peter will turn from infidelity to fidelity and is given the leadership mandate to "strengthen your brethren."

We might expect that this realization is all the apostles need in order to cement the relationship. We might further expect that the climax is reached in this fourth dialogue (v. 32), where the apostles are assured of leadership that will strengthen their relationship with the Lord. Yet, the fifth dialogue (vv. 35–38) seems to make an abrupt break with the evidently deepening relationship. There is yet another reversal and a return to transgression. In answer to Jesus' command to buy a sword, the apostles enthusiastically produce two, thus indicating that they have already in fact put aside Jesus' earlier injunction (Lk 10:1f).[46] This not only suggests the stubbornly enduring consequences of a lack of true table service but it also shows that— although the promise of reward is imminent for those with a right relationship with the Lord—nothing guarantees this relationship or reward. We remain disciples who are ever faithful and unfaithful, reckoned with the righteous and reckoned with transgressors.

The import of this linear structure reminds us that we are never to be smug in our service or the reward it entails, that we are always those in need of turning from infidelity to fidelity. Just when we think we have cemented our relationship with the Lord and are ready to sit at his table, we are confronted with our own transgressions. These bring us back full circle to the question about who is the traitor and the worst and the uncertainty of relationship that is apparent when we are traitors.

Jesus' teaching in Luke's earlier meal pericopes draws a parallel between the distractions of this life and the wisdom of life with God. By the linear structure of Luke's five dialogues at the Lord's Supper we are given a glimpse of the wisdom of life with God, a life of table service rewarded by sitting at the table in the Kingdom. We are still very much caught up in the distractions of this life even while we already share in that table.

We now take up a second analysis of the five dialogues. Rather than search for a thematic progression, we focus this time on textual indications that link the dialogues in our suggested concentric structure.[47] Four of the dialogues are rooted in the theme of humanity's transgression that we traced in the linear structure. The first and last dialogues accent betrayal, more specifically betrayal that "has been determined" (v. 22a; "this scripture must be fulfilled in me," v. 37a). The second and fourth dialogues highlight a boastful bearing and a misconceived confidence on the part of all the apostles in their relationship to the Lord ("which one of them was to be regarded as the greatest," v. 24), or on the part of Peter ("Lord, I am ready to go with you to prison and to death," v. 33). Luke shares an ironic insight into the human condition: though we are traitors and transgressors, we *perceive* ourselves as faithful to Jesus and expect our just rewards. Nonetheless, the real irony is exposed at the center.[48] In the third dialogue, Jesus assures the apostles of exactly that reward by appointing them to the Kingdom where they will sit at his table (vv. 29–30). While the dialogues reveal human frailty and seem to weigh us down, the concentric structure shows that frailty is overcome by the fidelity of the Lord and his promise of glory. The concentric structure helps us to focus on the Kingdom realized.

Luke is consistent in always favoring fulfillment. But in both the linear and concentric analyses, eschatological fulfillment is realistically tempered by human infidelity. In the linear structure, the emphasis circles back to human frailty and reminds us that table fellowship is never a guarantee either of right order or right relationship. In other words, we have a poignant reminder that the salvation Jesus' redemptive fidelity offers always remains a choice (for the arbitrary will) either to accept or to reject. The linear analysis points to a critique of our response of "turning." Ultimately, it is a reminder that the Kingdom is "not yet" in spite of the Lord's fidelity in bringing it about.

By a focus on the middle dialogue as center or turning point, the concentric structure allows us to bracket the very evident human frailty and instead give ourselves over to Jesus' promise of the Kingdom and thus to embrace it as a Kingdom already present to us. The concentric analysis witnesses to Jesus' fidelity to his promise. It is a reminder that the Kingdom is "already" and the redemptive actions of Jesus (distinguishing a normative will) remain forever stronger than the lures of human frailty.

These two analyses point to two different conclusions about the Kingdom: "not yet" and "already." Luke's Lord's Supper table talk juxtaposes these two seemingly disparate realizations into a single structural whole. The soteriological "not yet" confronts the eschato-logical "already" and releases a dynamic tension that—we sug-gest—actually defines the very meaning of the meal.[49]

In our discussion of the meal pericopes in Luke, we suggested that the Lord's Supper connects the first six meals and the last two meals of the Risen Christ. The structure of the meal pericopes taken together shows how soteriological criteria for realizing the Kingdom shown in the first six meals pave the way for the eschatological real-ization of the Kingdom in the last two post-Resurrection meals by means of sharing in the Lord's Supper.

The Supper, then, is the bridge between the distractions of this life and living in the wisdom of life with God in the Kingdom realized. Further, the structure of this larger body of Lucan meal material par-allels how the table talk of the Lord's Supper mediates the two sides of the dominical actions as redacted in Luke's Passion Narrative. The soteriological import of the meals, and in particular that of Sup-per, gives way to the eschatological import of the Passion, death, and Resurrection.

The five dialogues of Luke's table talk compose a masterfully constructed text, affording us a unique insight into the meaning of the events lying on either side of the unit. It is Luke's way of linking the dominical actions at the Supper with those events later that evening and the next day. In addition, it is his way of interpreting the substance of those actions for us. The historical event is revealed in Christ, but the thrust of Luke's interpretation refers essentially to us, to our response to that event.

Paschal Mystery: A Structural Interpretation

We delineate two dynamics in our structural analyses of Luke's Sup-per table talk: the "not yet" and the "already." We suggest that this prompts an approach to the Jesus events—the "Paschal Mystery"—that places its meaning in the structural dynamics or dialectic con-cretely experienced as a tension of living in the two kingdoms. To say this in another way, the meaning of the Paschal Mystery can be understood as a redemptive tension between soteriology and escha-tology.

This tension gives the pattern of our possible response to the Jesus event, a pattern characterized by the dynamic functioning as a vital *dialectic* played out in the ongoing realization of the Paschal Mystery. This dialectic is a constant reminder that we are both redeemed and still cooperate in the work of redemption, or that

Jesus has fulfilled his mission and still invites us to participate. This dialectic between soteriology and eschatology belongs, we further suggest, to the very heart of the Paschal Mystery itself, that is, this dialectic is structurally constitutive of the meaning of the Paschal Mystery.

Paschal Mystery as Dialectic

Christian living is a constant play between being confronted with the weakness of our own humanity and realizing the fruition of the divine plan to invite all to share in the Kingdom. The dialectic enables us to distinguish between the reality of evil, on the one hand, and the loving fidelity of God to us, on the other, regardless of our weakness. Particularly, this dialectic teaches us that as humans we have a genuine choice in the face of God's actions on our behalf and that God at no point threatens our freedom.

To understand the Paschal Mystery in terms of a soteriological-eschatological tension brings us face-to-face with the fact that the Paschal Mystery cannot be relegated to a past historical event. Hardly, for the Paschal Mystery has very much to do with our own relationship to God and to others in the concrete, everyday here and now. There is nothing "automatic" about Jesus' redemptive activity; that activity always demands an interaction with our own activity. While Jesus' fidelity to his Father remains the constant model for shaping our own fidelity, we can never be free from the necessity to make constant choices to enter more fully into the paschal event.

Luke's placement of the table talk *between* the Lord's Supper and Jesus' subsequent death and Resurrection directly links the Supper with those events.[50] One is interpreted by the other. For us, the soteriological-eschatological tension by which we might interpret those events is operative in our own remembering by taking, blessing, breaking, and sharing. This means that our ongoing appropriation of redemption is played out in the choices we make in our everyday lives. *That* is what we celebrate when we do Eucharist "in memory of me." The structure of Jesus' death and Resurrection is not only interpretive of his actions at the Lord's Supper, it is also a perfect analogue to our Christian living.

At the Lord's Supper there is a prior participation by the apostles in the death-Resurrection events. The table talk outlines the characteristics of that participation: misunderstanding but willing, weak but turning with strength, unfaithful but sustained by a relationship with the Lord. The Paschal Mystery holds all these realities of life in dynamic tension.

The originality of this dialectical approach to the Paschal Mystery lies in its accounting for human frailty as well as divine fulfillment, wavering infidelity as well as absolute fidelity, incomplete realization of the Kingdom as well as messianic fullness. The dialectic finally overcomes dualism because it holds all these polarities in a dynamic tension. The dialectic contains the whole of human-divine reality. The promise of the Paschal Mystery is the utter fidelity of God's proffering of the Kingdom and our sitting at the table of the Lord. The reality of Christian living is that this promise is ours to fulfill, and it remains our choice to work it out.

Paschal Mystery as Imperative of Praxis

In Part 2: Pastoral Interpretations, we shall address more adequately the broad ramifications inherent in interpreting the Paschal Mystery in terms of a soteriological-eschatological dialectic. Suffice it to say here that we see the embrace of both ministry and mystery as a single expression of the dialectic that reminds us that Christian living demands both action and passion; the two are simply different expressions of the same Jesus event. The liturgical interplay between Word and Sacrament—between the challenge of prophetic utterance and the timelessness of narrative proclamation—is indicative of the unfolding of the soteriological-eschatological tension of the Paschal Mystery.

The Paschal Mystery is the life, suffering, death, Resurrection, Ascension/Pentecost, and promised coming of the Lord. It is the whole Jesus event. It is tempting, though, to maintain a focus on the Lord and sometimes specifically on the earthly ministry of Jesus. But by drawing on Luke's unique composition of his account of the Lord's Supper, Passion, and Resurrection, and especially by noting the table talk as the link between them, we are able to expand the focus to include its meaning *for us*.

When we reflect on the Paschal Mystery in terms of a dialectical tension between soteriology and eschatology, we are certainly neither denying nor trying to minimize the Jesus event. We *are* focusing on it as *memorial*, as events that call the same response from us that Jesus called forth from his disciples. The real import of this dialectic is to recognize ourselves in that Jesus event. An imperative of praxis is only possible because of a prior appreciation of the Paschal Mystery as the foundation of our self-understanding. This is the source of our good works.

Interpreting the Paschal Mystery as a dynamic tension that cannot be resolved so much as lived brings us back to a link between liturgy and life. As the table talk interprets the Supper, Passion, and Resurrection, so does our life interpret liturgy and Kingdom. In other words, real liturgy can never merely be an appendage to life because it is only truly appreciated as the structure of Christian living itself—as a mimesis of the Lord's actions and promise and of our response. Nor can Christian living be an appendage to the celebration of liturgy because liturgy provides the ideological framework—in the best sense of the word "ideology"—that enables our Christian living to be meaningful human action. Ultimately, the Paschal Mystery is truly a celebration of our life in the Lord.

Part 2
Pastoral Interpretations

5

Christian Self-Understanding

In Part 1 we laid out a methodological framework to guide the pastoral interpretations of this second part. Ricoeur's methodic textual hermeneutics and his theory of meaningful human action have rarely been applied to the practical activity of actually interpreting texts. With only an occasional reference to interpreting the Word of God for preaching, Ricoeur could hardly be considered a liturgist; indeed, he even denies being a theologian. However, philosopher though Ricoeur is, his analytic framework offers much to the theologian and especially to liturgists who deal so specifically with texts. The manner of our application of Ricoeur's work to the liturgical milieu breaks new ground. In doing so, we postulate an innovative use of his insights. With respect to Ricoeur's methodic textual hermeneutics, we take the position that Christian living is connected to the two ontological moments of participation and appropriation, and the celebration of liturgy is connected to the critical moment of distanciation because we consider liturgy a text that is a window onto the meaning of Christian living. Similarly, with respect to Ricoeur's theory of meaningful action, we take the position that the ethical-political sphere is indicative of a participatory textual moment, a critique of ideology is essentially a distancing moment, and an imperative of praxis is redolent of an appropriative moment.[1]

A heuristic tool to help us shift from philosophical language to liturgical language and ultimately represent what we want to say about liturgical spirituality is the tryptich Life–Cultus–Life.[2] From the perspective of our model, religion and life are two expressions of our self-understanding, not dualistic entities. It is Christian living (life) that we celebrate in liturgy (cultus). As "cultus," liturgy is the work and care that prepares, brings to fruition, and celebrates our Christian living. It is a celebration of who we are and are becoming. Liturgy is God's work bringing us to perfection. There is a curious paradox here: we speak of liturgy as worship, as praise and thanks we give to God. And surely it is that. Nevertheless, liturgy is God's work to which we give ourselves. Without God's initiative, liturgy is devoid of the Spirit's fruitful dynamism. Without self-surrender, liturgy is devoid of meaning.

What is the soil and seed of the Christian life that we celebrate during liturgy? Or, to ask this question in methodological terms, what are the Christian originary events in which we participate? In this chapter on Christian self-understanding we focus on the moment of participation as shaping our Christian identity and on the ethical-political sphere and freedom as indicative of our self-understanding.

The mystery of God's relating to us constitutes a moment of participation whereby we locate ourselves within the ongoing tradition of those who have in all times and places had their eyes opened and recognize that the Divine is at the very core of our self-understanding. However, that mystery could never be fully revealed by individuals or by the community. It remains a quest for the Divine in which we enter ever more deeply into the Life proffered as our very identity. The Mystery, however, is fully revealed in God's Son, Christ Jesus.

The Jesus event (i.e., Paschal Mystery) was that meaningful moment originary to Christian tradition that conditions the intra-connectedness out of which Christians live. It is still remembered, still comes alive, as our community response within tradition to "do this in memory of me," as ever new possibilities still form, shape, and redefine the tremendous Life that we embrace as our very identity. Christian living is a journey toward Life; the Good News is that we are not alone on our path because we are already armed with the presence of the risen Christ.

Visages of Christian Identity

In order to capture the breadth and mystery of our self-understanding, we probe several visages of our Christian identity. Some of these have become popular catchwords for the Christian community, sometimes to the detriment of the richness of the identity we are trying to grasp. We examine the depth structure of who we are to see how the various visages interconnect into a profound identity that discloses who we are.

Paschal Mystery

All too freqently the Paschal Mystery is limited to the historical Good Friday–Easter Sunday events that liturgy celebrates during the

Easter Triduum. Certainly, the Jesus event is originary to Christian tradition. The critical question is, What constitutes that event? The Paschal Mystery? The death and Resurrection are central, no doubt. Each has something particular to contribute to the meaning of that originary event.

Jesus' death witnessed his relationship to the Father and his absolute fidelity to God's will. Jesus showed us that the Kingdom will come not when we do our will but when we do the will of the One who sent him. Jesus' death makes a difference because he showed us the germinal relationship between the coming of the Kingdom and fidelity to God. Jesus showed us that we must take the overtures of God seriously, often at great price. Yet, "cost" could hardly constitute such an enduring tradition as ours. If we add the Resurrection to the equation, we still have questions. Would we, then, have enough to constitute the tradition? The Resurrection as historical event occurred, not so much as a proof that Jesus is God but as a pledge that *Jesus lives!* In fact, the Resurrection made another event, Ascension/Pentecost, possible. By ascending to the Father, Jesus assured that he would be present in a new way. It is that presence that finally initiates the community and founds the tradition. Pentecost, the coming of the Spirit, completes the Jesus event as an event *for us*. The Spirit of the resurrected Christ—who descended upon the disciples—guarantees the presence of the risen Christ in the Christian community. The presence of the risen Christ means that the community has the power to live Life as Jesus did. In other words, the presence of the Spirit is originary to Christian tradition and enables our living the Paschal Mystery.

Pentecost can hardly be stressed enough. It is the event that unleashes the durable meaning of the Paschal Mystery. Without the descent of the Spirit, salvation would come from outside ourselves; we would be "acted upon." Moreover, the Jesus event would be relegated to historical time and space. Pentecost bridges the distance between Divine and human and invites us to be subjects in the unfolding drama of redemption. The Spirit within the Christian community is an ontological dimension that shatters the confines of time and space and lends an authentic historicity to Christian tradition. The Spirit is indicative of Christian identity and ensures that Christian activity leaves traces recoverable as a text objectifying the Paschal Mystery.

The Paschal Mystery is the complex revelation of the Father's wondrous plan in Jesus Christ that constitutes our Christian tradition. The soteriological-eschatological dynamic[3] that concretizes the Mystery in the here-and-now reality of everyday Christian living is the trace of the Paschal Mystery from which we recover its meaning. The constitution of a tradition, however, does not guarantee participants. To be Christian includes a public declaration of our participation in the tradition. Liturgically, we celebrate this at baptism.

Baptism

Sacramental reality is far more comprehensive than its ritualization. In fact, the reality of sacraments is not coextensive with their celebration. *Liturgy explodes the cultic occasion.* We celebrate baptism and Eucharist (and other sacramental moments) as ongoing realities that express our living the Paschal Mystery. Baptism [and confirmation] and Eucharist are sacraments of initiation because they are so closely connected with Christian identity. In particular, the renewal of baptismal promises and the weekly celebration of Eucharist remind us that Christian identity is more than a cloak we wear. It embraces an ontological dynamism into which we constantly grow by means of the choices we make concerning our Christian activity.

At the root of our Christian identity is an ongoing YES that is first ritualized at baptism.[4] Baptism is no magic moment. The celebration of the ritual of baptism is the manifestation of a faith dimension in our life that has only begun and will continue throughout our coming to full stature in Christ. One way to describe faith is as a YES before God: an enthusiastic readiness and reaching for fullness and conformity to God's will. Faith can never be definitive; it is a profession that unceasingly requires a full-throated chorus of YES. Faith has more to do with response-activity than it has to do with truth or doctrine. Faith is a constituting and a "texting" of Christian identity.

We publicly commit ourselves through baptism to be members of the Body of Christ who constitute and participate in Christian tradition. The rite opens us to a process that is *begun* at some point in our life and is *continued* by our saying YES to the various opportunities we have for making the Kingdom present for ourselves and others. Our life is characterized by saying YES over and over again; every time we say YES we realize more deeply what that means. (Or, we say NO and thereby weaken our commitment. We can even reject the process that was celebrated at baptism.) Curiously enough, in the practice of Christian doctrine we have always referred to faith as a "theological virtue," a disposition that is a gift from God. We are now stressing faith as a *response,* which seems contradictory. This obstacle is overcome, however, when we recall that our Christian identity is an ontological participation in God's life. All Christian activity—including our YES response to God's will—derives from our share in that life. There is no meaningful Christian action apart from that gift of life. The profound revelation of Jesus is that by calling us "friends," we share uniquely in Jesus' own identity.

Body of Christ

In our present day celebration of Christian rituals, we tend to minimalize the richness of the symbols we use. Baptism is certainly a case in point. Not so in the early church. Chapter 6 of Paul's letter to the Romans is one early expression of a baptismal theology that was effectively symbolized in the actual celebration of baptism. The one to be baptized was led down into a tomblike baptismal font where she or he, through a powerful use of symbol, experienced the death-dealing force of water. By means of this symbolic participation in death the catechumen died to the old self. The ritual itself veritably created an experience of death. Nevertheless, for baptism death is the door to life. The neophyte was brought out of the water and clothed in a white garment, an action symbolizing resurrection unto life. Now a new self lives, one who is a living icon of the risen Christ.

Drawing on the imagery and theology of Romans 6 (which has customarily shaped the baptismal theology of the western Church), we can say that baptism is a death/resurrection experience that discloses our participation in Christian tradition. Baptism is a sacrament of radical (root) identity: by dying to self we become someone new. We are the presence of the risen Christ when we profess YES to the Father's will and cooperate in the establishment of the Kingdom. In the prescribed actions of the baptismal rite, we symbolize a shift in identity from the old self who stands outside Christian tradition to a new self who participates in the tradition as a member of the Body of the risen Christ.

As Body of Christ, we all share a common Christian identity. Who we are—Body of Christ—is what our life is all about. Thus, our identity is also our ministry. In this sense it is useful to talk about a ministry of the assembly.

Ministry of the Assembly

When we say YES, when we identify ourselves with the Jesus event, we become the Other who is an expression of the risen Christ. This is why it was so important for the Spirit to come at Pentecost. Without the Spirit we could not share a common identity. As we enter more deeply into this identity and realize who we are, all our actions flow from it. To speak of a "ministry of the assembly" is first to speak of members of a community who *express their Christian identity in all they do.* By this exercise of who we are, we are better able to recognize Christ in the other. Literally, we *live into* our identity. We recognize ourself in the other. This identity has both a "being" and a "manifestation."

Priesthood of the Faithful. Jesus came *for us* in a most radical way: by giving himself over to death he made life possible for us. On our own we could never dare hope for or even imagine the wonderful identity made possible by God's initiative and our YES response. The baptismal call-response announces the radical graciousness of our God and expends God's inexhaustible lavishness. The Paschal Mystery makes actual what had only been possible. Jesus Christ the high priest enables us to say with Paul, "and it is no longer I who live, but it is Christ who lives in me" (Gal 2:20, NRSV). We, too, are sharers in the priesthood of Christ.[5] Our basic responsibility is to be holy. To share in the priesthood of Christ means that each of us, in our very selves, is an epiphany of the risen Christ.

The New Testament use of the term "priest" refers to Christ or to all the faithful.[6] It was only later that "priest" came to be applied to those ordained to preside at liturgy and who embodied the authority and leadership of the community. Even though the latter use has been so steeped in tradition that "priest" today is virtually equated with ordained ministry, the earlier notion of the participation of the baptized in the priesthood of Christ never quite died.[7] This is affirmed especially in *Mediator Dei*[8] and in Vatican II's *Lumen Gentium* and *Presbyterorum Ordinis*.[9] These documents reprise the characteristics of priesthood from the First Letter of Peter: We are chosen, holy, possessed by God, and given the task to proclaim God's mighty deeds.

Gifts of the Spirit. There are a variety of gifts. Baptism celebrates the presence of the Spirit and by it each of us is given a unique gift of the Spirit for the sake of building up the Body.[10] The Spirit confers gifts on each community according to what the community needs. Each of us, by being given the gift of the Spirit in baptism, is immediately faced with two tasks: to discern what our unique gift is and to minister it for the sake of the community. Ministry is a manifestation of our self-understanding by the exercise of our unique gift. Thus, ministry has less to do with choosing a task or getting a job done (although it obviously also includes that) than it has to do with who we are and our self-expression for the sake of others. The ministry of the assembly, then, is essentially a self-expression as and to the members of the Body. Without this ministry

Christian community fails to be an authentic presence of the Spirit of the risen Christ.

Each local Christian community has whatever gifts are needed to manifest the presence of the risen Christ today. If Christ is not present, then we have not discerned our gifts or we have not exercised them. When we are open to the Spirit and embrace our basic Christian ministry to be the Body of Christ, life-giving community is possible.

Community

Our remarks on baptism suggest that we are "bound together" ("religion" = to bind, to be in relationship). Often, the word we use for this is "community" although we generally use it in a rather narrow sense. What do we mean by community? One way to grasp this is to draft two distinctions.

Liturgical Community. The Hebrew word for community, *qahal*, suggests a helpful approach for an understanding of "liturgical community." This word, translated by the English word "community," is most frequently used of Israel when Israel is a community before the Lord; that is, when Israel is at worship and is a cultic assembly. The gathering of the assembly is a sign of what God is doing in and with God's holy people. The liturgical community is a locus of the revelation of God's presence.

We Christians are most clearly "one with" ("community" = *cum unus*) each other when we are standing before the Lord as a worshiping community. This is the deepest meaning of community because it is at liturgy that we are most able to recognize ourselves as the Body of Christ and therein express our common identity, our "one with" each other in Christ. Liturgical community is an expression of our very identity.

Sociological Community. An enduring reality of a sharing and caring Christian community is really only possible when we have truly experienced liturgical community. We have tended to put the cart before the horse. We seek something very worthwhile: a just, loving, and caring community. We suggest this cannot be a logically prior goal. A caring community is enabled and manifests itself most strikingly when the members recognize themselves first and foremost as belonging to each other because they first belong to Christ, because they first are a community before the Lord. When we stand before the Lord knowing ourselves for who we are and knowing others share this same identity, then and only then are we *compelled* to respond to Christ in the other and bring about just and loving relationships. In other words, the Kingdom is present to us when we live out our identity as Body of Christ.

This is our primary goal: we need to grasp more fully the reality of ourselves as the presence of the risen Christ for each other. This, in turn, becomes an impelling motivation for actually reaching out to others in need. If we recognize the other as the Body of Christ, then we cannot not love, we cannot not be just, we cannot not forgive. The motivation for right relationships is weak if it is only legislated. Right relationships falter as soon as circumstances highlight ever-present human weakness, ambition, and greed. Effective and lasting concern rests in the realization of our own shared identity as the risen Christ. Once we begin to live out of that identity, the world cannot help but be different.

The relatives of an extended human family share common ancestors and traditions. Often they share common values and customs. In many cases, there is even a physical "family resemblance." The shared identity characteristic of the members of the Christian community, however, goes beyond these collective traits. Relatives still remain separate, individual persons no matter how close they are to each other. Christians, on the other hand, may know little about each other and lack "closeness." Nevertheless, a bond unites Christians even more strongly than family ties. The Christian shared identity is Life; this is unique.

Our choice is not to opt for one or another notion of community. Our preliminary choice is to be the Body of Christ; the sociological notion of community with its imperative of right relationships flows from our identity. If we seek a community of right relationships without first recognizing and embracing our shared identity as Body of Christ, we have little motivation for sustaining the right relationships, and we quickly grow weary of trying.[11] A vital liturgical assembly will make a difference in the world because it is a community of right relationships. The point to stress is that our relationships to each other additionally concern our relationship with God.

Prayer

The realization of who we are in Christ really quite exceeds what we can grasp. Left to our own resources, we would probably become rather quickly discouraged. But we are not left alone. The God who chooses to love us is a God who reaches out and enables us. The only way we can begin to grasp what this means is to stand in awed silence before our God. Silence is a way to break out of ourselves and be attentive to God's overtures. That silent awe before God, none other than a basking in divine presence, is one way to describe prayer.

For many of us, "prayer" is "prayers." These formulae serve the important function of initiating us into God's presence and enabling several members to pray together. They are good stepping stones on the path toward a fruitful prayer life. For others, prayer may be "talking" to or with God who is a "silent" dialogue partner. This conversational approach to prayer highlights the very intimate nature of God's presence to us. While prayer has both of these aspects, the real objective of prayer is to enter into and become attentive to God's presence, to give ourselves over to God, rest in God, recognize God's love, and open ourselves to God.

We cannot command this opening to God's presence. True, we can practice. And we are able to secure conditions that foster attentiveness to God's presence. But in the last analysis it is always God's initiative that enables communion of presences.

An atmosphere of "silence" is one important condition for prayer. We are not a very silent society. Noise surrounds us. Activity surrounds us. "Things on our minds" is a way of life for most of us. God's overtures can easily be missed in all of this. So we must hush the noise, quiet our bodies, and still our minds so God may enter. When we become that comfortable with ourselves—and with each other—prayer in the sense of "awed silence before the Lord," basking in the Lord's presence, can happen.

Our remarks could leave the impression that prayer is a highly individualistic and passive exercise. This could not be farther from the truth. Even during our times of "private" (individual) prayer, we are still members of the Body, and our prayer touches various facets of accepting our self-identity as Body of Christ. We make a further distinction. Prayer is both liturgical and devotional.

Liturgical Prayer. We restrict the term "liturgical" prayer to refer to those ecclesial celebrations of the Paschal Mystery that have come down to us through tradition. In the Roman tradition this includes the celebration of the Liturgy of the Hours and the sacraments.

The privileged manifestation of the Paschal Mystery is characteristic of liturgical prayer. Liturgy celebrates the enduring meaning of the life-death-Resurrection-Ascension/Pentecost event so dynamically that we can assimilate that event as our own identity. Liturgy is why the Paschal Mystery pertains to us as well as Jesus; liturgy is why the Paschal Mystery is actualized here and now.[12] Further, liturgical prayer is always communal (though there are "private" moments during these celebrations) because the Body of Christ is manifested "where two or three are gathered." The gathered community is a symbol (sacrament) for the risen Christ. Since the Paschal Mystery pertains to all, no one individual can effect the Paschal Mystery event. Another characteristic of liturgical prayer is that its ritual expression is handed down through a tradition of celebrating communities. Liturgical rituals are the cumulative experience of the community's celebration of the Paschal Mystery.

Ritual is necessarily defined by a structure that manifests the Paschal Mystery and resists adding ceremony or components that would eclipse its fundamental meaning. Ritual is repeated action that concretizes aspect(s) of a people's originary events and their ongoing encounters with the mysteries of life in the here and now. It has the inherent capacity to enable us to assimilate the dynamic of the action. Because it is repeated, ritual can endure through tradition. It is important that we distinguish, however, between the deep dynamic that defines the ritual and the surface structure or specifics of the celebration that may change with time and cultures. We often confuse these. Ritual is a way for us to remember our origins and the mysteries of life. Ritual always transforms and marks changes in our self-understanding. It makes available the depth meaning of our common story as a people. This is why ritual is so structured and why it resists change. Ritual draws us into the action in such a way that we are free to give ourselves over to its meaning. Ritual creates us not vice versa. Ritual frees us to enter into defining events that are larger than life.

Liturgical prayer is ritual that belongs to the whole church and is a celebration of the efficacy of the Paschal Mystery of and by the whole church. It is a necessary critical moment in our Christian living. If we reshape liturgy to our own likes and purposes, we run the risk of bringing Christian ideology to a moment of disillusionment. Probably the more "enjoyable" and nonthreatening liturgy is, the less authentic it is. To permit liturgy to shape us is to underscore the absolute truth of the Paschal Mystery as authentically positing Christian ideology.

Devotional Prayer. Devotions have long been a part of Christian tradition. They are a necessary and healthy complement to liturgical prayer although they have sometimes supplanted it, especially in periods when liturgy was considered the domain of clerics performing a service on behalf of the community. It is important that devotional prayer be both private and communal because each has its own special benefits to contribute to Christian growth in prayer.

Private devotions are necessary in order to attune ourselves to God's overtures of presence. Those are the prayer times when we realize God's abiding love for each of us in a very personal and intimate way. They are the times when we encounter ourselves in Other; this in itself is a valid reason for praying. Private devotions are a way to confirm our self-understanding as Body of Christ, for we encounter in Other who we are. It opens the possibility of a genuine love affair between our God and ourselves. *Private devotional prayer is practice in the art of loving.*

Communal devotional prayer, on the other hand, helps us become comfortable with a response to God's presence in the company of other members of the faith community. It helps us to be attentive to each other at the same time that we open ourselves to God. Even more important, it is a reminder that we share a common identity. *Communal devotional prayer is practice in the art of responsiveness.*

Private or communal devotional prayer may be either spontaneous or structured. By spontaneous we mean a free-style structure that allows the prompting of the Spirit to shape the dynamic of the prayer. Prayer groups often pray in this way. A structured prayer may include formulaic prayer such as the Rosary or Novenas or it may be a structured prayer such as a Word service. When people are inexperienced with praying together, structured prayer can help them overcome initial discomfort and encourage them to be attentive and loving to one another. When people are more practiced in the art of prayer, spontaneous prayer becomes easier. Structured prayer can ease the way of burdened hearts during times of anguish or crisis; it may hinder spontaneity during times of great joy and exuberance.

These visages of Christian identity—Paschal Mystery, baptism, Body of Christ, ministry of the assembly, community, prayer—help manifest the Christian tradition in which we participate. Belonging, according to Ricoeur, is always effectively communicated through the tradition. Christian identity is more than a static given; it is a dynamic that is lived. Identity has to do with who we are; it is an ontological category.

Christian Self-Understanding

We have been considering some visages of Christian identity that help us describe who and how we are as Christians.[13] It becomes clear that the risen Christ is present to the extent we live out of this identity. Embracing and giving expression to our Christian identity is closely bound up with making the Kingdom present and with our ongoing cooperation in the redemptive mystery.

Each of these visages must be perceived as belonging to a whole.

The Paschal Mystery, originary to the tradition, is absolute in its promise and integrating in its effects. Baptism is originary to our own incorporation and continuance in the tradition and must be interpreted in terms of our public response to the Paschal Mystery. In this sense baptism brings the Paschal Mystery to concrete expression *for us*. That mystery *for us* is the reason for our common identity as members of the Body of Christ. Further, each differentiation of who we are as members of the Body—ministry, community, prayer—is an articulation of our own self-awareness in Christ. Though our fidelity along the way may be less than perfect at times, the whole—symbolized by God's proffer of Self to us—nonetheless remains intact.

Just as life itself is a gift, so too is the Life we share as a common Christian identity. If we approach this mystery as anything other than gift, we cannot even begin to grasp the breadth of the reality offered to us. True, to open ourselves to the gift of God's presence and recognize ourselves as members of the Body of the risen Christ is utterly beyond our own initiative.[14] The marvel is that our common identity in Christ does not depend upon our initiative but upon Jesus' utter fidelity to his Father; we are already assured of that by the death/Resurrection event. What is more, even our individual YES response is a collaborated response given within the context of and facilitated by the impetus of a tradition.

Participation in Christian tradition already identifies the ethical-political sphere of meaningful Christian action. Further, the tradition—particularly in its liturgical expression—embodies the normative will that confronts our arbitrary wills. The confrontation reminds us we are a subject who must affirm the act of Christian existence. No mere intellectual process, the affirmation of the act of existing is manifested in concrete human actions. In other words, Christian self-understanding is *acting* that ratifies and continues the tradition by its very nature. Christian freedom is radically living within the tradition. The novelty of Christian freedom is that it derives from Christian identity (the Body of Christ). Freedom is an ontological order, and its reality is an expression of who we are.

These interpretations of visages of Christian self-understanding remind us of the commitment of early Christians. The response of martyrs in the face of persecution makes little sense until we realize the extent to which their radically new identity guided their actions. Outsiders to the community exclaiming "see how they love one another" is another indication of the parity of Christian identity and Christian action.

As Christians who participate in a tradition, the very expression of our identity constitutes the tradition. That expression is what we have specifically called a "text."[15] In other words, Christian identity is expressed in meaningful human action that leaves traces in the tradition that endure through the tradition as texts and become available for interpretation. To interpret the *documents* of human action is to interpret human action. To interpret the *documents* of Christian existence is to interpret Christian existence. Because liturgy is a privileged document of Christian living (since both liturgy and Christian life share the same Paschal Mystery referent), the interpretation of liturgy is actually an interpretation of who we are as Christians.

We point out again that this is a reversal of the customary tendency to see life as a witness to how well we have been open to the "grace" of liturgy. We are reversing the logical order of liturgy and life and suggesting that liturgy is a celebration of Christian identity. Without a sense of our self-understanding, authentic celebration is impossible. This reversal is critical: unless it is grasped, the methodology underlying our approach to liturgical spirituality cannot be understood. The interpretation of liturgy is more than an intellectual exercise for scholars. The interpretation of liturgy is the life task of Christians because no other interpretation can help us understand ourselves as Body of the risen Christ.

We have used the methodological considerations presented in chapter 3 to interpret what we have called visages of Christian self-understanding. In so doing, we have explored the content of the first term of our Life–Cultus–Life tryptich. In Ricoeur's terms, our interpretations at this point can only be a "guess" about Christian reality that must yet be validated. Validation is a critical task, a reflective moment, a function of distanciation. We propose that all celebration of liturgy is a critical reflection on our Christian self-understanding.

6
Liturgy of the Hours

In the previous chapter we surveyed different visages of our Christian identity. We propose that these visages circumscribe a participatory moment given as a Christian tradition in which we find ourselves and out of which we live. Christian living discloses a shared identity that is known through and continues the tradition. Because our shared identity as Body of Christ is so generously at hand (God is the ever faithful One), there is always a risk that we take it for granted. The moment of distanciation precludes any such uncritical stance toward our self-understanding.

Even though we never completely stand outside our participation in this shared identity, we Christians nonetheless build on and build up our self-understanding by critical reflection. Methodically speaking, we might say that one function of liturgy is to fulfill this critical, reflective requirement of Christian living. Liturgy, in this methodological framework, is a moment of distanciation.

These next three chapters examine and interpret Christian liturgy as methodic moments of distanciation. The format for all three of these chapters is the same. Each chapter begins with some introductory remarks about the liturgical reality covered in the chapter, proceeds with a detailed analysis of the structure of the particular liturgy,[1] and concludes with a pastoral interpretation of that structural analysis from the viewpoint of the soteriological-eschatological dialectic developed in chapter 4.

Since the Liturgy of the Hours still is not part of the regular schedule of liturgical activities in the average parish, it is germane at the outset of this chapter to reiterate some basic liturgical concepts with regard to this particular prayer: (1) Liturgy of the Hours is a celebration of the Paschal Mystery; (2) it is a public, communal celebration; (3) it is a text (icon, objectification) of Christian self-understanding; (4) Liturgy of the Hours is a ritual that is prescribed, it comes out of the tradition; and (5) it leads to change in self-understanding and meaningful action.

For a very long time in the Roman tradition, Liturgy of the Hours has been the private prayer of ordained clerics and the members of those religious Orders who pray it as prescribed by their Constitutions.[2] This historical development, however, is a far cry from its origin as the daily prayer of the Christian community celebrating its identity as members of the Body of Christ living the Paschal Mystery. Because it is liturgy, the celebration of the Liturgy of the Hours should not be something that a local community constructs; it is neither private nor even community devotional prayer. We reiterate that liturgy is a privileged manifestation of the Paschal Mystery, a door to our own self-understanding. Liturgy functions as a text, a concrete object enabling us to do a certain kind of critique of ourselves. We must keep in mind that a text is a document of human living and meaningful human action. It is a document, an icon, of our own self-understanding. Consequently, a text is not studied for its own sake but for the sake of the text producers and text readers (both of whom form the tradition that gives rise to the text).

Liturgy differs from most kinds of other texts because liturgy is constantly being produced. Liturgy is never a fixed text as are, for example, classic works of literature or art. The text of liturgy is necessarily fluid because its "authors" are subjects who live through a tradition. We celebrate liturgy as a part of a tradition that we, in turn, are helping to constitute.[3] Tradition refers to the moment of participation. When we critique that tradition, we have entered a reflective moment of distanciation.

The Liturgy of the Hours is a moment of distanciation whether we are engaged in an abstract exercise such as reading this chapter or prayerfully involved in its celebration. In both cases we step back from living the tradition (bracket the moment of participation) in order to take a fresh look at our response to the Paschal Mystery. It is a critical moment in that it invites us to make a judgment about the transparency of our self-understanding vis-à-vis the Body of Christ. The Liturgy of the Hours is the privileged daily celebration of the Paschal Mystery.

Structural Analysis

As with most Christian practices, the actual beginnings of the Liturgy of the Hours are hazy.[4] The structure and prayers of the earliest liturgical celebrations of the Christian community—from the time of Pentecost to the earliest texts with differentiated structure and prayers—are unknown. Although we can make some intelligent guesses from hints in text sources and reconstruct at least the main lines of the basic structure, we can conjecture very little about actual prayer style.

Overview of Development

No doubt, early Christians prayed daily. In the Jewish-Christian communities, daily prayer probably continued the familiar Jewish prayer practices of the synagogue gatherings. The structure of synagogue prayer was quite simple, consisting at least of psalmody and the *Tefillah* (or Eighteen Blessings, which basically function as intercessory prayer).[5] Quite significant for our inquiry is that the simplest structure of synagogue prayer—psalmody and intercession—is exactly the basic structure of the earliest examples of the Liturgy of the Hours. At whatever point in history Christians were dismissed from Jewish communities and began to develop in a uniquely Christian way, they obviously continued some kind of daily prayer together. It would have been instinctive for them to draw on the format they had used when they were still attached to the synagogue.

As Christianity grew and became more structured, so, naturally, did daily prayer. The community gathered morning and evening—the two natural times of the day when people of all cultures seem to gather for prayer—in a common location presided over by the bishop.[6] As we said above, the structure of their daily prayer was similar to Jewish daily prayer in its main lines—psalmody and intercession.

From the end of the second century, there is evidence that the celebration of daily prayer had specific Paschal Mystery thematic overtones. Morning prayer was always prayed as the sun rose, as a greeting to the resurrected Son. As the sun rises, we greet the risen son. Morning prayer has always had a strong Resurrection theme, a strong praise theme, a strong Paschal Mystery focus. Evening prayer, as we might expect from the time of day at which it is prayed, is a "dying" prayer. It focuses on how we have lived our Paschal Mystery identity during the day just ending. This is why Psalm 141[7] with its penitential theme is appropriate and why thanksgiving is offered for the light and blessings of the dying day. Evening prayer is a preparation for a period of waiting and emptiness during the night when we enter into the tomb with Christ. We might think of this prayer as occurring during the lower half of the daily ebb and flow of life and as containing low or quiet points as opposed to the high and jubilant points more appropriate to the first prayer of the day. While the overall themes of morning and evening prayer are harmonious with the time of day and with the appropriate Paschal Mystery emphases, the basic structure in both is psalmody and intercession.

Daily prayer was originally simple, ceremonial, and largely invariable: it was *liturgical*. Now commonly referred to as "cathedral" style office,[8] it was a prayer of praise and thanksgiving.[9] As time went on, monastic practice encroached on the celebrative, parochial practice of cathedral style morning and evening prayer where Christians sandwiched the ordinary activities of their day between specific times devoted to remembering God's redemptive deeds. These two natural prayer times of the day gave way to a mystique of "praying always." The monks had time and energy to devote numerous periods of the day to longer stretches of prayer. With more available time for prayer, the very simple structure proper to the cathedral office was necessarily modified because the monastic community could not sustain the celebrative quality of this kind of structure all day, every day.

The adaptations were structurally explosive. Rather than rely on the largely invariable psalmody of cathedral morning and evening prayer in which the psalms were specifically chosen for the time of day and congruent theme, monks prayed the psalms sequentially, covering the entire psalter of 150 psalms over a determined course of time.

The style of praying the psalms also changed. In cathedral prayer, the psalms were sung responsorially: a cantor would sing the strophes (stanzas) of the psalm and the assembly would "punctuate" the unfolding message of the psalm with a simple sung response. Because their response was vital, the members of the assembly were drawn into the prayer. Since there were no pews, people were free to move about and to make liturgical gestures that enabled them to participate in the prayer in body as well as in mind.[10] This simply does not work in monastic prayer style. Since the monks multiplied the number of times they prayed during the day to be consistent with their desire to pray without ceasing, they developed a prayer style that would sustain their prayer for longer and more frequent periods of time throughout the day. Invariable but thematically and temporally appropriate psalms gave way to larger numbers of sequential psalms so that the entire psalter was covered over a given period of time. Further, the responsorial style of praying the psalms gave way to a recitative mode. A monk (who could read—not a universal skill in those times) would pray a psalm aloud while the other monks kept themselves physically occupied with some kind of handiwork (like weaving mats out of bullrushes) and mentally joined with the psalmist in meditation. Monastic style is much more reflective or meditative.[11] There is the stimulation of the human voice of the one praying the psalms aloud, but each individual was engaged in a private prayer activity.

Even more structurally explosive is the introduction of a regular reading of Scripture: a *lectio continua* in which the Scriptures were read in their entirety, usually in the course of a year. With this innovation, the prayer of pure praise so characteristic of cathedral style very definitely gives way to a Word service that is more devotional in character. A difficulty is that, even though there is a gathering of the community, the clear perception of the daily prayer of the church as liturgical celebration of the Paschal Mystery is dimmed in favor of individual communion with God and edification.

The structural anomalies instigated by the monastic office impaired the very meaning of the prayer. The monastic office runs the risk of depriving daily prayer of its critical function as an objectification—a text, a document—of Christian living by turning it into a resource for communion with the divine. Critical reflection on Christian self-understanding gives way to devotional prayer that is more edifying in import. To put it another way, Liturgy of the Hours shifts from being God's presence and service of fidelity to humanity to being our service (cf. "office") of God. When the structure changes to what is, in effect, a Word service, the relationship between psalmody and intercession gives way to a much more reflective kind of prayer. The differences between cathedral and monastic prayer are structural, not just stylistic.[12]

The 1971 revision of the Liturgy of the Hours, sensitive to the *canonical* requirement for ordained ministers to pray the "office,"[13] includes both monastic and cathedral structural elements. For example, cathedral elements include antiphons and psalm prayers and the *Gloria Patri* at the conclusion of each psalm; monastic elements include the sequential arrangement of the psalms over a four-week cycle[14] and a (short) Scripture reading and response. In general, the revised office may be characterized as private, devotional prayer because of its present stylistic features as well as the fact that the Liturgy of the Hours has not been widely introduced in parishes as the daily prayer of the entire church.[15] A basic problem with the celebration of the Liturgy of the Hours has persisted even after the 1971 revision: the Liturgy of the Hours remains principally the prayer of clerics and some religious.[16]

Fourfold Structure

We now turn to examining the structure of morning and evening prayer as it is given in the revised Roman rite.[17] There are introductory rites (invitatory or introductory versicle and response, hymn) and concluding rites (blessing and dismissal) that help us to enter into and exit from the heart of the prayer, psalmody (including antiphons and psalm prayer as well as Old or New Testament canticles) and intercessions (including the Our Father and a collect). Also, reading the Word of God and response was retained as well as a gospel canticle (*Benedictus* in the morning and *Magnificat* in the evening). We see here a fourfold structure that is similar for all liturgical prayer: introduction, two central components that form the heart of the prayer and disclose the depth meaning, and conclusion.

Analysis of Introduction and Conclusion

The elements of the introduction and conclusion are so few and brief that it would be easy to miss them altogether.[18] Structurally, they supply the ritual components—simple though they may be—that enable us to bracket and then unbracket our participation in tradition through meaningful Christian living. This bracketing of self-understanding allows us to step outside the tradition in order to critique it. In other more pastoral terms, the introduction and conclusion help us enter into and leave the ritual action. They aid transition from life to cultus and then from cultus to life.

The introduction includes a short versicle with response and hymn. The hymn serves well to set a mood, both in terms of situating the prayer for its appropriate time of day as well as drawing the assembly into the ritual action.[19] Though there is no rubrical indication for a formal signing of self with the Cross at the beginning of each Hour, it has been customary to sign oneself on the lips with the cross (at the invitatory) or with the customary sign (at the other Hours) during the opening invitatory or versicle. Thus, the Liturgy of the Hours is a prayer sandwiched between signing ourselves "in the Name," similar to the eucharistic liturgy as we shall see in chapter 7. The conclusion incorporates blessing and dismissal. Our signing ourselves with the Cross establishes a trinitarian context for living the day. It also reminds us that our prayer is celebrated as a response to God's call to presence.

The introduction—brief though it is—promotes a transition from the human activities that precede the prayer to the special ritual activity that marks it. The conclusion transposes us out of liturgical time and back to the cares and concerns of everyday living. Their brevity ought not obscure the important role they play in breaking open the depth meaning of the Liturgy of the Hours. Without these bracketing and unbracketing activities, ritual is not set apart from ordinary human activity. Because of the bracketing of the ontological moment, a reflective critique is possible that opens up new possibilities for Christian living.

Analysis of Psalmody

A helpful description of the psalms for our present purpose is that they are the *poetic discourse of Israel*.[20] We break this description down into its three component parts and work with each one in the next three paragraphs.

Poetic **Discourse of Israel**. As poetic, the psalms have both a literal and a figurative reference.[21] They do speak of concrete situations within concrete historical situations, but they say more than this. They speak *for us*. The psalms are not only a human prayer, they are also *response*. The psalmist was quite comfortable in responding to whatever situation gave rise to the psalm. To speak of the psalms as poetic is also to enter into them in such a way that the language is a timeless and therefore always a timely language. We often find use of the word "today" in the psalms.[22] The psalms are more present than past or future tense. They enable us to be in touch with our originary events in our own time, which is quite removed from that of the psalmist.

Poetic *Discourse* **of Israel**. Here it is helpful to make a distinction between what may be called first and second level discourse. The psalms are essentially first level discourse, that is, unreflective and uncritical. This means that the psalms use the language of *response* and *prayer*, not the reflective language of theology. The psalms are a way for us to relate to God and to each other. Further, the psalms are essentially story. They are a constant recitation of the history of Israel. The psalms are one stylized way in which Israel recited its sacred history. The psalms symbolize the history of Israel's response to God's presence and celebration of God's mighty deeds. The praying of psalms in Liturgy of the Hours is a key structural element precisely because psalms objectify originary events. The performance[23] of the psalms, then, best serves a structural purpose when the movement (dynamism) proper to story or narrative is enhanced.[24] The very performance of the psalmody (whether as recitation, responsorial, or other manner of praying) is most helpful when it highlights the dynamism proper to each psalm. Far from mere edification, the praying of the psalms concerns an ontological dimension in terms of the transformation of self-understanding.

One way to think of the psalms is that they were to Israel what the Eucharistic Prayer is to Christians today. The psalms tell Israel's story just as the Eucharistic Prayer tells our story. This is an important point for a number of reasons. First of all, every time we pray the psalms we are reciting our originary events. The psalms liturgically commemorate God's salvific presence that continually constitutes Judaeo-Christian tradition and endures for all people at all times.

Christians have tended to pray the psalms within a Christological frame of mind. We look to how Christ prayed the psalms or to how his life was a reflection of what the psalmist longed to see.[25] But we must come to understand the psalms as the story of Israel in its own right. The psalms are an important connection between us and the very beginning of God's dealing with humankind. We are praying our relationship with God and experiencing God's response. Those originary events are ours as well. The Christological events are a moment in the tradition of God and God's people, but they neither erase the events that came before nor even require a reinterpretation of those events. To pray the psalms Christologically is to distort them because we have taken them out of their cultural context. It also shortchanges us because Israel's history stands on its own as our history. The psalms allow us to pray a much longer history and to clearly recognize that God's relationship from the very beginning of humanity is important for us today. What is said about Israel and God is what we are saying about ourselves and God. Our history begins with creation.[26]

Poetic Discourse *of Israel*. Even though the psalms are frequently attributed to an individual, especially David, we should realize that they are the stylized songs of Israel as a people.[27] The psalms are a communal response, handed down through a tradition that captures concomitant moments in that tradition. There is a dynamic in the psalms, then, that draws us into a larger framework. Psalms are neither private nor devotional prayers but cultic prayers that celebrate the making of a people. As cultic they are liturgical prayers. Therefore, they are a text or objectification of Israel's self-understanding.[28] The psalms remind us that the history of Israel is also our own. But more: they enable us to enter into the fullness of identity between God and Israel, the fertile soil from which our own Christian identity grows.

The psalms are a preferred invitation to share in the fullness of God's overtures of presence and God's continual invitation to share in a personal relationship that knows no limits. The psalms empower a messianic presence that proclaims God's love and fidelity.

Structure of Intercessions

The restoration of a Liturgy of the Word to each sacramental rite suggests that the scripture reading and response is the structural complement to the psalmody of the Liturgy of the Hours. However, since earliest examples do not invariably include a proclamation of the Word, we suggest its omission cannot simply be a structural anomaly unique to a particular period of history. On the contrary, from a structural vantage point, the lack of a Word service and the invariable inclusion of (at one time, lengthy) intercessions endorse this latter component as the structural counterpart to the psalmody. This is easier to accept when we realize that the intercessions are not a "shopping list" of needs presented to God.[29] Their liturgical function is quite different from this.

Structure. In morning prayer the intercessions are essentially invocations customarily addressed to Christ.[30] Given the Resurrection character of morning prayer, this is a natural structural pattern; our language addresses the very presence of the One to whom we are praying. Morning prayer is a prayer of risen presence; vocative language reminds us of this. At evening prayer the intercessions are more properly petition and include specific requests. This is structurally appropriate if we consider that at night we enter into emptiness and waiting by acknowledging our dependence on God and by asking God to bring us safely through the night. The final petition is always one for the dead, which captures very well the passion/sacrifice character of evening prayer.[31]

The basic structure of invocation consists of a short attribute of praise addressed to Christ and a response. For example, "Christ, you are the light of the World." "May your light dispel darkness." Invocation lends itself nicely to litanies. Intercession as petition, on the other hand, consists of an announcement of an intention, a time for prayer (this is usually omitted in actual pastoral practice), response, and collect.[32] If the invocations and petitions were restored to their proper structural form and more adequate expression, intercession could more readily function as the structural complement of the psalmody. As they presently occur in the revised rite, they are perceived more in terms of concluding rites. This veils their dynamic flow.

Function. Instead of listing needs, the intercessions function as a litany of praise.[33] The structural format of invocation/petition followed by a response is important in this regard. The intercessions serve to draw the assembly into deeper engagement with the prayer and generate deeper awareness that liturgical prayer is larger than the local assembly. The intercessions remind us that liturgical prayer is the prayer of the whole church, and they enable us to configure ourselves to the larger community sharing a common identity. Further, as the psalmody helps us remember God's originary deeds on behalf of the Chosen Ones, so the intercessions help us remember God's Chosen Ones in the here and now.

As mentioned above, in actual practice of celebrating the Liturgy of the Hours the intercessions take on the character of being part of its conclusion. This is especially apparent when the intercessions are quite short. Since we suggest that the intercessions are a major structural element in their own right and complement the psalmody, it would be better pastoral practice to pray the intercessions as a litany in a more extended and solemn manner.

Pastoral Interpretation

The relatively simple ritual of the Liturgy of the Hours may deceive us. This liturgy embraces all the dynamism of the Paschal Mystery as more structurally complex liturgies do. In the Liturgy of the Hours we have a compact, well-rounded rite. To return to our Life–Cultus–Life tryptich, the Liturgy of the Hours is a cultic moment that concretizes and critiques the Paschal Mystery as expressed by our daily Christian living.

A ritualized introduction facilitates a transition from everyday life to liturgical activity (from life to cultus). A ritualized conclusion facilitates another transition, this time from liturgical activity to everyday life (from cultus to life) whereby we venture forth to complete the interpretive act in the methodic moment of appropriation. The introductory and concluding rites expedite the transition back and forth between temporal time and liturgical time. Structurally, then, what we have is an introduction that helps us bracket the moment of participation and a conclusion that removes the brackets and allows a new participation through the appropriation of alternative or new possibilities for daily Christian living. These two structural divisions facilitate the movement to and from the critical moment of reflection. They frame and focus attention on the psalmody and intercessions. By so doing, the introduction and conclusion set in motion a structural dynamic that suggests a specific relationship between psalmody and intercession. More is at stake, then, than moving progressively through a ritual from beginning to end. The ritual is constructed in such a way that the relationship of the central divisions lays bare its deep structure.

The Paschal Mystery is the referent of all Christian liturgy. If we are correct in saying that psalm and intercession carry the freight of the deep structure, then their relationship makes present the soteriological-eschatological dialectic (which, we saw in chapter 4, describes the Paschal Mystery), the content from which flows a critique and offer of new possibilities to be appropriated for living. In the case of Liturgy of the Hours, this dialectic plays itself out in the "tension" between psalmody and intercession.

Psalmody—an idealized and comprehensive recitation of the relationship between God and God's people—captures an *eschatological* moment in which we liturgically experience the fullness of God's love and fidelity. Psalmody is a reassuring moment of hope in which we identify with all the promises God has already fulfilled. Their narrative genre, therefore, is essential to grasping the eschatological character of the psalms. By drawing us into God's story of relationship with God's people, the psalms bracket chronological time and enable us to enter into liturgical time during which God's past, present, and future deeds on our behalf are all experienced as "at hand" and fulfilled. The eschatological hope that can be released by the psalms has as its basis the witness to God's unwavering love and fidelity.

The intercessions, on the other hand, bring us back to a soteriological "need" in which we liturgically embrace the brokenness and interdependence of humankind. The intercessions—the invocations in terms of a recognition of who we are still becoming and the petitions in terms of a solidarity with those in need—open to us the content of each day's living. Choosing new possibilities for living the paschal events is no willy-nilly venture but a carefully crafted presentation of challenges to be embraced.

We hold the position that the dialectic of soteriology and eschatology plays itself out in the relationship between psalmody and intercession in the Liturgy of the Hours. We enter the dialectic in a moment during which we are immersed in eschatological fulfillment; we begin with a psalmodic sense of fullness, a sense of God's presence and utter fidelity, a sense of well-being. Only then do we move toward a sense of un-finishedness, a mandate, a sense of our own need to cooperate in redemption, a sense of what we still have to do that is brought home by the intercessions.

The deep structure integrates the introduction, eschatological-soteriological dialectic, and conclusion of the Liturgy of the Hours into a single liturgical act. A single dynamic thrust is at work; the key to disclosing this deep structure lies in the subtle shifts in a fuller revelation of God's presence. The movement is from (1) introduction:

God as *Other* who calls us to praise and worship; to (2) psalmody: God as *faithful* who acts on our behalf and brings us to fulfillment; to (3) Intercession: God [Christ] as *immanent* who hears our needs; to (4) conclusion: God as *guardian* who transforms and accompanies us on our daily journey. Each successive shift in presence draws God ever closer to our lives and invokes God as a subject of our human activity. The meaningful human action that is the imperative of the Liturgy of the Hours is not only *our* activity but *God's*.

In daily liturgical prayer the weight of the dialectic comes down on the side of soteriology. Eschatological psalmody—with its emphasis on our ideal identity, on disclosing the ideology that shapes our originary events, on messianic hope being realized—does indeed offer a moment of fulfillment, but this can only be fleeting in our everyday experience. In the celebration of the Liturgy of the Hours, the moment of eschatological fulfillment is chronologically first. This sense of fulfillment, however, gives way to an urgency to establish more earnestly the presence of God's reign that is captured in the soteriological import of the intercessions. Fulfillment yields to promises yet to be completed. The lingering strain of the Liturgy of the Hours is a confrontation with the work of God still to be accomplished. The soteriological intercessions that emphasize our solidarity with others and their consequent imperative of praxis demonstrate that a prophetic awakening to new and better possibilities is indeed what marks our days.

A close reading of an actual text of Liturgy of the Hours would uncover themes, symbols, and movement that could be further analyzed according to various structural methods. These surface meanings enrich and fill out our understanding of liturgy. Our purpose in this chapter, however, has been otherwise. We have looked to the larger structural division—the fourfold division of introduction, psalmody, intercessions, and conclusion—to give us clues to the dynamic that unfolds the depth structure. The soteriological-eschatological dialectic that we use to describe the Paschal Mystery suggests a framework for interpreting that depth structure. The "already-not yet" rhythm that is embedded in the relationship of psalmody and intercessory prayer mirrors a cadence of fidelity-infidelity that marks all of our lives.

When structural components follow one another with little regard for dynamic rhythm, ritual prayer quickly becomes tedious. When the manner of celebration enhances this depth dynamic, liturgy optimizes the prophetic critique of Christian ideology that is proper to it. Short though they may be, the introductory elements invite us to pause (bracket life) in order to respond to God's call to cultic presence. The psalmody and intercessory prayer afford a glimpse of fulfillment and incompleteness that defines Christian existence. The concluding elements bless our transformation of self and the choice to live new possibilities that make a difference in the world in which we live. Of such is the daily rhythm of Christian liturgical prayer.

7

Eucharist

If you are to understand what it means to be the Body of Christ, hear what Paul has to say: "Now you are the body of Christ and individually members of it" (1 Cor 12:27). If you are the Body of Christ and members of it, then it is that mystery which is placed on the Lord's table: you receive the mystery, which is to say the Body of Christ, your very self. You answer Amen to who you are and in the answer you embrace yourself. You hear Body of Christ and answer Amen. Be a member of Christ's body, that your Amen will be true.[1]

These words of Augustine uttered so long ago sound very much like they could have been penned by a post-Vatican II liturgist. Indeed, the realization that we "feast" on who we are brings this tremendous mystery of ourselves as Body of Christ within our grasp. This is no new or contemporary theology; its seeds were sown early on in our Christian tradition. Our very self-understanding is bound up with the tremendous love and beneficence of our God.

The metaphor "Body of Christ" has its most profound articulation in Paul. For him, this was more than a way of speaking. When he described the Corinthian community as the Body of Christ, he used this organic metaphor to explain exactly how closely related with each other we Christians are. The reality for Paul is that we are the Body because we share in the one Life. We call ourselves the Body of Christ because we share in the common food, the one loaf. Eucharist most eloquently symbolizes our self-understanding as Body of Christ. It is the "summit and fountain" of all Christian living. This now-familiar image from *Sacrosanctum Concilium* recalls our earlier Life–Cultus–Life tryptich, which we have been using to illustrate how the depth structure of Christian living is the same as the depth structure of its ritual enactment. The depth structure is accessible through a critical reflection on cultus (in this chapter, Eucharist) because cultus is a document of life. Eucharist celebrates the Paschal Mystery, and in so doing discloses that Mystery most profoundly unique to Christian living. Eucharist celebrates the Body of Christ.

The enduring meaning of Sunday Eucharist is disclosure of this Mystery. We truly celebrate Eucharist when that paschal reality truly defines our Christian existence. We hardly just "go" to Mass; this kind of language is indicative of a duality between liturgy and life. It is indicative of religion as "practices" rather than religion as "relationship." Rather, we come together in a symbolic action to remind ourselves what our life is all about. When we live liturgically, our everyday life is a living of the Paschal Mystery that we celebrate when we gather for liturgy.

In terms of what is radically important, the depth meaning of Christian life is the same as the depth meaning we celebrate at liturgy. When we celebrate Eucharist, we are not doing something out of the ordinary or something different (which is not to minimize the sacredness of the act), but we are celebrating that which our life as Christians is all about.[2] Eucharist captures the reality of who we are and can become and what our life is. We never "leave" life when we gather for Eucharist (though we do "bracket" it). We gather for Eucharist to join with others in a full and visible expression of Christian living as Paschal Mystery. Worship—in terms of offering what is "due" the deity—is most sublime when the offering is the Body ever conforming itself more closely to God's Son.

Structural Analysis

Four major divisions make up the eucharistic rite: Introductory Rites, Liturgy of the Word, Liturgy of the Eucharist, and Concluding Rite.[3] Each of these divisions has a number of components, but here we are primarily interested in the dynamic that runs through the rite as a whole and constitutes it as an integral celebration. Each individual component serves the purpose of the depth structure and can be understood only in terms of the meaning of the division as a whole. We do dissect the rite for analytic purposes and the ritual does actually unfold during celebration as a great number of discrete words, actions, and postures. Nonetheless, liturgy is a celebration disclosing its depth meaning as a whole, its complexity refined into a dynamic flow that carries the worshipers into sacred time and sacred space where God is encountered.

The various components of the eucharistic ritual as well as the style of celebrating them have changed throughout the tradition of the church. But from earliest times the basic structure has been observable. By examining each major division and pointing to links that integrate the rite as a whole, we begin to grasp the depth structure and meaning of Eucharist.

Prologue to the Rite

It has become fashionable among some pastoral liturgists to refer to the Introductory Rites as a "gathering rite." When we talk about a gathering rite for Eucharist within the framework of our Life–Cultus–Life tryptich, however, we suggest we are actually referring to the meaningful human actions of Christian living that are prior to the celebration and to which the celebration is linked. A "gathering rite" cannot be contained at a given moment and includes more than physically coming together. The gathering rite moves the undulations of everyday Christian living toward their climax: liturgical celebration. Meaningful human actions are the "stuff" of our celebration. The offering of Jesus to the Father incorporates the whole Body. The gathering—which is a *prologue* to the cultic occasion and of all meaningful human actions—serves as a focus and brings to closure a certain stage in our own self-understanding. The entrance procession of the ministers, with its accompanying song, may be interpreted as a ritual conclusion of the whole activity of Christian life itself readied for a cultic moment.

Introductory Rites

After completion of the gathering, the beginning of Eucharist itself invites a shift in focus from our action to God's action, from our worldview to God's purview. That opening gesture is one undertaken together: we sign ourselves in the name of the Father, Son, Spirit. The greeting by the presider is a further indicator of this shift, for the greeting is a declaration of trinitarian presence to the assembly.[4]

The rite proper begins with the Sign of the Cross. Grammatically, we begin with a series of prepositional phrases, which function in sentences to define a context, to situate, or to clarify. The Sign of the Cross, then, sets the stage for our "sentence"—indeed, the entire eucharistic action—that we are about to utter. When we begin "In the Name" we remind ourselves that this action we are entering is God's action. Our very first ritual gesture and words invite a bracketing of activities during which we put aside the demands of everyday Christian living and enter into ritual activity where God beckons us to abide in Presence. From the very opening gesture and words, we give ourselves over to God in an action that manifests the very Mystery we are. This action and these words symbolize God's calling us into cultic presence; our collective action and utterance are a response to that call.

When we celebrate Eucharist, we are called into God's always dynamic presence, a presence that touches us at the very core of our being and invites a transformation of self-understanding. The purpose of all ritual is transformation, and we enter liturgy's transforming process when we respond to God's call to do this action "In the Name." Response is our acknowledgment that we wish to embrace new possibilities for living in Christian existence, that is, for living the freedom of the daughters and sons of God. If we neglect to open ourselves to the mystery of God—to God's Presence—we cannot be open to the transformation that might happen. The kind of transformation that the Introductory Rites launch is a deepening of our own self-understanding as Body of Christ and a realization of how that can better be nourished. In addition, the Sign of the Cross that accompanies the Blessing at the conclusion of the whole rite is another indication of this transformation. The cultic occasion is set between two Signs that function as an *inclusio* between which presence is given over to Presence.

As we unpack the implications of God's call and give ourselves over to God's presence in the ritual action, we set a dynamic in motion that draws us ever deeper into the mystery of God's Presence. Ultimately, the transformation appropriate to Christian liturgy is a self-understanding in terms of becoming God's Presence for the world. By our presence, God is present. The Introductory Rites, then, are a critical moment to encounter God's Presence as call and invitation to Presence. God offers Self to us and asks that we answer the call by an openness to transformation that embraces divine Presence.

At the very beginning of our communal rite, we join together in Signing ourselves as Christians. The other components of the Introductory Rites can be interpreted as initial utterances of our response to God's vocative Presence. An integral and consistent celebrative dynamic would best be served by Introductory Rites accommodating a Sign and Greeting, a pause to recognize God's call and to prepare ourselves for a communal response to God, and a concluding prayer.

Liturgy of the Word

At first glance, the Liturgy of the Word appears to be primarily a cognitive moment. The change of posture from standing during the

Introductory Rites to sitting during the first part of the Liturgy of the Word suggests a "settling in." Yet, the structural components of the Liturgy of the Word, like the elements of the Introductory Rites, are many and varied and encourage more than mere hearing. In our analysis we begin with a central axis, the Gospel, in order to see how evangelical proclamation and the other components of the Liturgy of the Word encompass a reflective moment that is more ontological than epistemological.

Gospel. A number of ritual indicators point to the Gospel as central to the Liturgy of the Word: gospel procession, optional use of candle bearers and incense, ordained proclaimer,[5] standing posture. An even more telling indication of the importance of the Gospel for identifying the current at work in the Liturgy of the Word is the dialogue between proclaimer and assembly that precedes and concludes the proclamation.

The evangelical proclaimer does not begin by simply announcing the citation of the gospel text, as is the case with the first two readings. The dialogue begins with the liturgical formula "The Lord be with you" and its response. This formula occurs only four times during the eucharistic rite: It is one of the options for the apostolic greeting at the beginning of the Introductory Rites, it opens the Eucharistic Prayer as the first of the Preface dialogues, and it introduces the Concluding Rite. In all these cases, "The Lord be with you" begins a new major structural division[6] and serves to call our attention to a change in focus, usually accompanied by a change in posture as well (from sitting to standing). But this formula does not begin the Liturgy of the Word (when posture changes from standing to sitting). Instead it is delayed until the time for evangelical proclamation (when our posture changes from sitting to standing, the same pattern that accompanies "The Lord be with you" at the beginning of the Liturgy of Eucharist and the Concluding Rites). "The Lord be with you" readies us for the proclamation and points to its centrality, but even more than this, it alerts us to the centrality of the Gospel.

The gospel citation is announced by the proclaimer ("A reading from the holy Gospel according to N.") and, unlike the citation announcement for the first two readings, here the assembly gives a response: "Glory to *you*, O Lord." This response is significant in that it changes pronominal person, to second person direct address. The one being addressed is "*you*, O Lord." The same grammatical pattern is repeated at the conclusion of the proclamation: "Praise to *you*, Lord Jesus Christ." We use direct address pronouns ("you") only when we are speaking to someone who is actually present to us. The language surrounding the proclamation of the Gospel suggests that something far more strategic is happening with the proclamation of the Gospel than with the first two readings: proclamation constitutes a *personal Presence* of the One being proclaimed.[7] Moreover, this hints that proclamation is hardly a "speaking-hearing" activity; proclamation is an exchange of presences that motivates to action.

The very language of our responses to the proclamation of the Gospel acknowledges a personal Presence of the One we address. The Word is present in the very act of proclaiming. Evangelical proclamation is that of a Person. When we become aware of the current that is unfolding, we gain insight into what Good News is all about: the subject of the Gospel, Our Lord Jesus Christ, is present to us. Our direct address language does not take us back to the historical person and events of two thousand years ago. Rather, our language evidences an "im-mediate" encounter with Someone here present. The subject of the Paschal Mystery, the One whom we claim to be as Body of Christ, is present to us. In the very proclamation of the Gospel, we are confronted with the fullness of who we are: the Lord Jesus Christ. In the very proclamation of the Gospel we are confronted with the ideal self-understanding for which we strive.

During this moment in the unfolding eucharistic dynamic, God's vocative Presence encountered at the Introductory Rites shifts and is deepened to a personal, ideal Presence. We are faced with an Ideal Self who we are becoming. We are called deeper and deeper into the mystery of Presence. The Liturgy of the Word is showing us, here and now, what being the Body of Christ entails. The Gospel shows us the Christian ideal: be and do as Jesus was and did. In this way liturgy constantly makes the ideal of our self-understanding and the goal of ritual transformation available to us. Proclamation offers us a world of possibilities to be appropriated. These new possibilities are an enticement for transformation.

Other Components. The other components of the Liturgy of the Word serve to break open this personal, ideal Presence encountered through the proclamation of the Gospel. The first reading is usually from the Old Testament (the Sundays of Easter excepted when we read the account of the early Christian response to the Resurrection as recorded in the Acts of the Apostles) and is thematically related to the Gospel and liturgical season.[8] This is an important innovation of the revised *Lectionary* that enables us to experience God's relationship to Israel and God's relationship to us through Christ as a single tradition. The Responsorial Psalm is an opportunity for us to savor and respond to God's interventions in human history and connect them with the Gospel. The Second Reading is a semicontinuous reading of the New Testament letters. It is not usually thematically related to the Gospel and Old Testament reading.[9] The homily breaks open the Word, explores new possibilities for living the ideal, and helps us to face the prophetic/soteriological import of the ideal Presence with a personally receptive attitude. The Profession of Faith publicly acclaims our YES to living the ideal; it extracts an initial response to the ideal Presence.[10] The General Intercessions unite our acceptance with that of the whole church and engage us in a community response. God's Word invites response. Word and response synopsize the disparate elements of the Liturgy of the Word and shape this division of the eucharistic rite into a whole.

The prophetic judgment inherent in the proclamation of the Word has salvation rather than condemnation as its purpose. Its soteriological import confronts us with the fact that we are called to open ourselves continually to new possibilities. Response to the Word makes a difference in the world because it has first made a difference in self. Response is an ontological category that transforms our self-understanding. Far from an illusion of ideology, the content of the Liturgy of the Word is the Person who is Head of the Body. This cultic pole of the Paschal Mystery dialectic reminds us of our solidarity as a pilgrim people and breaks us out of solipsism. The Liturgy of the Word excites assembly to be community.

Liturgy of the Eucharist

Just as paying attention to language use helped us interpret the Liturgy of the Word, it can also help us grasp the depth meaning of the Liturgy of the Eucharist. This division of the eucharistic rite is preceded by the preparation of the altar and the presentation of the gifts.[11] The operative word here is "preparation." These are minor rites that have the import of "housekeeping tasks." At the same time, these activities of preparation and presentation should not be taken lightly. They can function in a very pointed way to ease the shift in posture, spatial focus, and thematic content from the Liturgy of the Word to the Liturgy of the Eucharist. And, if the Liturgy of the Word has been particularly challenging, some time of quiet and silence[12] could be beneficial.

Eucharistic Prayer. The core of the Great Thanksgiving and the axis of the Liturgy of the Eucharist is the recitation of our Christian story. Though the Eucharistic Prayer is addressed to God (usually to the Father) in prayer language, much of this prayer uses the third person pronouns and past tense verbs characteristic of a narrative genre.[13]

We learn a great deal from little children about the way stories work on us. Most children have a favorite story, and they can hear it over and over again, sometimes even in the same sitting, and never tire of it. What is more, each time a child hears a favorite story it is as if s/he hears the story for the first time: the child laughs or becomes frightened or squeals with delight at the very same lines each time the story is read.[14] When children hear stories, they enter into them in such a way that they live *in* them. So each time they hear a story, it is truly new. They pass beyond their temporal time and physical space and enter into the story's time and space. It is a new adventure, a brand new story with brand new insights. We might relate what Jesus meant when he said "Unless you become as little children" (cf. Mk. 10:15) to this childlike, trusting attitude of being caught up in the events of the story. Jesus invites us to enter into our own Christian story as it is told and retold in Eucharist with the same childlike attitude, to live in God's time and space so that each time the story is new for us, with new possibilities.

After meeting the ideal we are to become in the Liturgy of the Word, we are given the opportunity to hear the Christian story and give ourselves over to it in such a way that the story becomes our own. In this way—within the very shape of the ritual action—we are invited to *become* that Ideal. Entry into the story/narrative of the Eucharistic Prayer lends an immediacy to the Christian tradition that is characteristic of liturgical time and space. Ideal Presence gives way to a Presence characterized as *We are.* God's Presence in the dynamic of the eucharistic action is now such that we recognize ourselves as the Presence.[15]

By entering into the story, we live the story. This is a *ritual* rather than an intellectual activity. We enter into God's story in such a way that the response God called forth in creation, called forth from the Israelites, called forth from Jesus, and called forth from the church through the ages is our response. When we remember—tell—the Jesus story, we live in the same event. We hear the Christian narrative in such a way that, by being drawn into the story, we give the same response as did the historical respondents.

Three acclamations punctuate the unfolding of the Christian story during the Great Thanksgiving and help us to experience it as a deepening dynamic: the Holy, Holy, Holy, which responds to a recitation of creation, salvation, and redemption as related in the Preface; the Eucharistic Acclamation, which responds to a recitation of the Jesus event; and the Great Amen, which not only concludes the last part of the Prayer that remembers the church and her needs but is also a climactic acclamation for the whole Eucharistic Prayer. These acclamations are performatives that function to draw us deeper and deeper into the story. They are *our* initial response to the story that draws us into its narrative world. The world of the Eucharistic Prayer is God's world in which the fullness of possibilities for Christian living are ready at hand. The story is always proffered to us. The wonder of our God is that we are invited to respond ever more deeply, to come face to face with our identity as the Body of Christ.

Communion. The communion rite is a complex set of words and actions, evolving from our identity and witnessed to by eating and drinking as a sign of our having given ourselves over to that identity by entering into the Christian story. We *dare* to pray "Our Father" as Jesus did because we recognize ourselves as united with the Head of the Body. We exchange a Sign of Peace as a greeting to each other who is the Body of the resurrected Christ.[16] We receive the Body of Christ because we know ourselves *to be* the Body of Christ.

The ministerial exchange during the communion procession—"Body of Christ." "Amen."—is a faith declaration of our newly experienced identity. When communion is anything other than this, we "eat and drink to our own condemnation" (cf. 1 Cor 11:27). Communion is a confirmation of our entry into the Paschal Mystery. It is our personal and public proclamation that we are the Body of Christ. It is only because we know ourselves to be the Body that we dare eat the Body. We are nourished on the Body and Blood of the Lord because we have lived who we are in the story and this nourishment is all that will satisfy us. Communion, then, makes sense only within the dynamic flow of the whole Liturgy of the Eucharist. In this context, communion is our response to the story. When detached from the proclamation of the Christian story, receiving communion risks being little more than devotional practice.[17] When integrated with the Liturgy of the Eucharist, communion is a profound manifestation of who we are and are becoming.

Concluding Rite

At the Concluding Rite, the "We Are" that characterizes the Presence of the Liturgy of the Eucharist gives way to a Presence characterized as "for others." We are sent forth by blessing to "go in peace to love and serve the Lord."[18] Our identity cannot be contained. Having been sent forth, we burst the timelessness of the ritual and, fortified by a new self-understanding, we are eager to share our identity with others and to make a difference in the world. The blessing reminds us that we live "In the Name" and are sent forth as such.

We are sent to live the dynamic of Presence into which we have entered and have become. Clearly, liturgy explodes the cultic occasion. Presence, then, is a key not only to understanding the deep dynamic of Eucharist but is also a key to how we live the Paschal Mystery in our daily lives. Each time we reenter the ritual celebration of the Paschal Mystery, we try to open ourselves so that more of that Mystery is apparent in our life. Sometimes, when we celebrate Eucharist, we are more aware of this dynamic of Presence than at other times. This statement of simple human reality reminds us of the basic thrust of the Introductory Rites: eucharistic action is God's action in us and on our behalf. By giving ourselves over to that action we need not be overly concerned with what is happening. Our chief concern is to lose self in the dynamic of Presence, to lose self in the deepening Mystery. The transformation unique to the eucharistic rite directs us to the heart of the Paschal Mystery originary to us as God's holy people.

Pastoral Interpretation

There is no absolute pastoral guarantee that we will come to a deeper self-understanding by taking part in the eucharistic rite. No foolproof formula exists that automatically brings transformation in our self-understanding. That, too, is part of the mystery and part of our "incompleteness." What is guaranteed—because of the witness of God's fidelity through time—is God's proffer of divine Presence. It ever remains our challenge to open self to that Presence, no matter how imperfectly we may do so.

We have considered a structural analysis of the eucharistic rite shaped by a realization that Eucharist is essentially about a deepening Presence of God to us that transforms our very self-understanding. That Presence was traced through the four major structural divisions of the rite. The movement is from (1) Introductory Rites: God as the One who *calls* us to cultic Presence; to (2) Liturgy of the Word: Christ as *Ideal Self* whom we are becoming; to (3) Liturgy of the Eucharist: we enter the story and live the reality that *We are* the Body of Christ, the Bread of Life; to (4) Concluding Rite: We are Presence *for others*. This analysis is a moment of distancing ourselves from participation in Christian tradition so that a new self-understanding for living our identity as Body of Christ may emerge. What happens on the other side of the Rite, consequent upon realizing our new self-understanding as "Body for others," is a moment of appropriation in which we actually live the dynamic of Presence as our Christian existence. The cultic moment, the moment of distanci-ation, is dialectically related to participation and appropriation. In our basic Life–Cultus–Life tryptich, our manner of Christian living before the cultic, distancing moment of interpretation is bracketed—set aside, held in abeyance—at the Introductory Rites. Life on the other side of the cultic moment is assumed as a new participatory moment when we "unbracket" the life that was suspended at the beginning of the cultic occasion and ready ourselves to live new pos-sibilities. Thus, the Introductory Rites and Concluding Rite have more to do with the transposition of self in and out of the cultic occasion than with the import of the moment of distanciation itself.

The critical work of distanciation, we suggest, is uncovered in a dialectic between the Liturgy of the Word and the Liturgy of the Eucharist. That dialectic is one between Ideal Presence and Self Presence; between a prophetic announcement of who we are to become as the ideal self and who we can actually be as messianic Presence when we give ourselves over to the story and recognize *ourselves* in the breaking of the bread. It is a dialectic between the "not yet" and the "already"; between soteriology and eschatology unfolding as the deep dynamic of the cultic moment that is the text of our own Christian lives.

As the ritual proceeds from the Liturgy of the Word to the Liturgy of the Eucharist, the rhythm of that dynamic moves from a soterio-logical toward an eschatological moment. The "stuff" of our every-day lives—and of our own pre-understanding—is challenged by the prophetic confrontation with our Ideal self, the Lord Jesus Christ. We are confronted with the "not yet" of our existence: We are still weak humanity always in need of embracing the grace of salvation. This soteriological moment flows into an eschatological moment that discloses the full riches of what it means to be Body of Christ. Eucharistic feasting invites satiated rest in the Lord. On Sunday, the day of Resurrection,[19] the dis-ease of our own unfinished selves finds rest in the messianic fullness of the Banquet of the Lord. We sit at the Lord's table and share in a lavishness quite beyond imagi-nation or deserts.

Both baptism and Eucharist are sacraments of Christian identity. Baptism objectifies the radical identity of those who call themselves Christian. Eucharist objectifies the depth possibilities of that identi-ty. The transformation characteristic of eucharistic ritual involves no change in identity. Transformation invites an ever growing open-ness to the Mystery of who we are. In other words, the new possibil-ities available for appropriation make a difference in living our relationship with God and with each other. The term "new possibilities" refers less to ethical injunctions and concrete behaviors than to changed patterns of living the covenantal relationship that defines how we are bound to God and to each other.

Eucharist is perhaps the potentially most rewarding sacrament and also the most dangerous with respect to Christian ideology. It is dangerous because the unmitigated recognition of ourselves as Body of Christ and the bid to rest in that identity might entice us to the greatest illusion. There is but a small step from shared identity to idolatry. A taste of messianic fullness may lull us into forgetting that fullness is always in dialectical relationship to soteriological need. The unmitigated recognition of ourselves as Body of Christ may so satisfy our human requirements for social integration that we may become an exclusive community that truncates or even entirely ignores the demands of appropriation. The rubrical and ministerial requirements necessary for authentic eucharistic celebration may legitimate an authority that is too narrow and self-serving and promote illusion instead of critique.

Eucharist is methodically explosive when it critiques Christian ideology in such a way that illusion is shattered and all are indeed equal sharers in the One Body. Eucharist is most rewarding when its fruit is reconciliation with each other and creation because our shared identity is more motivating than our ambition for wealth or success or power. Eucharist is most rewarding when the availability of new possibilities for living our Christian self-understanding is an opening of Christian freedom, a living *in* Christian existence that is continually creative of the tradition. Eucharist is most rewarding when the taste of messianic fullness prompts us to make a difference in the world in which we live.

Eucharist is a celebration where we live in the fullness of who we are becoming. It is a moment of hope and finality that balances everyday despair and contingency. The eucharistic dynamic of entering into and living God's faithfully proffered Presence invites us to place ourselves on the table and become the One we eat and drink to the glory of God and the coming of the Kingdom.

8

Liturgical Year

The object of inquiry for this third and final chapter in our analytic interpretation of the structure of liturgical texts is different from that of the previous two chapters. Both the Liturgy of the Hours and Eucharist are specifically defined rituals actually celebrated by Christian communities. The Liturgical Year is hardly available in quite the same way, at least in terms of how we usually think of ritual as a distinct cultic occasion. Nevertheless, we propose that the Liturgical Year *functions* like ritual texts because like all texts it, too, is structured, the product of purposeful formation, bears the stamp of human existence, and reflects the various styles of differing traditions. Furthermore, the Roman Calendar and *Roman Lectionary* are documents that shape and give meaning to the Liturgical Year even though they are not rituals as such. Therefore, the Liturgical Year lends itself to the analytic moment of distanciation and functions as a kind of quasi-ritual text.

Earlier, we underscored the Liturgy of the Hours as the daily liturgy of the church and Sunday Eucharist as the weekly celebration. In this there is an opening up, a broadening of the reach of the Paschal Mystery. The consolidated intensity that characterizes our daily living with its morning/Resurrection and evening/dying rhythm opens onto the restful rhapsody of Sunday that crowns our week. With the Liturgical Year we are beckoned into an even larger, integrating venue of the Paschal Mystery.

The celebration of liturgy brings home our need for constant reinterpretation in order to enter into the depths of the Paschal Mystery. This reinterpretation happens on a daily, weekly, yearly basis: each different time frame cues us into a distinct experience of the Paschal Mystery. We begin with something manageable, a daily celebration, and advance to ever more expansive celebrations. As we enlarge the venue, however, the Paschal Mystery is more focused on a specific aspect or event that may foster a greater awareness, but we also risk losing sight of the whole. The daily and weekly celebrations keep bringing us back to that whole. On the other hand, the recurrent yearly celebrations permit us the luxury of a longer preparation to savor and experience a particular moment of who we are and what our Christian living is really all about. The yearly cycle allows us to concentrate on one element or other of the dynamic in a focused way and encourages a heightened sense of celebration.

From the viewpoint of our Life–Cultus–Life tryptich, the Liturgical Year functions as a quasi-cultic moment. This is another reason why we treat it as a moment of distanciation. The Liturgical Year is able to bring home to us how our everyday living is liturgical and how the import of our whole life is cultic. The Liturgical Year clearly parallels our experience of life as a cadence of festivity (high points) and ordinariness (ebb points). It, too, unfolds as high points (the two festal cycles) and ebb points (the two periods of Ordinary Time).[1]

The ebb and flow of rhythm is harder to recognize in the daily celebration of the Paschal Mystery because it is concentrated in such a short time span. For "night people" morning prayer is hardly a good time to celebrate a festive occasion (though it is just that). For "morning people" evening prayer may hardly be celebrated with the attentiveness it deserves for they have already "retired." Sometimes, one or the other (or even both) of these prayers is omitted. A natural rhythm is perhaps a little more easily experienced in the weekly cycle where there can be an obvious celebrative difference between weekdays and Sunday. But the contrasts become most apparent during the yearly unfolding of the Paschal Mystery where, parallel to our human experience of festivity and ordinariness, we experience the cadence of the cycles of liturgical celebrations.

Our assertion that "liturgy explodes the cultic occasion" makes particular sense in light of the whole Liturgical Year. The cultic occasion, which is scarcely confined to a ritual moment, extends beyond the ritual celebration into the very living of life. Now we can see the importance of the context of the quotation from Augustine with which we began chapter 7. This quotation is actually from a post-Pentecost sermon, and its power and meaning flow from this festal context. Pentecost assures that the Spirit of the risen Christ is among us. It is only possible to speak of ourselves as the Body placed on the table because we are a Spirit-filled community. It is only with Pentecost, which brings the Spirit to dwell among us, that the paschal event touches us in the here and now.[2] The Spirit is the "enduring meaning" of the Paschal Mystery. Because of Pentecost, the paschal work becomes our work, our life.

Structure

The Liturgical Year is arranged by cycles of festivals and by the schedule of Scripture selections given in the Sunday *Lectionary*. If we omitted the Liturgy of the Word from our liturgical celebrations, the Liturgy of the Eucharist itself would hardly account for the Liturgical Year.[3] The riches of the proper (changeable) components of liturgy are derived from and/or colored by the Liturgy of the Word. Thus, the *Lectionary* selections for the two festal cycles of Christmas and Easter are ordered to those cycles. Obviously, at Christmas we hear about the coming(s) of Christ and at Easter about the Resurrection. The *Lectionary* assignments for Ordinary Time, undistinguished by a specific Paschal Mystery event, are a semi-continuous reading of a Gospel.

Overview of the Liturgical Year

The Liturgical Year, as we have it today in the Roman tradition, is given in the 1969 revised Roman Calendar, yet another work of liturgical revision in the wake of Vatican II. One principle at work during the construction of this revised calendar is the simplification of the Liturgical Year in such a way that the temporal calendar—that is, the list of festivals and seasons that are proper to the regular unfolding of the Paschal Mystery during the course of a calendar year—is quite clearly primary.[4] The sanctoral calendar, on the other hand, lists the various festivals that support and help us break open the meaning of the Paschal Mystery and contributes to the basic dynamic underlying the Liturgical Year. When we interrupt the temporal calendar with too many saints days and special festivals—a problem that historically recurs with predictable regularity and requires periodic calendar revision—the unfolding of the Paschal Mystery during the course of a given year tends to be obscured. Even the fourteen solemnities retained on the 1969 calendar are there only because they have a direct relationship to the Jesus event and help bring out the Paschal Mystery import of the entire Liturgical Year. The feasts (twenty-five of them, mostly of gospel incidents such as the Transfiguration and feasts of the Apostles) and memorials (a few over a hundred of them, mostly optional) that remain on the 1969 calendar are there to help the faithful enter into the Paschal Mystery; they are not foci unto themselves. The point of this simplification is to enable the Paschal Mystery to stand out as that which shapes the meaning and celebration of the Liturgical Year.[5]

The two festal cycles of the Liturgical Year are Advent/Christmas/Epiphany, with which it begins, and Lent/Triduum/Easter. These two cycles are counterbalancing intensifications of specific aspects of the mystery of salvation celebrated during the Christian year. They are those festal times when we are particularly keyed into the originary events that gave rise to the Paschal Mystery. In addition to these two festal cycles, all those other weekly celebrations of the Resurrection make up the Sundays of Ordinary Time. Ordinary Time is divided into two parts: a shorter time coming between Epiphany and Ash Wednesday and a longer period between Pentecost and the First Sunday of Advent. Altogether, Ordinary Time fills thirty-four weeks of the year; it is the longest season of the calendar, taking up about two thirds of the entire year.

Advent/Christmas/Epiphany Cycle

Although attention at the beginning of the church year popularly tends to be on Christmas Day, this cycle is not a one-day celebration with a passing thought given to Advent and with Epiphany missed almost entirely. Instead it is a *season* consisting of a preparatory period (Advent) that leads to a Solemnity (Christmas) that leads to an appropriating period (Epiphany).[6] The readings for this season are chosen specifically to bring out its dynamic meaning.

The initial theme of this cycle is already apparent even prior to the first Sunday of Advent[7] in the last Sundays of Ordinary Time, reaching a climax with the Solemnity of Christ the King. The semi-continuous reading of a synoptic Gospel (which marks Ordinary Time) builds in a crescendo toward a strong parousia/eschatological thematic focus that is carried into the Advent season. This eschatological focus does not completely shift until the third Sunday of Advent when it gives way to a more soteriological one as we look specifically toward the celebration of the Incarnation. Another shift occurs with Epiphany and the Baptism of the Lord,[8] two festivals that direct us toward Mystery being celebrated as a here-and-now event and which point to our own work in manifesting the coming of the Kingdom. While the cycle sustains its own internal eschatological integrity, there is a forward movement toward soteriological import, reminding us that we are the Body of Christ continuing the mission inaugurated by Jesus.

We thematically divide the Advent/Christmas/Epiphany cycle into three parts according to the *Lectionary* selections. The first part of the cycle includes the last three Sundays of the Liturgical Year and the first two Sundays of Advent and focuses on the final events that will usher in eschatological fulfillment (stay awake, be watchful, be on guard). We begin this festal cycle with a clear concentration on the eschatological pole of the Paschal Mystery dialectic. As we near the middle of Advent, this theme takes on a definite preparatory leitmotif (one is coming who is greater than I) that shatters our yearning for parousia and eschatological fulfillment and shifts our temporal focus to the immediacy of God's Presence and involvement in human affairs. Even the feasts that come on the heels of Christmas—the martyr Stephen, Holy Innocents, Holy Family, and Mary, Mother of God—remind us that our taste of eschatological fulfillment is flavored by the exigencies of human existence. Finally, the third part of the cycle (Epiphany and Baptism of the Lord) shifts theme again, this time to a clear manifestation of Christ's mission. The end of this cycle leads to Ordinary Time and the proclamation of the beginning of Jesus' public ministry; the Advent/Christmas/Epiphany cycle leads us to a soteriological moment. Within the festal cycle itself, the predominance of the eschatological motif is never eclipsed; it remains dialectically related to the soteriological pole.

The delineation of these divisions is determined by a thematic progression in the readings from Sunday to Sunday and may be uncovered by a synchronic reading of these seasonal texts.[9] The following table gives one thematic interpretation of the Advent/Christmas/Epiphany lectionary readings. The word(s) given in italics are key to recognizing our suggested thematic progression.

Sunday	Theme
32nd Sunday of Year	Beginning of *heightened expectation*
33rd Sunday of Year	How will we know when to *ready ourselves*?
34th Sunday of Year (Solemnity of Christ the King)	*Presence of the Kingdom* in Jesus' actions
Advent 1	*Be ready*, stay awake, be on guard
Advent 2	John *prepares the way*, awareness heightens
Advent 3	*One is coming* who is greater
Advent 4	Annunciation: beginnings of the *manifestation of the Messiah*
Christmas	God's *Presence is made flesh* and dwells among us
Holy Family	Hidden life: *transition*
Mary, Mother of God	Meaning/cost of *salvation*
Epiphany	*Manifestation* of salvation for all
Baptism of the Lord	Beginning of *public ministry*

The Advent/Christmas/Epiphany cycle is a celebration of the comings of Christ: second coming at the *parousia*; first coming at the Incarnation; and every day in our living the Paschal Mystery and at celebration of liturgy. As we move through the Advent/Christmas/Epiphany cycle, the liturgies integrate these comings into a single Paschal Mystery event. The focus shifts from Christ to us as we move through the cycle of celebrations. The presence of Christ at the end of time and at the beginning of the Christian era is enfolded in a presence of Christ in us. This dynamic is most apparent when our celebration does not isolate the festivals into different historical events or realities. To fixate on one celebration to the diminishment of any of the others is to eschew the dynamic mystery of Christ's coming. Further, this cycle reminds us that, finally, the coming of Christ is an event into which *we* enter and are absorbed.

Lent/Triduum/Easter Cycle

Again, our attention tends popularly to be on Easter Sunday as an individual day but this cycle, too, is a season. Similar to the Advent/Christmas/Epiphany cycle, we have a preparatory time (Lent), a Solemnity (the Easter Triduum), and an appropriating period (Easter/Pentecost). The readings for this season, too, are chosen specifically to bring out its meaning.

Lent. Until recently, the emphasis during Lent was on more negative aspects of sacrifice and sin, hence our tendency to approach it as a penitential season separate from Easter. This serves to isolate Lent from the dynamic of the whole cycle. However, since the current emphasis is to see Lent as a time for bringing baptismal preparation to closure, its direct relationship with the Easter Vigil and, in this sense, with the whole of the Easter Season is made more clear. We must be careful here to realize that baptismal preparation concerns more than those who will be baptized at the Easter Vigil and others involved in the baptismal preparation program.[10] Actually, Lent is a time when the whole community prepares (with the candidates) for baptism so the renewal of vows by all at the Vigil is, indeed, a significant component of the rite. The early practices of asceticism—especially fasting and almsgiving—are directed toward conversion, not toward "punishing" ourselves. Differing from a mere devotional practice, the renewal of baptism at the Easter Vigil is a solemn entry into the Mystery being celebrated. It is a public avowal of our self-understanding as Body of Christ. In this sense penance has quite a positive thrust and is an external sign of the interior promptings of the thematic movement of the Lenten season. Thus, Lent carries a baptismal import for the whole Christian community.

We note four thematic shifts in the Lenten *Lectionary*. Ash Wednesday, predictably, sets the tone for Lent: all the external practices in the world, if not directed toward interior conversion, reap no lasting reward. The first and second Sundays of Lent emphasize the two natures of Jesus: the human nature triumphing over weakness is a model for our own Lenten objective; the divine nature revealed in glory is a promise of what awaits the faithful. We begin Lent on a note of hope, encouraged by the fidelity and glory of Jesus the Christ. The next three Sundays evince a thematic shift. Year A Gospels emphasize water symbolism and its meaning for risen life in Christ.[11] In these Gospel selections pertaining to living water, the movement is from desire to having our eyes opened to the new life that living water promises. Each week draws the assembly into an encounter with living water that marks the way an individual responds. Years B and C confront us with our own weakness and recommend that *we* must choose to act and to change. They encourage our conversion process by reminding us that Jesus is present to us as we grope for salvation. We overcome blindness to embrace salvation and identify with the Jesus who acts. Another shift occurs on the sixth Sunday of Lent, Passion (Palm) Sunday, which eloquently testifies to Jesus' salvific activity as we are beckoned to enter into the passion events; Jesus acts and we are saved. Only by giving ourselves over to the Cross can we enter with him into glory. The following table lays out a thematic progression through Lent.

Sunday	Theme
Ash Wednesday	True religious practice is *interior*
Lent 1	Temptation in desert: *triumph over human weakness*
Lent 2	Transfiguration: *harbinger of divine glory*
Lent 3	Year A: *desire* for living water
	Years B,C: *blindness* to own weaknesses; fickleness of heart
Lent 4	Year A: living water *opens our eyes*
	Years B,C: Action taken toward *embracing redemption*
Lent 5	Year A: water *brings new life*
	Years B,C: evil is exposed and *Jesus acts*
Passion (Palm) Sunday	Ultimate meaningful human action: *do the will of God*

Overall, Lent is an opportunity to face our abiding human weakness and to turn from self toward God. It continues the soteriological thrust that marks Ordinary Time, but there is a clear movement toward wholeness. The dynamic of this preparatory season, then, carries us toward the Easter events, the high point of the whole Liturgical Year.

Easter Triduum. The Easter Triduum is so powerful its message hardly needs comment. Its structural elements, however, deserve some careful scrutiny.

The Easter Triduum begins with the Mass of the Lord's Supper on Holy Thursday and concludes with evening prayer on Easter Sunday. Originally there was only one Eucharist on Easter Sunday, the one celebrated at sunrise on Easter morning that concluded the great Vigil. Our attention in this section is directed toward three liturgies that—as far as is pastorally feasible—are to be considered as one celebration: Holy Thursday Eucharist, Good Friday liturgy, and the Easter Vigil. One structural indication of this tripartite but unified Triduum celebration is the singing of the Gloria (optionally accompanied by ringing of bells) at Holy Thursday Eucharist, a doxology that has been suppressed during Lent. The Gloria is also sung (again, optionally accompanied by ringing of bells) at the Eucharist of the Easter Vigil. The Gloria functions as an *inclusio* and helps us grasp the integrity of these three rituals as a single cultic celebration of the Paschal Mystery.

Two (convergent) themes mark the eucharistic celebration of Holy Thursday. One derives from the second reading and concentrates our attention on the Lord's Supper and the "institution" of Eucharist. The other theme derives from the selection from John's Gospel portraying Jesus as a servant who washes the feet of his disciples. The Easter Triduum begins with a liturgy that summarizes the meaning of the Paschal Mystery in terms of nourishment for life and model for service. Two ritual accretions to the usual eucharistic ritual highlight the two themes: the footwashing that replaces the Creed and functions as a profession of faith, and the procession with and adoration of the eucharistic elements that concludes the liturgy and draws attention to the Lord's giving of his Body and Blood for us. The stripping of the altar that customarily takes place at the conclusion of the Holy Thursday ritual prepares the assembly for the sober simplicity of the Good Friday liturgy.

The Good Friday liturgy consists of a mix of liturgical and devotional elements. If we would omit the devotional elements (adoration of the cross and communion)[12] from the liturgy, we would be left with a structure consisting of an introductory rite (entrance of the ministers in silence and an opening prayer), a Liturgy of the Word with a vortex at the *solemn proclamation* of the Passion, the solemn Prayers of the Faithful (the intercessions), and a dismissal. This adjusted, familiar fourfold liturgical structure sustains a soteriological import throughout. Especially since the proclamation of the Passion stops short of a Resurrection account, the liturgy underscores a soteriological moment without an eschatological, dialectical counterpart. The Solemn Prayers of the Faithful, prayers for all the peoples of the world, are a primary means for entry into a profound soteriological moment during which we experience solidarity with all of humankind, whatever their various needs. Good Friday is a prolonged entry into the "not yet" of redemption. This liturgy leaves us hungry for the hope that only life can bring. Death has its sting.

The Easter Vigil is the most solemn as well as the most complex of our Christian liturgies. The entire Liturgical Year converges on this most sacred of nights, during which we spend the hours of darkness in expectant waiting for the glorious moment of sunrise Resurrection. The structure of the Vigil is fourfold and consists of the Service of Light, the Liturgy of the Word, the Liturgy of Baptism, and the Liturgy of Eucharist.

The Easter Vigil, too, would benefit from some structural adjustments. Rather than begin with the proclamation of the Easter light—a joyful and eschatological moment—the Vigil would more fittingly begin with the Liturgy of the Word. This would ease the transition from the essentially soteriological moment of Good Friday suffering and death. Its transitional function would then be more apparent, especially since the Liturgy of the Word unfolds as a proclamation of salvation history. By entering into our great story of salvation, we spend the long night of waiting by reflecting on the various faithful and unfaithful responses of God's people through our history. Baptism is a joyous faith response to this proclamation. After this takes place all the assembly—both the newly baptized and those already baptized—then greet the Light of Christ and recognize therein their own identity. Proclamation of salvation history, celebration of rebirth in baptism, and proclamation of the risen Light of Christ *all* lead toward sunrise when we proclaim the Easter joy and celebrate Eucharist.[13] The whole dynamic of the Vigil ushers in a thoroughly eschatological theme that is taken up by the celebration of the "Great Sunday."

Easter and Pentecost. One of the many significant changes of the 1969 Roman Calendar is to call the Sundays between Easter and Pentecost the Sundays *of* Easter. This is the time of the "*Great* Sunday" that accents the eight Sundays of Easter in terms of a single celebration. It is easier to see this singularity when we uncover the thematic movement connecting these eight Sundays.

Our attention during the first three Sundays of Easter is on the appearances of the Risen Christ. More than mere repetition of Resurrection encounters, even these Sundays have a deepening realization: the appearances advance from *seeing* to *touching* to *eating*; in those ever more concrete sense actions they unmistakably bring home the reality of the Resurrection. The fourth Sunday of Easter is a kind of pivotal Sunday. Customarily called "Good Shepherd Sunday," it serves as a reassurance that although Christ has conquered death and risen to new life, the love and concern and care that Jesus had for his disciples during his earthly life has not changed. What has changed is that the love and care and concern are now taken up by *those disciples* as *their* mission. Thus, the Gospels for the next three Sundays—all from John's Supper discourse—concentrate on the disciples but, again, with an ever-deepening realization. There is a thematic progression from a statement of our relationship to Christ and each other, to a promise that the risen Presence will be with us, to a prayer for those who accept to be disciples. All of this culminates in the eighth Sunday of Easter, Pentecost, where we experience a new Presence of the risen Christ: the Spirit. With the descent of the Spirit amidst the community, the work of redemption is to be taken up by the community's realization of itself as enspirited Body of the risen Christ.

The following table makes the thematic progression of the Easter Season more apparent.

Sunday	Theme
Easter	*See* Jesus and respond with wonder and joy
Easter 2	Thomas: *touch* transforms doubt to belief
Easter 3	Jesus is recognized and known to be alive in the *eating*
Easter 4	Jesus is the Good Shepherd who *continues his care*
Easter 5	Metaphors describing our close *relationship to Christ*
Easter 6	Promise that the Risen Lord will be *with us* in the Spirit
Easter 7	Prayer assures *continued presence*
Easter 8 (Pentecost)	Spirit: *new Presence* of risen Christ

Four thematic shifts move us through the eight Sundays of Easter. Reassurance that the Lord is alive (1) is bolstered by a reminder of Jesus' abiding care and concern (2). Further, we ourselves are invited to be disciples (3) and given the means—the Spirit—to fulfill our mission (4).

The deepening sense of Presence in the Advent/Christmas/ Epiphany cycle moved from an eschatological to a soteriological Presence marked by mission to the world. In the Lent/Triduum/Easter cycle, the opposite movement occurs. Lent begins with a soteriological Presence that calls us to conversion and moves us toward an eschatological Presence celebrated in resurrected Life.

Sundays of Ordinary Time

There are two periods of Ordinary Time, one between Epiphany and Ash Wednesday, which is very short, and the other between Pentecost and the first Sunday of Advent, which is quite long. During Ordinary Time there is a semicontinuous reading of a Gospel beginning with the initial events of Jesus' public ministry. Each year we hear the inaugurating events of the mission before we hear about the consequences (the Passion, death, and Resurrection) of that mission that are taken up in the Lent/Triduum/Easter cycle. Immediately following Epiphany, then, we begin a Gospel and hear such early manifestations of Jesus and his public ministry as the Baptism of the Lord (the First Sunday of Ordinary Time), the call of the disciples, and the first miracles. This narrative is suspended at the beginning of Lent but continues after Pentecost. The longest period of Ordinary Time is a semicontinuous proclamation of the Good News through the summer and fall months, and it leads to the Passion events as recorded in the Gospel account that culminates at the end of the Liturgical Year.

Ordinary Time is a kerygmatic (teaching) time of the church. It is as if we Christians need a long period of time to reflect on and digest the evangelical message. The semicontinuous reading connects the Sundays of Ordinary Time into a narrative pattern that discloses our Christian identity and invites us to take up our mission. This narrative pattern, whereby we travel with Jesus through his public ministry and gradually recognize the implications of his mission to establish the Kingdom,[14] is a description of our own ordinary, everyday living. As such, it is largely soteriological in import and stands in dialectical relationship to the two festal cycles. The manifestation of God's Presence that characterizes Ordinary Time is one of abiding with us as we ever take up anew our own mission to spread the Good News.

During two thirds of the Liturgical Year we ponder the Good News. The synoptic Gospels each have their own structure and purpose, but parallel each other at least in terms of recording Jesus' initiation into public life, his preaching the message of Good News, and finally submitting to the Passion/Resurrection events that resulted from his prophetic words and deeds. The longest portion of the Gospels—and, hence, covering the greatest portion of the Sundays of Ordinary Time—relates Jesus' prophetic words and deeds. Week after week, the Good News is that Jesus changed the world. Ordinary Time challenges us to appropriate the Good News and change our world. It is during Ordinary Time that we hear the words and deeds that critique most pointedly the illusions of Christian ideology we yet entertain.

Pastoral Interpretation

The two festal cycles are celebrative focal points of the Liturgical Year. But there is more to the dynamic of the Liturgical Year than these high points. Both of these two great festal cycles open toward periods of "ordinary" time when we are afforded the opportunity to "catch up" with ourselves in order to digest, appropriate, and live out what we have experienced through celebration. We anticipate and celebrate eschatological rest which always opens to soteriological mission. The two essentially eschatological festal cycles stand in a dialectical relationship with the two essentially soteriological periods of Ordinary Time. Our Liturgical Year, then, is divided into four periods of time that alternate between the "already" and "not yet." But because of the shared dialectical thrust, we have a single season of Ordinary Time and a single season of festal time. This enables us to see the relationship between Christmas and Easter as two sides of the same Mystery and the two periods of Ordinary Time as continuous.

The Paschal Mystery integrates the rhythm of the Liturgical Year into a whole. Each festal cycle is related to the other, and the two periods of Ordinary Time are connected. Furthermore, a fluidity of theme precludes ruptures so that the four divisions of the Liturgical Year flow smoothly one into the next. The eschatological meaning of the coming(s) of the Lord celebrated in the Advent/Christmas/Epiphany cycle is more fully disclosed by the context of mission, a soteriological theme proper to the first Sundays of Ordinary Time. Before we come to Lent, with its undertones of baptismal preparation, there is already a shift toward Lenten themes. Easter itself is so central that it is celebrated over eight Sundays, culminating in Pentecost. Pentecost opens onto the Sundays of Ordinary Time when we return to the salvation narrative put aside at the beginning of Lent and once more enter into the "not yet" of our life. Rather than abrupt changes from eschatology to soteriology, the Liturgical Year has undulations within seasons that prepare for the next phase of the yearly unfolding of the Paschal Mystery.

Christmas and Easter are two complementary celebrative facets of the one Paschal Mystery. Indeed, Christmas derives its eschatological look from a post-Easter perspective.[15] Easter remains the primary season but the shared dialectical pole shows how Christmas is tied to Easter.[16] This permits a greater interrelating between these two great cycles: actually, the festal cycles are two celebrative expressions of paschal events, originary and enduring. These festive events are the source of hope that sustains us during Ordinary Time.

The constant fluidity between eschatology and soteriology, re-entry into eschatology and return to soteriology, brings out two facets of divine Presence: a *coming* Presence and a *realized* Presence. There is a recurring shift between these two presences, each couched within the other. During the festal seasons there is an eschatological thrust that is evidenced in celebration, rest, hopefulness, sense of fullness to come. During Ordinary Time the emphasis is on mission and ministry, especially since it draws us into relationship with others. In spite of the regular change in seasons that characterizes the Liturgical Year, Sunday remains the core celebration. In this sense, Ordinary Time assumes a meaning beyond "filling in time" between the two great temporal celebrations. Sunday after Sunday we are being drawn deeper and deeper into the Good News, so that by the time we begin one of the festal cycles we are already steeped in its mystery and are "primed" to celebrate the fullness of redemption.

We see from the above remarks that the soteriological-eschatological dialectic functions at the level of the Liturgical Year as a whole. It also functions within each festal cycle and Ordinary Time so that there is a continual play throughout the Liturgical Year between the "not yet" and the "already." Thus, the Easter and Christmas cycles have a primary eschatological focus, but both also show a soteriological leitmotif. Ordinary Time is primarily soteriological, but there is an eschatological leitmotif in the solemnities and feasts that gives hope and promises fulfillment. The entire sanctoral calendar, in fact, can be seen in this eschatological light.

Additionally, the dialectic operates among the daily, weekly, and yearly celebrations of the Paschal Mystery. The Liturgy of the Hours celebrates a daily dialectic between eschatology and soteriology, the latter sending us forth to our daily tasks. Eucharist works in the opposite direction, assuming the soteriological import of our daily lives into the eschatological fulfillment and rest of the weekly celebration of Resurrection. Similarly, as we have seen, the soteriological-eschatological dialectic marks the dynamic of the Liturgical Year. The two great festal cycles are times of participation; Ordinary Time is a time of appropriation, hence the basic soteriological-eschatological dialectic exposed in the course of the Liturgical Year is appropriation related to participation.

Although much of our life is characterized by the dis-ease of our own "unfinishedness" and a yearning for the fullness that we know can be ours, this dis-ease is mercifully extenuated by a reassurance that only Christian hope can bring. Giving ourselves over to the dynamic rhythm of the Liturgical Year exposes us to a successive experience of the soteriological-eschatological dialectic over a long period of time, permitting a prolonged savoring of the Presence of Mystery. The Liturgical Year discloses God's Presence in festivity and ordinariness, in both joy and longing. The Liturgical Year is, indeed, a rich feast.

9
Liturgical Spirituality

In the three previous chapters we analyzed the structure of liturgical texts in order to uncover the depth structure of the text as a means of revealing its depth meaning. Much of our work has been *integrating*; we have been examining what draws the ritual together as a dynamic whole. Since our particular texts have been liturgical ones, it is not surprising that a common thread of dynamic divine "presence" emerged from each of the three texts as different openings of God's Presence to us and our possible responses to that Presence.

A desire to integrate human presence within divine Presence can ultimately describe the motive for the Jesus event (Paschal Mystery), the fruit of celebrating liturgy, and the impetus for Christian living. What is more, the integrating process leaves the utter freedom and radical "otherness" of both God and humanity intact. *Process* is a key word.

So far in our pastoral interpretations of Part 2 we have accounted for two of Ricoeur's methodological moments in text interpretation: in chapter 5, Christian Self-understanding, we identified our *participation* in the Christian mystery and in chapters 6, 7, and 8 we analyzed ritual (i.e., text) structures and their pastoral interpretation as moments of *distanciation*. This final chapter draws out the ramifications of these prior observations in terms of authentic Christian living, the completion of the hermeneutical process. That is, chapter 9 describes liturgical spirituality as completing the *hermeneutical process* in the act of *appropriation*.

We propose that a liturgical spirituality is the fruit of entering into an ongoing hermeneutical process grounded by our *participation* in the Christian tradition. It begins with our self-understanding as Body of Christ and, submitted to liturgy's critical moment of *distanciation*, is completed only when we *appropriate* one or more of the new possibilities for self-understanding proffered in liturgy. This, in turn, becomes a new moment of participation and Christian living. Liturgical spirituality is a completion of the hermeneutic process we begin when we open ourselves in faith to the saving work of God. Yet this hermeneutic process is unique because its "completion" is never final. The text we interpret is a *memorial* of the Paschal Mystery. Our response to that Mystery is ever creative and creating. Liturgy is a text to which we constantly return because the possibilities for entering ever more deeply into God's Life are inexhaustible.

In this chapter we work with three interweaving structures. There is the infrastructure of Ricoeur's three methodic moments of participation, distanciation, and appropriation that has shaped all of Part 2. There is the structural dialectic of soteriology and eschatology by which we have described the Paschal Mystery and have seen how it unfolds during various cultic occasions. Finally, there is our original problematic of the relationship of liturgy and life. We are now in a position to address this in terms of synonymous deep structures (our dynamic of "presence") that have a common referent (the Paschal Mystery). The methodic infrastructure is a heuristic tool that provides us with an interpretive method. The structural dialectic of soteriology and eschatology supplies the content or data for interpretation. Method and content come together in liturgical spirituality, a constant communication of the experience of the dialectic at work in liturgy as the ritual counterpart of the experience of the dialectic at work in our everyday life.

As we live from Liturgy of the Hours to Eucharist to Liturgical Year, from daily to weekly to yearly temporality, we enter into a successively larger experience that permits a deeper penetration into the Paschal Mystery. There is something of a paradox here, for we would naturally think that the celebration of the Paschal Mystery in the course of a single day would be more concentrated and therefore more within our grasp than when the dynamic of the celebration of that Mystery is fragmented over a year. Yet, we suggest that with each advance to the next time frame (from daily to weekly to yearly), we are able to come to a more central, focused, concentrated, simplified, core experience of the Mystery. This depends, however, on whether our daily and weekly celebrations are what they should be and whether there is a discernible progression in celebrative style. The Paschal Mystery really breaks open in each successively larger time frame only when these two conditions are met. It is precisely in progressing toward a larger cultic opening of the Mystery that we promote a prayerful, nonreflective, "im-mediate" response. Each larger opening facilitates an experience of the whole because it enables a longer time for anticipation and celebration of the Paschal Mystery.

The necessary connection between daily, weekly, and yearly celebrations suggests a pastoral need to gather the community specifically at these times and with an increasingly festive style of celebration. This approach to an interpretation of liturgy precludes an isolated Sunday worship service as the only religious expression. It also precludes ignoring the structural relationships and thematic connections between daily and weekly celebrations and between weekly and yearly celebrations. More important, this approach reminds us that liturgical celebrations are never moments separate from daily life but *celebrations of our Christian living*. To celebrate liturgy is to celebrate life.

If we consider "liturgical spirituality" at this point in our study, the phrase may seem redundant. "Spirituality" implies a way of living. We have seen that "liturgy," too, implies a way of living. If we begin to conceive of liturgy in this holistic, real-life way, we become aware that it is impossible to live as a Christian and not live liturgically because our very living has as its *raison d'être* making the Paschal Mystery present. Liturgy also accomplishes this. More to the point, when we begin to conceive of liturgy as an objectification of the Paschal Mystery in terms of a structural dynamic between soteriology and eschatology, then we have begun to grasp the depth meaning of liturgy itself. We perceive that our Christian life, too, is a matter of living this soteriological-eschatological dynamic of the Paschal Mystery. Christian life, therefore, is itself really a kind of liturgical expression to the extent that our life is a response to—a specific objectification of—the Paschal Mystery.

Given this point of view, when we refer to "spirituality" as a way of life we also mean "liturgy." The celebration of liturgy objectifies the baptismal reality of ourselves as Body of Christ and the enduring meaning of the Jesus event is carried through the tradition by our *living* the Paschal Mystery. To be Christian means to *live* a liturgical spirituality for that is how we define ourselves. Liturgical spirituality belongs to us as Christians; it is the common way of life we share.

Structure of Christian Living

In this first part we want to spell out the structural dynamics we have uncovered in the three previous chapters and see how they connect with and complement one another. The dynamic between soteriology and eschatology that we have been spotlighting unfolds in a number of different ways. To appreciate both its complexity and integrity, we must understand the different levels on which the dynamic operates and discern the connectedness.

Ritual Experience of the Dialectic

Each of the ritual occasions we have considered has its own way of unfolding the soteriological-eschatological dialectic and holding it in dynamic tension.[1] During Liturgy of the Hours we move from an eschatological pole (experienced during the psalmody, a resting in the story of God's utter fidelity to us and continued involvement in the affairs of humankind) to a soteriological one (played out by the intercessions which remind us that we are citizens of the whole church and the whole world). In Eucharist this dynamic is reversed, for Eucharist begins with a soteriological moment (Liturgy of the Word) and moves to an eschatological moment (Liturgy of the Eucharist). The Liturgical Year begins with the Advent/Christmas/ Epiphany festal cycle, a primarily eschatological moment that moves toward a soteriological moment in Ordinary Time I. This, in turn, moves toward yet another eschatological moment unfolding during the Lent/Triduum/Easter cycle and, finally, ends with another soteriological moment in Ordinary Time II. During the liturgical year we alternate between festal time and Ordinary Time, between the eschatological and the soteriological poles.

Each successively larger ritual occasion begins the dynamic at the same pole where the previous one left it. Daily living is characterized by a soteriological import, with which the Sunday Eucharist begins at the Liturgy of the Word. Sunday is characterized by the eschatological import introduced by the Liturgy of Eucharist that also characterizes Advent, the first liturgical season. Each of the seasons progresses toward the opposite pole of the dynamic and the whole liturgical year builds to an eschatological note upon which it ends. The tension between the dialectical poles is, therefore, not experienced as rupture but as a fluidity as one pole of the dynamic leads toward the other.

Rituals objectify the Paschal Mystery dynamic; participation in daily, weekly, and yearly ritual occasions promotes the transition from one pole to the other. Ritual keeps intact both the "not yet" and the "already" aspects of our human existence. At the same time, the objective predictability of ritual keeps us from being discouraged when we are living the "not yet" of our existence. It also keeps us from being overly confident when we are living the "already" of our existence. The sure movement from one pole of the dialectic to the other brings out the unity of the Mystery we live. *Ritual summons an awareness of the radical sameness between the poles of the dialectic.*

Temporal Experience of the Dialectic

Three different temporal experiences of the Paschal Mystery dialectic mark progressively larger temporal periods. The first temporal experience is a daily one; each day evening and morning[2] are held in dialectical tension. The focus of evening prayer is passion, death, entry into the tomb, waiting, emptiness, and longing: themes appropriate to a dying day that serve as a reminder of our human condition and the alienation from self, others, and God that we are constantly trying to overcome. Evening leads to morning and the greeting of the rising sun (Son) with its appropriate Resurrection theme. Our daytime is lived in Resurrection time and is characterized by Christian hope in promises fulfilled. The "dark night," traditionally the time of sin and alienation, is the shorter, soteriological part of our daily cycle.

There is also a weekday/Sunday play of the dialectic in which the weekdays (marked by the soteriological import of the Liturgy of the Hours) are lived primarily as a soteriological moment while Sunday (marked by the eschatological import of the eucharistic celebration) is lived as an eschatological moment. All our weekday "not yets" are the content of our self-understanding that begs a new and focused confrontation with the Christian Ideal Self proclaimed and made present during the Liturgy of the Word. During the Liturgy of the Eucharist we are invited to share in the messianic banquet and rest in an eschatological moment during which we "com-mune" with Christ our Ideal Self.

A third experience of the temporal dialectic is a play between a Sunday/yearly temporality. The import of a Sunday experience of the Paschal Mystery is eschatological. During festal seasons there is a kind of "double rest" whereby the "already" of Sunday is reinforced by the "already" of the eschatological import of the festal seasons. During the most of the year, however, we live in Ordinary Time, which has a soteriological thrust. We noted above how the ritual experience of the soteriological-eschatological dynamic is a fluidity, each pole being taken up into the next ritual moment. The temporal experience of the dynamic, however, does not bear out such a fluidity, but, on the contrary, evidences a rupturing or radical shift from one pole of the dialectic to the next.

The fullness of morning Resurrection is disrupted by the "not yet" of our everydays. This soteriological import of our weeks is disrupted by the eschatological rest of Sunday. And for most of the year, the rest of Sunday is disrupted by the "not yet" of Ordinary Time. *Temporality summons an awareness of the radical difference between the poles of the dialectic.*

Intersection of Ritual and Temporal Experiences

The point to our analytic is not to play word games; something far more important is at stake. Only by speculating on a number of different emphases can we begin to grasp the various rhythms of the dynamic that play on us at different moments of Christian living. The soteriological-eschatological dialectic cannot be resolved but it is lived to the fullest extent of objectifying the Paschal Mystery when we are most aware that at any given moment, no matter what the emphasis, the other pole of the dialectic is also operative. Herein lies the *integrating* principle of liturgical spirituality. Though we may experience the Paschal Mystery with different emphases, now with more intensity and then with less, the whole is nonetheless always operative.[3]

There is an inexorable connectedness within the dynamic that we locate exactly in the permutation from one dialectical pole to another. The progression in the eight Gospels of the Great Sunday is paradigmatic and suggests a pattern of movement from one pole to the next (in this case, from the eschatology of the Resurrection appearances to the soteriology of discipleship). Within each season there is a movement toward the opposite pole of the dialectic so that there is no disruption when a change of season occurs because we have already been prepared and have begun to live another emphasis. The development within the season itself leads us forward to a new living of the dynamic.

The relationship between the poles of the dialectic is also brought out by the sanctoral calendar (though this part of the Roman Calendar has not figured significantly in our analysis). Most of the solemnities on the sanctoral calendar occur during times of soteriological import. Thus, they afford us an opportunity to reenter eschatological, festal time. This eases us through our ordinary human life but does not take us out of it. Indeed, the solemnities are celebrations *of* ordinary life. The very movement within eschatological periods still suggests the "not yet." This is where the depth of the dynamic begins to really come alive. We experience fulfillment, an eschatological moment, but *that rest* is still an *unrest*. Even within rest we are being brought to the reality of our human living and its unfinished business, to the reality that we are still cooperating in the ongoing act of redemption.

Ritual experience, temporal experience. Sameness, difference. Fluidity, rupture. The intersection of these opposite dimensions of our living and celebrating the Paschal Mystery dialectic demands an integration that is a gain in meaning.[4] At one level we are living out of one emphasis or another so that we are acutely reminded of the differences. At the same time we always celebrate both emphases as a reminder of the wholeness of the Mystery so that we are acutely aware of the sameness. This analysis of the dialectical structures proper to Christian living is a challenge to an ever more dynamic way of living that shapes our very experience of life and Mystery. We now turn to the task of interpreting this gain in meaning.

Pastoral Interpretation

Our main issue in this volume is the juncture of liturgy and life. What we experience in our own life as a dialectic of anguish and hope, of weakness and glory, is what we celebrate in liturgy as promise and fulfillment, hunger and satisfaction. To put it conversely, what we celebrate in liturgy is none other than the same dynamic we play out daily at a very human level. Our humanity is not in dualistic opposition with divine life but is our way of revealing (i.e., objectifying) the gift of divine Life.

The structural synonymy of liturgy and life has the same meaning as the structural dialectic that we have identified as the Paschal Mystery. This essentially says that the "not yet" and the "already," the promise and the fulfillment, are available to us and are played out in our living the Paschal Mystery. What Jesus gave us by his life was a pattern of living our own life: a Paschal Mystery pattern of carrying out the mission of making the Kingdom available in our lives and yet recognizing that the Kingdom is not yet fully realized.

The participation-distanciation-appropriation infrastructure of Part 2, while an abstract and analytical exercise here, nonetheless has its practical import. For us Christians, interpretation is a way of life. This is to say that Christian living as participation in the Paschal Mystery is in dialectical relationship with Christian liturgy as distancing ourselves from life in order to enter more deeply into that life. The liturgical moment of distanciation, in turn, is in dialectical relationship with appropriating new possibilities for a new Christian self-understanding. We have, then, a dialectic between life and liturgy and between liturgy and life.

Liturgy and Life

The dialectic between life/liturgy/life (Life–Cultus–Life) requires interpretation since we open the expectation of renewed, graced living each time we celebrate liturgy. Interpretation allows expectation to be brought to fruition. To be out of touch with this interpretive process is either to miss our own interaction with life and liturgy or, worse, to miss their interconnectedness and risk falling into a dualistic approach to religious expression and life. In the latter case, we dismantle liturgical spirituality and revert to two spheres (liturgy versus life).

The content of the dialectic between liturgy and life is given in the soteriological-eschatological dialectic we teased out of the Lucan account of the Lord's Supper. To describe the Paschal Mystery in terms of such a dialectic is to describe our Christian living in the same terms. Both method and content help us distinguish the sameness and difference of liturgy and life. The interrelationship of method and content as well as reflective analysis and dialectics trigger new insights into the relationship of liturgy and life.

The ongoing immersion of one pole of the soteriological-eschatological dialectic into the other in both its ritual and temporal dimensions is a key concept. This functions as a constant reminder that both poles are always operative even while granting that the emphasis may be on only one of them at any given moment in time. This is important in order to grasp how liturgical living is a whole rather than a grab bag of fragmented temporal moments or isolated ritual moments. In liturgical living, the fullness of the dialectic—that is, the fullness of the Paschal Mystery—is readily at hand.

Living the fullness of the Paschal Mystery does not come automatically by "being good" and "going to Mass." We are suggesting that the relationship between liturgy and life is far more radical than such literal interpretations would have us believe. At stake is the realization that how deeply we articulate the Paschal Mystery in our own everyday living determines how deeply we can enter into liturgical celebration. Liturgy does not happen in a vacuum. It is celebrated out of the rich experience of the depth dimension of Christian living. The interconnectedness of liturgy and life as logically prior makes demands on our everyday living.

The relationship of liturgy and life is a broad framework for the more trenchant relationship of liturgy and social concerns. The interest that liturgists have for liturgy and justice and liturgy and ethics demonstrated by the flurry of recent publications indicates both their conviction that liturgy demands right living and a desire to explore the meaning of this basic stance further. If we perceive the structure of liturgy as the Paschal Mystery dialectic of soteriology and eschatology and recognize the structure of Christian living as the same, then it is impossible to truly live Christian life without being in right relationship with others (and God). This is just living. Justice is characteristic of authentic Christian living. Justice is not an entity unto itself to be sought, but a fruit of living the dialectic that helps us break open the depth meaning of the Paschal Mystery.

From within the framework that we have been considering, the interconnectedness of liturgy and justice must be displaced to a different problematic. It is not a question of adjoining them. This posits them in two different spheres of human activity and results in a dualism that simply does not (or ought not) exist.

If we understand liturgy in its deepest sense as a celebration of our own identity as Body of Christ and our own cooperation in making the Paschal Mystery fruitful by making the Kingdom available, then the doing of justice is located at the very core of our identity. Doing justice is not an "add on" undertaken by those who have the gift of being "socially committed," though specific types of engagement may derive from particular gifts. When we connect liturgy and life at the level of depth structure and maintain that both are disclosures of the Paschal Mystery in the here and now, then to live the Paschal Mystery (that is, to be Christian) is to be in right relationship: "He [the Lord] has told you, O mortal, what is good; and what does the Lord require of you but to do justice, and to love kindness, and to walk humbly with your God?" (Micah 6:8). Right relationship and God's Presence make authentic worship possible. The new problematic for comprehending the relationship of liturgy and justice is located at the depth level where the sameness and difference of liturgy and life as constitutive of Christianity's originary metaphor, the Paschal Mystery, are identified and so are concretely and knowingly expressed in liturgy.

A frequent interpretation of justice borrows from the scholastic categories of distributive and retributive justice and tends to obscure the relationship between liturgy and justice in terms of a shared depth meaning. While these are helpful distinctions and offer a concrete way to live justly, they fall short of a larger dimension that promises rich fruits. If we consider the actions of the God of justice of the Old Testament, we see a God who is concerned with right relationship, love, and mercy. We see a God who is lavish, who shares divine largess. Liturgy and justice can be another dualistic way of speaking, can be another way of setting up an opposition between the kingdom of this world and the Kingdom of the next. Or, liturgy and justice can be expressed in terms of an understanding of liturgy as a celebration of who we are as Body of Christ, a celebration of God's Kingdom. Dualism can be shattered in this way, for when we more deeply enter into this understanding of why Christian living demands right relations, the more our own imperative is to live in the lavishness of God. Our response, then, can only be one of lavishness and largess, love and mercy that emulates God's relationship toward us.

Liturgy is a radically personal undertaking during which we put our life and self on the line. By taking the stance that authentic Christian living is logically prior to liturgy, we are risking the comfort and security borne of routine and are placing conscious choice about the meaning of liturgy and life squarely on our own shoulders. Everyday decisions and the behavior that follows from them open us to the reality of who we are and, therefore, what we live: the Paschal Mystery.

But the dialectic also works in the opposite direction. Although logically second, liturgy retains its significance as *source* (fountain) and *summit* of Christian living.[5] Without this reminder we run the risk of proceeding as if doing good is *our* work rather than ultimately an expression of God's work *within us*. As critical moment, liturgy contributes a corrective and/or encouragement for everyday decisions and prompts us ever to give ourselves over to God so that our human activity is really an expression of God's dwelling within. In other words, our human activity is an expression of our self-understanding as Body of Christ. Then, and only then, can we truly perceive not only the inexorable relationship between liturgy and justice but also the more fundamental relationship between liturgy and all of life.

Principles of a Liturgical Spirituality

A number of principles upon which we might base a liturgical spirituality are dictated by our analytic and interpretation. The basic principles operative in the methodology give the basic principles operative in a liturgical spirituality.

Liturgical spirituality is a dialectic of interpretive moments. This principle integrates the celebration of liturgy into Christian living (and, integrates Christian living into liturgy) as one of its interpretive moments. It is a methodological statement of our Life–Cultus–Life (participation-distanciation-appropriation) tryptich. At stake here is a dualistic approach to liturgy and life that keeps them external to each other and isolates them as two distinctive spheres of living. This principle shatters that dualism by accepting liturgy and life as interpretive moments of one sphere of living where the divine and human merge and are celebrated.

The depth structure of Christian living is the same as the depth structure of Christian liturgy. Underlying this synonymy is Ricoeur's notion of text as a document of life. Liturgy is a document of Christian living. Since liturgy functions like a text, it is more readily available as an object for interpretation at the analytic moment of distanciation than is the whole of Christian living. At stake here is an access to the meaning of the Paschal Mystery as having import *for us* here and now. This principle not only gives insight into the meaning of the Paschal Mystery for us in the very celebration of liturgy, but it also ensures a certain objectivity to that meaning because the text that we celebrate as liturgy is a document of the tradition formed by the interaction of divine Presence and God's people. Liturgy functions as a kind of normative will that shapes the meaning of Christian living without hindering our own freedom of choice (arbitrary will).

The Jesus event is originary to the tradition. Jesus' life, death, Resurrection, and continued Presence are historical events that gave rise to the Christian tradition. Just as significant, though, the actual experience of that resurrected presence continues the tradition and is constitutive of it. At stake here is the realization that Christian living and liturgy are first and foremost God's action on our behalf. This principle eases the yoke and lightens the burden of right Christian living so that Christian tradition is a bearer of hope. We are never alone when we embrace the responsibilities of the Paschal Mystery dynamic. We are members of the Body of Christ and share in its collective strength as a mutual embrace.

The Jesus event is communicated through a tradition by an authority (the Spirit) resting within the community. The Spirit, the continued Presence of the risen Christ, authors the creative (creating) response of the Body to its Head. At stake here is the dynamism that carries the tradition forward in authentic and faithful ways. This principle gives credence to the liturgical changes that necessarily occur from time to time. It also brings us to expect these changes because texts are not dead documents, but documents of life. Liturgy is a document of a living, vibrant Christian community.

Koinonia **is constitutive of liturgical spirituality**. Christian truth can only be known in its community expression. No one person is Body of Christ, but together we are members of the one Body with Christ as Head. Our participation in the tradition is as community, that is, as Body of Christ. At stake here is any individualistic approach to either Christian living or liturgy.[6] This principle builds up the whole Body through the various actions of its members. This suggests that an individual is more than just "one among many"; an individual holds the Body in the palm of her/his hand by the works s/he performs. Each of us is responsible for the whole Body. Each of us is co-author of the Christian text, the living document we call "liturgy."

Kerygma **is constitutive of liturgical spirituality.** The ongoing revelation of the meaning of the Paschal Mystery that is lived in our everyday lives and celebrated in liturgy has as its source God's continuing desire to be involved in the affairs of humankind. God's Word is unceasingly spoken in a chorus of deeds on our behalf that reveal an ever-deepening Presence to us. Critically distancing ourselves from our own everyday deeds sensitizes us and readies us to recognize God's actions for our sake. At stake here is liturgy's built-in critique of our Christian living as well as its documentation of originary events. This principle reminds us that God's Word will never be silent as long as we celebrate authentic liturgy and thereby open new possibilities for Christian living and echo that Word in our everyday living.

Metanoia **is constitutive of liturgical spirituality.** Christians can never rest; they can never be satisfied; they are always seeking more from the well of inexhaustible Presence. Since liturgy is a vibrant document of Christian living, each celebration of liturgy always brings new possibilities. Liturgy is dynamic and creative. At stake here is the fact that interpretation demands change in self, a new self-understanding, if it is to be complete. The liturgical celebration is finalized in the appropriation of new ways of Christian living that build up the Body. Embracing change is a way of life for Christians, and it is constitutive of liturgical spirituality, an interpretive process that is only completed by new self-understanding. Appropriation becomes, in turn, a new moment of *koinonia*. This principle points to Christian tradition as a never-ending response to the promise "and remember, I am with you always, to the end of the age" (Mt 28:20). Our appropriating the new possibilities proffered in liturgy pledges unfathomable depths of Presence.

A Liturgical Spirituality

Interpretative moments, dynamic depth structure, Paschal Mystery, communication of tradition, community as Body of Christ, new possibilities, change—these are the hallmarks of liturgical spirituality. The synonymy of the structures of everyday Christian living and Christian liturgy indicates to us that authentic liturgical spirituality derives from within and is dependent upon our openness to God's Presence. Liturgical spirituality is hardly the juxtaposing or adjoining of two spheres of living, the human and divine. Liturgical spirituality helps us recognize deep within the core of who we are that our life is grafted onto God's Life.

The Paschal Mystery is the meaning-content of our liturgical spirituality. We have described this in terms of a soteriological-eschatological dialectic. That is to say, we actually live in terms of the "not yet" and the "already." The "not yet" is never a negative stance toward ourselves but is a way to acknowledge that our entry into the depths of God's Presence is always a dynamic that beckons us to a larger embrace. Nor is the "already" a tantalizing illusion but a way to live hope sprung eternally and celebrated now. To open ourselves to the dialectic is to give ourselves over to the Source of the Life we live and celebrate.

The more completely we embrace liturgical spirituality, the more deeply we are able to enter into the movement that connects weekdays and Sundays and seasons as a point in time pregnant with meaning and as a kind of living "timelessness" of God's movement within us. The fountainhead of liturgical spirituality is within, is Godself. God co-authors with us the text we celebrate that documents divine Presence to us in our everyday lives. To be sure, like all spiritualities, certain external signs witness to the interior promptings of God. Liturgical spirituality lends credence to popular devotions that increase our fervor and help us recognize God's Presence and the demands of that Presence. But more than this, authentic liturgical spirituality precludes any friction between liturgy and devotion for they have a common aspiration: to open ourselves to the divine Mystery within.

Defining our lives in terms of the Paschal Mystery favors an approach to Christian living that takes seriously our identity as Body of Christ. No less than the reality of the Presence of the Risen Christ is at stake. Does the dynamic of presence inform all liturgical rites and, therefore, liturgical spirituality? We think it must. Each liturgical action extends its own unique disclosure of the many modes of God's presence.

The Liturgy of the Hours begins with God as Other (invitatory, hymn) and moves toward God as faithful presence to immanent presence to God who is with us as guardian as we reach out to others. Eucharist unfolds as God's call to presence and moves toward our being that presence for others. The Liturgical Year unfolds as an eschatological, realized presence to a soteriological, anticipated presence. There is a parallel between the expression of presence at the beginning and at the conclusion of both the Liturgy of the Hours and Eucharist: We begin with a transcendent presence that seeks us and conclude with a thrust outward whereby we seek others.

God's Presence is experienced liturgically in many ways. Each is an opportunity to open ourselves to a fuller Presence. No matter where we stand in *our* relationship to God, the Lord is an ever faithful Presence to us.[7] So much so that through the varied moments of liturgical expression and their accompanying communications of presence, God offers in myriad ways according to our own needs whatever we require to open ourselves to an appropriation of ever deeper Mystery.

Liturgical spirituality interprets through living and celebrating the meaning of the Paschal Mystery from the depths of the One who dwells within. It expresses the synonymy of life and celebration through consistency with the Christian tradition in the concrete works of meaningful human action. Liturgical spirituality is not something we can possess; it is a way of life to be lived. This way of life is an ongoing interpretation of the meaning of the Paschal Mystery for our everyday living and its celebration in liturgy.

With so much stress on divine Presence, we might be tempted to view liturgical spirituality as a wholly interior attitude. This could hardly be farther from the truth. Because of the dialectic of liturgy and life, authentic liturgical spirituality always leads to concrete activity on behalf of society, especially the downtrodden. There is nothing passive about this approach; it is demanding. Liturgical spirituality bids us to take up the Cross of Christ by responding to the exigencies, misunderstandings, and risks consequent on doing the will of the One we embody. Liturgical spirituality admits to our sin and weakness and our inability at times to respond. It puts our own suffering into perspective and requires that we do all we can to alleviate the suffering of others. Liturgical spirituality is an emptying of self. It prepares for and appropriates death as a new vision into what is possible.

At the same time, liturgical spirituality celebrates the fidelity of our responses and brings hope into perspective. Liturgical spirituality bids us to live as Resurrection people and rejoice in life that is fulfilled.

There is no way of measuring the extent to which a Christian has "put on" a liturgical spirituality. Nor does liturgical spirituality preclude embracing elements of other spiritualities as well. However, basic to all Christian living is liturgical spirituality as the ground of Christian existence because its content is the Paschal Mystery. The promise of liturgical spirituality is wholeness of the Body because the Head has been vindicated. And just as surely as the Father raised Jesus to new life, so, too, will God raise us to new life. O death, where is your sting?

Notes

Introduction

1. See, for example, L. Bouyer, *Life and Liturgy* (London: Sheed and Ward, 1965); N. Pittenger, *Life as Eucharist* (Grand Rapids, Mich.: William B. Eerdmans Publishing Company, 1973); A. Schmemann, *Liturgy and Life: Lectures and Essays on Christian Development Through Liturgical Experience* (New York: Department of Religious Education, Orthodox Church in America, 1974); C. Kiesling, "Liturgy and Social Justice," *Worship* 51 (1977) 351–61; D. E. Saliers, "Liturgy and Ethics: Some New Beginnings," *The Journal of Religious Ethics* 7 (1979) 173–89; M. Searle, *Liturgy and Social Justice* (Collegeville, Minn.: The Liturgical Press, 1980); W. H. Willimon, *The Service of God: How Worship and Ethics Are Related* (Nashville, Tenn.: Abingdon Press, 1983); P. Gibson, "Liturgy and Justice," *Toronto Journal of Theology* 3 (1987) 3–13; K. R. Himes, "Eucharist and Justice: Assessing the Legacy of Virgil Michel," *Worship* 62 (1988) 201–24; J. F. Henderson, K. Quinn, and S. Larson, *Liturgy, Justice and the Reign of God: Integrating Vision and Practice* (New York: Paulist Press, 1989); J. L. Empereur, S. J. and C. G. Kiesling, O. P., *The Liturgy That Does Justice* (Collegeville, Minn.: The Liturgical Press/A Michael Glazier Book, 1990); J. Dallen, "Liturgy and Justice for All," *Worship* 65 (1991) 290–306; K. Hughes and M. R. Francis, eds., *Living No Longer for Ourselves* (Collegeville, Minn.: The Liturgical Press, 1991).

2. Previous works on liturgical spirituality include such diverse authors and works as L. Bouyer, *Liturgical Piety* (Notre Dame: University of Notre Dame Press, 1955/1983); A. Schmemann, *The World as Sacrament* (London: Darton, Longman & Todd, 1966); N. Pittenger, *Life as Eucharist* (Grand Rapids, Mich.: William B. Eerdmans Publishing Company, 1973); K. W. Irwin, *Liturgy, Prayer and Spirituality* (New York: Paulist Press, 1984); L. Boff, *Sacraments of Life, Life of the Sacraments*, trans. J. Drury (Washington, D. C.: The Pastoral Press, 1987); T. Keating, *The Mystery of Christ: The Liturgy as Spiritual Experience* (Amity, N.Y.: Amity House, 1987); S. Madigan, *Spirituality Rooted in Liturgy* (Washington, D. C.: The Pastoral Press, 1988); E. Bernstein, C.S.J., ed., *Liturgy and Spirituality in Context: Perspectives on Prayer and Culture* (Collegeville, Minn.: The Liturgical Press, 1990). Each of these works shares a common concern that liturgy is more extensive than the cultic occasion that focuses the ritual. The authors use various approaches to describe the relationship of liturgy and everyday Christian living. These efforts differ from this volume in that I am interested in addressing the methodological questions that take us beyond demonstration of the relationship of liturgy and life that liturgical spirituality captures; I wish to propose an ontological rationale for such a relationship.

3. This fine little work by M. Hellwig, *The Eucharist and the Hunger of the World* (New York: Paulist Press/Deus Book, 1976) takes its title from this Congress.

4. Here I want to make the point that I am not doing structural analysis in the manner of semioticians. My use of "structural analysis" is as an analysis of the structure of the text. I ask the very important questions, What is going on in the text? What is the movement? What is the dynamic? What makes this text integral? What holds the text together? While these questions are important for the semiotician as well, my way of approaching the text uses a different set of analytic tools.

5. By "depth meaning" I mean the integral structural dynamic that holds a work together and makes a text a text, a living document of human existence.

6. I limit myself here to Ricoeur's text theory. In some of his later work Ricoeur looks at the relationship of narrative and time, and a very precise notion of history is operative there. This does not figure into the present work.

7. This is my own innovative application of Ricoeur's method.

8. This gives us an insight into the relationship between God's proffering of gifts and our freedom in face of those gifts. God offers an abundance of possibilities, but we freely choose. I suggest that the celebration of authentic liturgy cannot leave us unchanged.

9. Again, I remind the reader that this is my application of Ricoeur's textual method to the liturgical domain.

10. Political here means *polis* or society and excludes our usual connotation of political as "politics," especially if understood pejoratively.

11. Ideology, then, is a positive force within a society even though ideology often comes to disillusionment and certainly needs a critique.

12. The first cup mentioned by Luke is not mentioned in the other synoptic accounts.

13. The word "dialectic" is more consistent with Ricoeur's terminology.

14. Our point here is not that this is the only way to approach these Christian realities nor even necessarily the "right" way. Rather, *if* we accept the intimations of our methodological studies in the first part of this book, how might they help us think about these realities in a new light? What can we learn? The response to these questions gives birth to a new interpretation.

Chapter 1. Concern for Others: *Remembering*

1. This verb in its various forms also occurs frequently in Psalms (53x), Isaiah (26x), Ezekiel (21x), and Jeremiah (16x).

2. See Ex 13:3ff and Ps 74, for just two examples.

3. Though impossible to trace this theme here, two comments are in order. In the Lucan Lord's Supper tradition (cf. Lk 22:19 and 1 Cor 11:24), Jesus commands his disciples to "do this in remembrance of me." This is taken up below in chapter 4. Second, "to remember" occurs in the revised eucharistic prayers of the Latin Rite of the Roman Catholic Church (for example, Eucharistic Prayer 1 where it is used three times; Prayer 2 where it is used twice; and Prayer 4 where is is used three times).

4. In this context, we recall an unrelenting theme of the prophets: the pursuit of righteousness is a prerequisite for cultic observance (for example, see Is 1:11–17; 58:2–7; Jer 6:19–21; 7:8–11; 7:21–26; Am 5:21–24; Mic 6:6–8).

5. I use *Sitz-im-Leben* in the broad sense of "life context" rather than in the more technical sense employed by source critics, which would necessarily be subject to more strict exegetical examination of the passages in question.

6. The *qal* is the simplest Hebrew verb conjugation consisting of a root plus a stem pattern to indicate tense. Other conjugations are derived from the *qal*.

7. The remarks in the final section point not only to the necessity of doing this but also to the richness of the promised results for someone who takes up this study.

8. It should be noted that there are two noun forms of *zkr*. One is in the Book of the Law (25:19, zēker) and the other is in the Son of Moses (32:26, zik^{e}rām, with third person masculine plural pronominal suffix). They are simply translated in the NRSV as "remembrance." Another note needs to be made here: We are really only dealing with fourteen passages though there are fifteen occurrences of verb forms. Dt 7:18 has two verb forms: the infinitive absolute and the preformative future *qal*. Classical Hebrew grammar employs the convention of preceding a finite verb with an infinitive absolute to express emphasis. Hence, the meaning of 7:18 is "you indeed shall remember." See J. Weingreen, *A Practical Grammar for Classical Hebrew*, 2d ed. (Oxford: at the Clarendon Press, 1959), 79. Also, T. O. Lambdin, *Introduction to Biblical Hebrew* (New York: Charles Scribner's Sons, 1971), 158. These two occurrences are separated here only because of the two different grammatical forms. In the rest of the chapter they are treated together.

9. The second person masculine singular perfect afformative *qal* (w^{e}zākartā), all with *wāw* consecutive, occurs seven times (Dt 5:15; 8:2; 8:18; 15:15; 16:12; 24:18; 24:22). The *qal* infinitive *(zākōr)* appears three times (Dt 7:18; 24:9; 25:17). The second person singular preformative future *qal* (tizkōr) is found twice (Dt 7:18 and 16:3); and, finally, the second person masculine singular imperative *qal* (z^{e}kōr) occurs three times (Dt 9:7; 9:27; 32:7).

10. There is no pattern as to how the grammatical forms appear: all four grammatical forms show up in 4:45–11:32; three appear (the imperative excepted) in chapters 12–28.

11. G. Von Rad, *Problems of the Hexateuch and Other Essays*, trans. E. W. True-man Dicken, Intro. Norman W. Porteos (Edinburgh: Oliver & Boyd, 1966), 27. See also J. M. Schmidt, "*Vergegenwärtigung und Überlieferung*," *Evangelische Theologie* 30 (1970) 186, who sees all of Deuteronomy as having a cultic *Sitz-im-Leben*. For arguments *pro* and *con* a cultic *Sitz-im-Leben* for Deuteronomy, see R. de Vaux, *The Early History of Israel*, trans. David Smith (Philadelphia: Westminster Press, 1978), 401–19.

12. Von Rad, *Problems of the Hexateuch*, 33.

13. R. E. Clements, "Deuteronomy and the Jerusalem Cult Tradition," *Vetus Testamentum* 15 (1965) 301.

14. See M. Weinfeld, *Deuteronomy and the Deuteronomic School* (Oxford: at the Clarendon Press, 1972), 37ff.

15. S. Mowinckel, *The Psalms in Israel's Worship*, trans. D. R. AP-Thomas (Oxford: Basil Blackwell, 1962), 15. See also W. Eichrodt, *Theology of the Old Testament*, vol. 1, trans. J. A. Baker (London: SCM Press, 1961–67), 198: "The term 'cultus' should be taken to mean the expression of religious experience in concrete external actions performed within the congregation or community, preferably by officially appointed exponents and in set forms." For Eichrodt, the cult is secondary to the religious experience. For an extensive treatment of the cult in Israel, see R. de Vaux, *Ancient Israel: Its Life and Institutions*, trans. John McHugh (London: Darton, Longman & Todd, 1961), 271–518. Our use of "cultus" in chapter 5 below follows Eichrodt.

16. A. Weiser, *Introduction to the Old Testament* (London: Darton, Longman & Todd, 1961), 89; italics added.

17. B. S. Childs, *Introduction to the Old Testament as Scripture* (Philadelphia: Fortress Press, 1979), 212. See also E. W. Nicholson, *Deuteronomy and Tradition* (Oxford: Basil Blackwell, 1967), 47.

18. See Schmidt, *"Vergegenwärtingung,"* 182.

19. The phrase "Hear, O Israel," also occurs in Dt 4:1, 20:3, and 27:9. Note the proximity of "today" or "this day" to these occurrences, a point to be taken up below.

20. See A. S. Herbert, *Worship in Ancient Israel*, Ecumenical Studies in Worship 5 (Richmond, Va.: John Knox Press, 1959), 14ff. He gives five liturgical referents: cultic acts, ritual recitals, cultic objects, cultic persons, and cultic occasions.

21. See A. Klostermann, *Der Pentateuch: Beiträge zu seinem Verständnis und seiner Entstehungsgeschichte* (Leipzig: Al Derchert, 1907), 246.

22. See H. Zirker, *Die kultische Vergegenwärtigung der Vergangenheit in den Psalmen*, Bonner Biblische Beiträge 20 (Bonn: Peter Hanstein Verlag, 1964), 9.

23. W. Schrottroff, *'Gedenken' im Alten Orient und im Alten Testament, die Wurzel Zakar im semitischen Sprachkreis* (Neukirchen: Neukirchener Verlag, 1964), 172f.

24. Dt 5:22: *kal qᵉhālkĕm*: all your assembly; 9:10: *bᵉyôm haqqāhāl*: on [the] day of the assembly. See chapter 5 in which we discuss the implications of this for the meaning of Christian community.

25. See Appendix A in Weinfeld, *Deuteronomy*, 330, #20.

26. See S. Mowinckel, *Le Décalogue* (Paris: F. Alcan, 1927), 129 and 139. Also, A. Klostermann, *Der Pentateuch*, 344; and B. Gemser, "The Importance of the Motive Clause in Old Testament Law," *Supplements to Vetus Testamentum*, vol. 1 (Leiden: E. J. Brill, 1953) 62.

27. P. Buis and J. Leclercq, *Le Deutéronome* (Paris: J. Gabalda, 1963), 121.

28. See G. E. Wright, "Cult and History: A Study of a Current Problem in Old Testament Interpretation," *Interpretation* 16 (1962) 14. He gives four liturgical referents: hymnic forms, legal corpora, confessions, and liturgies. See also W. Eichrodt, *Theology of the Old Testament*, vol. 1, 102–76; his categories for liturgical referents are Sacred Sites, Sacred Objects, Sacred Seasons, and Sacred Actions.

29. Von Rad, *Problems of the Hexateuch*, 28. See also Schmidt, "Vergegenwärtingung," 183; Wright, "Cult and History," 8; Klostermann, *Der Pentateuch*, 340; and Nicholson, *Deuteronomy and Tradition*, 45. Weinfeld (*Deuteronomy and the Deuteronomic School*, 174), holds the position that the use of "today" is merely a rhetorical idiom intended to stress the solemnity of the occasion.

30. "Today" occurs twice at the beginning of the section (5:1, 3), three times in chapter 8 (vv. 1, 11, 19; "this day" *[hayyôm hezeh]* also appears in v. 18), and seven times in the conclusion of the section in chapter 11 (vv. 2, 8, 13, 26, 27, 28, 32; "this day" also appears in v. 4).

31. All *hayyôm*: 12:8, 13:18, 15:5, 19:9, 20:3. For 20:3, note the use of "Hear, O Israel," a liturgical utterance we mentioned above; see also 6:4–6.

32. *hayyôm*: 26:3, 7, 18; 27:1, 4, 10; 28:1, 13, 14, 15; *hayyôm hezeh*: 26:16; 27:9.

33. This could be due to the fact that Dt 12–28 is an older section and the terms "today" and "this day" are later insertions. We briefly address the redaction of Deuteronomy below.

34. Vv. 4, 9, 11, 14 (2x), 17, 28 (the *hayyôm hezeh* term); this chapter is a summary and actualization of the covenant.

35. Vv. 2, 8, 11, 15, 16, 18, 19; this chapter is a liturgical address to the community.

36. It is interesting to note that Weinfeld does not include these words in his Appendix A where he lists deuteronomic repetition.

37. See note 29 above.

38. J. Muilenburg, "A Study in Hebrew Rhetoric: Repetition and Style" in *Supplements to Vetus Testamentum*, vol. 1 (Leiden: E. J. Brill, 1953), 100.

39. Muilenburg, "A Study in Hebrew Rhetoric," 99.

40. Muilenburg, "A Study in Hebrew Rhetoric," 100.

41. R. L. Harris, et. al., *Theological Wordbook of the Old Testament* (Chicago: Moody Press, 1981), 241ff. For meanings of *zkr* in extra-deuteronomic writings, which have parallels with this presentation, see H. G. Reventlow, "Das Amt des Mazkir," *Theologische Zeitschrift* 15 (1959), 164ff. See, too, M. Thurian, *The Eucharistic Memorial*, Part 1: The Old Testament, trans. J. G. Davies (London: Lutterworth Press, 1960), 22ff for a broader interpretation; his first two meanings coincide with our presentation.

42. Dt 5:15 is given as an example of this level of meaning. It will be shown below that this falls short of what is implied because of the liturgical context of the passage.

43. The following list are these passages with the implied action and upon whom that action ensues, God or the people:

5:15	People are to keep the sabbath day.
7:18	God will take care of the people.
8:2	God tests the people.
9:27	God shall not regard the infidelity of the people.
15:15	People are to keep the commandments.
16:3	People are to keep the Passover.
16:12	People are to observe these statutes.
24:18	People are to keep the commandments.
24:22	People are to keep the commandments.
32:7	God establishes the people.

44. See Schrottroff, "*Gedenken*," 118, 119; Gemser, "The Importance of the Motive Clause," 55ff; J. Cogswell, "Lest We Forget: A Sermon," *Interpretation* 15 (1961) 45–46.

45. H. Eising, "*zkr*," in G. J. Botterweck and H. Ringgren, eds., *Theological Dictionary of the Old Testament*, vol. 4, trans. David E. Green (Grand Rapids, Mich.: William B. Eerdmans Publishing Co., 1980), 66.

46. See B. S. Childs, *Memory and Tradition in Israel* (London: SCM Press, Ltd., 1962), 75. See also Schrottroff, "*Gedenken*," 159f; F. J. Leenhardt, *Le Sacrement de la sainte cène* (Neuchatel: Delachaux & Niestle, 1948), 16; N. A. Dahl, "Anamnesis. Mémoire et commémoration dans le christianisme primitif," *Studia Theologica* 1 (1947) 72; Blair, "An Appeal to Remembrance," 43f; J. Pedersen, *Israel: Its Life and Culture*, vols. I-II (London: Oxford University Press, 1926), 106f; J. Muilenburg, "The Biblical View of Time," *Harvard Theological Review* 54 (1961) 244.

47. Eleven passages mention these categories of people: Dt 10:18; 14:29; 16:11, 14; 24:17, 19, 20, 21; 26:12, 13; 27:19.

48. For example, O. S. Rankin, *Israel's Wisdom Literature: Its Bearing on Theology and the History of Religion* (Edinburgh: T. & T. Clark, 1936), 3 and M. Weinfeld, "The Origin of the Humanism in Deuteronomy," *Journal of Biblical Literature* 80 (1961) 243, 245.

49. For example, W. O. E. Oesterley, *The Wisdom of Egypt and the Old Testament*

in the Light of the Newly Discovered 'Teaching of Amen-em-ope' (London: SPCK, 1927), 76.

50. G. Von Rad, *Wisdom in Israel* (London: SCM Press, 1972), 188.

51. Weinfeld, *Deuteronomy and the Deuteronomic School*, 290. See also Weinfeld, "The Origin of Humanism," 244. For a more extensive treatment of the widow in Israel, see de Vaux, *Ancient Israel*, 40.

52. "For *[ki]* you were strangers [sojourners] in the land of Egypt" (Dt 10:19; cf. Ex 22:21).

53. Oesterley, *The Wisdom of Egypt*, 77.

54. Or, in Thurian's terms, "as a thanksgiving to God, something that can be done for God," 27.

55. W. Eichrodt, *Theology of the Old Testament*, vol. 2, trans. J. A. Baker (London: SCM Press, 1961–67), 297.

56. We understand this phrase to be a symbol for anyone counted as the "downtrodden" of society.

57. See Weinfeld, *Deuteronomy and the Deuteronomic School*, Appendix A, 320–65.

58. The Psalms have the most frequent occurrence of the verb "to remember" as well; see note 1.

59. Admittedly, no attempt here has been made to separate preexilic, exilic, and postexilic material in the prophets. This would probably reveal further interesting results.

60. "Today" appears seven times and "this day" occurs six times.

Chapter 2. Concern for Others: *Diakonia*

1. This phrase is borrowed from the title of a handy little volume published over a decade ago but nonetheless still valuable as an introduction to an expanded notion of ministry: *The Ministry Explosion: A New Awareness of Every Christian's Call to Minister* by R. J. Hater (Dubuque, Iowa: William C. Brown Company Publishers, 1979).

2. See J. D. G. Dunn, *Jesus and the Spirit* (Philadelphia: The Westminster Press, 1975), 249.

3. Dunn, *Jesus and the Spirit*, 249.

4. See chapter 5 for our remarks on the ministry of the assembly.

5. To be sure, early in the church this service was formalized in an office. Already in Acts 6:1ff there is evidence of service being a formal office to which some are called by the community for special service: "Therefore, friends, select from among yourselves seven men of good standing, full of the Spirit and of wisdom, whom we may appoint to this task" (Acts 6:3; NRSV). To this first meaning of *diakonia* applied to the gift/responsibility incumbent upon all Christians, Dunn comments that "it should be noted however that the charisma of *diakonia* here does not signify a particular office (diaconate) or act of service as a community appointment or even at the community's behest" (*Jesus and the Spirit*, 249). When we begin to grasp *diakonia* in terms of self-expression, we are already on the road toward a conceptualization of the question raised at the end of chapter 1 that addresses dualisms and the relationship between being and action. For reflections on the relationship of ministry and self-expression within the context of "priesthood," see my article "Priesthood Through the Eyes of a Non-Ordained Priest" (*Eglise et Théologie* 19 [1988]), 223–40.

6. *Did* 15:3 from C. C. Richardson (trans. and ed.), *Early Christian Fathers* (New York: Macmillan Publishing Company, Inc. Unless otherwise indicated, all direct quotations from early sources are taken from this handy volume.

7. *1 Apology* 15–16.

8. See G. W. H. Lampe, "Diakonia in the Early Church" in *Service in Christ*, ed. J. I. McCord and T. H. L. Parker (Grand Rapids, Mich.: William B. Eerdmans Publishing Company, 1966), 50.

9. We need only to read the Infancy Narrative in Luke's Gospel to be convinced that Jesus was identified with the poor; for example, in Lk 2:7 we read "and she gave birth to her first-born son and wrapped him in bands of cloth, and laid him in a manger, because there was no place for them in the inn" (NRSV).

10. 1 *Clement* 38:1. Ignatius states this in a different way, but no less clearly: "Only what you do together is right. Hence you must have one prayer, one petition, one mind, one hope, dominated by love and unsullied joy—that means you must have Jesus Christ" (*Magnesians* 7:1).

11. *Plea Regarding Christians*, chapter 11; italics added.

12. On the relationship of fasting and almsgiving, see R. Grant's *Early Christianity and Society: Seven Studies* (San Francisco: Harper & Row Publishers, 1977), 130–31. See also 2 *Clement* 16:4. Fasting and almsgiving are frequent themes in the *Shepherd* of Hermas: *Vision* III, 10:6; *Parable* V, 1:4–5 and V, 3:5–8 (in *The Apostolic Fathers,* vol. 1, trans. Francis X. Glimm et. al., The Fathers of the Church, Gen. Ed. Ludwig Schopp [Washington, D. C.: The Catholic University of America Press, 1962]).

13. Hermas, *Vision* III, 10:6.

14. Hermas, *Parable* V, Intro.; also Hermas, *Parable* V, 1:1–4. See also Is 58:6ff.

15. *Clement* 16:4.

16. Hermas, *Parable* V, 3:6–8.

17. See, for example, *Didache* 11:12, 13:4, 15:4; *Barnabas* 19:9, 11; Hermas, *Mandate* II, 4; Hermas, *Parable* I, Intro. and I, 8 and X, 4:2; 1 *Clement* 34:7, 38:2.

18. Hermas, *Parable* II, 5. See also *Parable* II, Intro. and Polycarp, *Philippians* 10:2.

19. Torrance, "Service in Christ" in *Service in Christ,* 14. Cf. Ignatius, *Magnesians* 6:1: "and let the deacons (my special favorites) be entrusted with the ministry of Jesus Christ."

20. Lampe, "Diakonia," 59–60, beautifully summarizes the deacons' liturgical role as developed later in the church's history in terms of the link between the presider and congregation: 1) to instruct; 2) to reconcile differences so the community may be at peace; 3) to instruct "hearers" to withdraw before the prayer for the catechumens; 4) to ask all who are not baptized to leave before the liturgy of the faithful; 5) to call for silence and attention at the Scripture readings; 6) to announce the kiss of peace; and 7) to dismiss the congregation at the end of the liturgy.

21. Lampe, "Diakonia," 60. Cf. Ignatius, *Trallians* 2:3; Hermas, *Parable* I, 26:2.

22. Lampe, "Diakonia," 61.

23. Though this problem of limited eucharistic theology in early church writings does not directly concern us here, the arguments and explanations put forward data that is helpful for our inquiry.

24. In this context, Pelikan remarks that "against various heresies and schisms, the orthodox and catholic church defined as apostolic doctrine that which it believed, taught, and confessed. This doctrine, so it was presumed, had been *believed* and taught

by the church *before* heresy demanded that it be confessed" (J. Pelikan, *The Emergence of the Catholic Tradition (100–600),* vol. 1, The Christian Tradition: A History of the Development of Doctrine [Chicago and London: The University of Chicago Press, 1971], 121; italics added).

25. Pelikan, *The Emergence,* 123; also, 141–42, 166–67.

26. G. W. H. Lampe, "The Eucharist in the Thought of the Early Church" in *Eucharistic Theology Then and Now,* Theological Collections #9 (London: SPCK, 1968), 34.

27. Lampe, "Eucharist," 34.

28. Lampe, "Eucharist," 37.

29. J. E. Carpenter, *Phases of Early Christianity: Six Lectures* (New York and London: G. P. Putnam's Sons, 1916), 268.

30. See Ignatius, *Romans,* Intro.

31. See Irenaeus, *Heresies* II, 3:2: that Peter and Paul founded this church also contributes to its preeminence. See also 1 *Clement* 5:4–7 which mentions that Peter and Paul were martyred in Rome and Ignatius, *Romans* 4:3 where Ignatius indicates that Peter and Paul were apostles with authority. All quotations from Irenaeus will be taken from *Five Books of S. Irenaeus Bishop of Lyons Against Heresies,* trans. John Keble (Oxford: James Parker and Co., 1972).

32. Cf. 1 *Clement* 56:2, 58:2, 59:1, 63:2.

33. This is noted in R. C. D. Jasper and G. J. Cuming, trans. and ed., *Prayers of the Eucharist: Early and Reformed,* 3d revised ed. (New York: Pueblo Publishing Company, 1987), 25.

34. Ignatius, *Trallians,* 2:3; cf. Ignatius, *Smyrnaeans* 6:2.

35. Cf. Ignatius, *Ephesians* 5:2 and *Philadelphians* 4:1.

36. Cf. *Didache* 14:1–2; also, Irenaeus, *Fragment* III.

37. Cf. Pelikan, *The Emergence of the Catholic Tradition,* 168.

38. Ignatius, *Smyrnaeans,* 7:1; see also *Philadelphians* 4:1 and *Romans* 7:3.

39. Irenaeus, *Heresy* V, 2:2; see also IV, 17:5 and IV, 33:2 on real presence.

40. Irenaeus, *Heresy* V, 2:3; italics in original.

41. See T. B. Falls, *Writings of Saint Justin Martyr,* Fathers of the Church Series (New York: Christian Heritage, 1948).

42. Lampe, "Eucharist," 38.

43. *Dialogue* 41:2 quoting Mal 1:10–11.

44. See Pelikan, *The Emergence of the Catholic Tradition,* 146.

45. Cf. W. Rordorf et. al., *The Eucharist of the Early Christians,* trans. Matthew J. O'Connell (New York: Pueblo Publishing Company, 1978).

46. *Heresy* IV, 18:3. See also IV, 18:1 where Irenaeus quotes Mt 5:23–24 ("leave your gift there before the altar and go; first be reconciled to your brother, and then come and offer your gift."), and IV 18:3 where Irenaeus comments that Cain's sacrifice was not pure and acceptable to God because he harbored "envy and malice toward his brother."

47. For further references on Eucharist as sacrifice, see Ignatius, *Romans* 2:2; *Martyrdom of Polycarp,* 14:1; Athenagoras, *Plea* 13; 1 *Clement* 44; Justin, *Dialogue* 117.

48. *Romans* 7:3. On Eucharist as eschatological assurance, see also *Barnabas* 3:1–5 and 21:1.

49. Cf. Lampe, "Eucharist," 35.

50. Lampe, "Eucharist," 35.

51. Thus, the deacon not only *administers* the resources of the church for the needy, but this is also an *extension* of the deacon's ministry of distributing communion to those present during the Eucharist. See Lampe, "Diakonia," 60.

52. See, for example, Ignatius, *Philadelphians* 6:1 and 1 *Clement* 59:4; Justin, 1 *Apology* 67; Irenaeus, *Heresy* V, 33:2; *Barnabas* 3:1–5.

53. Cf. Grant, *Early Christianity and Society*, 130–33.

54. H. Conzelmann, *History of Primitive Christianity*, trans. John E. Steely (Nashville, Tenn.: Abingdon Press, 1973) 87.

55. See, for example, Ignatius, *Smyrnaeans*, 6:2; Justin, 1 *Apology* 67; 1 *Clement* 59:4.

56. Cf. Grant, *Early Christianity and Society*, 131. Liturgical formulae of those in need played extensively in chapter 1 with the phrase "the sojourner, the fatherless, and the widow. "

57. Lampe, "Diakonia," 48.

58. Torrance, "Service in Christ," 14.

Chapter 3. The Paschal Mystery: *Methodological Openings*

1. For a more complete treatment of Ricoeur's method of textual hermeneutics and the pertinent references to Ricoeur's works, see J. A. Zimmerman, *Liturgy as Language of Faith: A Liturgical Methodology in the Mode of Paul Ricoeur's Textual Hermeneutics* (Lanham, New York, London: University Press of America, 1988), 71–92 and especially pp. 88–90.

2. Immediately, I utter a caution: our object of inquiry is not limited to a printed sacramentary (though that is surely a text and, even what we usually think of as "text"), but includes the whole rite in both verbal and nonverbal dimensions as it is actually celebrated. Also, it should be noted that the closest Ricoeur comes to applying his method to what might be considered a liturgical text is in his occasional interpretations of scripture passages— especially Gospel parables—and comments on preaching.

3. "Understanding" has less to do with concepts and perception— epistemological categories—as it does with being and reality—ontological categories. In other words, understanding has less to do with the mind and more to do with the heart and will. This will become clearer as we continue to delve into Ricoeur's interpretation theory.

4. These points are taken up and expanded below in chapter 5.

5. This "riddle" of an interpretation already given in the object to be interpreted is referred to as a "hermeneutic circle." Ricoeur claims that interpretation gets us somewhere because interpretation changes our self-understanding. This will become clearer as we examine the other two methodic moments.

6. By "structure" Ricoeur means more than the observable configuration that makes something up. Biologists once thought they had cracked the essence of life by discovering DNA and RNA. Now they know there are even smaller building blocks of life and the search goes on. Liturgists once thought they had cracked the essentials of liturgy by thoroughly revising liturgical texts according to Vatican II's principles of renewal. Now we know these adaptations cannot guarantee authentic celebration of liturgy and the work of renewal goes on. "Structure" is a depth dynamic that makes something what it is. The closer we come to grasping a text's deep structure, the closer we come to entering into the human existence documented by the text.

7. Like text, "language" has a broad extension. More than words in a dictionary belonging to a particular language group, language can be any communicative expression.

8. See P. Ricoeur, "The Model of the Text: Meaningful Action Considered as a Text" in *Hermeneutics and the Human Sciences: Essays on Language, Action and Interpretation*, ed., trans. and intro. by John B. Thompson (Cambridge: Cambridge University Press, 1981), 218.

9. See Ricoeur, "The Model of the Text," 202.

10. Time and historicity are major themes that Ricoeur develops in works other than those upon which we are drawing. We are using this phrase "out of time" in a ritual sense to mean atemporal in which we are "caught up" in a "timeless" ritual moment.

11. Actually, its liturgical trace is most aptly expressed as profession and acclamation.

12. Note that these last five entries to the diagram—Self-understanding, Liturgy of the Hours, Eucharist, Liturgical Year, and Liturgical Spirituality—are the content of the last five chapters of this book.

13. The more properly philosophical term is "solipsistic."

14. See P. Ricoeur, *Sémantique de l'action* (Louvain: Université Catholique de Louvain—Cercle de Philosophie, 1971, polycopy), 129.

15. Ricoeur, *Sémantique de l'action*, 139; translation my own.

16. See Ricoeur, *Sémantique de l'action*, 130. Ricoeur claims that phenomenology and linguistic analysis see the will as solipsistic: *I* will, *I* decide, *I* evaluate my motives, etc. (see *Sémantique de l'action*, 131). Elsewhere, Ricoeur asks the question: "What kind of action makes sense?" (P. Ricoeur, "The Problem of the Will and Philosophical Discourse" in *Patterns of the Life-World, Essays in Honor of John Wild*, ed. J. Edie, F. Parker, and C. O. Schray [Evanston: Northwestern University Press, 1970], 277).

17. Ricoeur, *Sémantique de l'action*, 131. These new objects are possible because phenomenological reduction allows for a neutralization of the discourse (see ibid.), that is, "all the naturalist statements about things, facts, and laws are bracketed and the world appears as a field of meaning" (Ricoeur, "The Problem of the Will and Philosophical Discourse," 275).

18. Ricoeur, "The Problem of the Will and Philosophical Discourse," 277; italics added. On "norms," see also Ricoeur, *Sémantique de l'action*, 133 and "The Problem of the Foundation of Moral Philosophy," trans. D. Pellauer, *Philosophy Today* 22 (1978) 184–85.

19. Ricoeur, "The Problem of the Will and Philosophical Discourse," 283. Liturgy is a good partner with which to enter into a dialectic with respect to arbitrary and normative wills. The normativity of liturgy (the Paschal Mystery) is expressed cumulatively through a tradition of celebrations and is ever the recognition that the choices we make as the Body of Christ are both our own (arbitrary) *and* Another's.

20. See P. Ricoeur, "Nature and Freedom," trans. D. Steward in *Political and Social Essays*, ed. D. Steward and J. Bien (Athens: Ohio University Press, 1975), 32. See also J. W. Van Den Hengel, *The Home of Meaning: The Hermeneutics of the Subject of Paul Ricoeur* (Washington, D. C.: University Press of America, 1982), 162–64.

21. See Ricoeur, "Nature and Freedom," 43.

22. See P. Ricoeur, *The Rule of Metaphor: Multi-disciplinary Studies of the Creation of Meaning in Language*, trans. R. Czerny with K. McLaughlin and J. Costello, S. J. (Toronto: University of Toronto Press, 1977), 308.

23. See Ricoeur, "The Problem of the Will and Philosophical Discourse," 284. See also Ricoeur, "The Problem of the Foundation of Moral Philosophy," 176.

24. See Ricoeur, *Sémantique de l'action*, 136.

25. See Ricoeur, *Sémantique de l'action*, IX-8. The implication here is that freedom is recoverable in the structures of human experience. It should be noted that Ricoeur does not mean by "experience" a feeling or the inexpressible. For Ricoeur (following Husserl), experience "has a meaning, an essentially *expressible* structure and which, by this very fact, lends itself to an *essential* analysis" (P. Ricoeur, "Phenomenology of Freedom" in *Phenomenology and Philosophical Understanding*, ed. E. Pivcevic [London: Cambridge University Press, 1975], 183; italics Ricoeur's).

26. Note Ricoeur's remark: "all that is possible through freedom is practical" (Ricoeur, *Sémantique de l'action*, 141).

27. Ricoeur, "The Problem of the Will and Philosophical Discourse," 284.

28. Ibid.

29. Ibid. We must insert here, too, what Ricoeur has called "freedom in the second person" (see Ricoeur, "The Problem of the Foundation of Moral Philosophy," 178). The self-affirmation of freedom and the history conferred on one by that is complemented by a willing of the other's freedom (see ibid.) and her/his history.

30. See Ricoeur, "The Problem of the Will and Philosophical Discourse," 285.

31. Ibid., 288.

32. See P. Ricoeur, "Can There Be a Scientific Concept of Ideology?" in *Phenomenology and the Social Sciences: A Dialogue*, ed. J. Bien (the Hague: M. Nijhoff, 1978), 44.

33. See P. Ricoeur, "Science and Ideology" in *Hermeneutics and the Human Sciences: Essays on Language, Action and Interpretation*, ed., trans. Intro. J. B. Thompson (Cambridge: Cambridge University Press, 1981), 223. Actually, Ricoeur sees ideology as one pole of a dialectic, the other pole being utopia. Ideology is a generative, operative dynamic within society; utopia is neither a fantasy nor romantic ideal, but rather a literary genre that gives expression to the fullness a society may achieve within its ideology. Since the present discussion concerns a hermeneutics of action, only the first pole of the dialectic is developed here. For more on utopia as the second pole, see P. Ricoeur, "L'Herméneutique de la secularization: Foi, Ideologie, Utopie," *Archivo di folosofia* (1976), 56–68.

34. See Ricoeur, "Science and Ideology," 225–30.

35. See Ricoeur, "Science and Ideology," 225. See also Ricoeur, "Can There Be a Scientific Concept of Ideology?" 45.

36. Ricoeur, "Science and Ideology," 225.

37. Ibid., 243.

38. It is always risky to make a literal one-on-one correspondence between two such diverse disciplines as a philosophy of human action and a theology of liturgical celebration. But who could resist thinking of the Holy Spirit when Ricoeur suggests that ideology is characterized by "dynamism"?

39. See Ricoeur, "Science and Ideology," 226.

40. See Ricoeur, "Can There Be a Scientific Concept of Ideology?" 46.

41. Ricoeur, "Science and Ideology," 226.

42. Ibid., 227. See also Ricoeur, "Can There Be a Scientific Concept of Ideology?" 47.

43. Ricoeur, "Science and Ideology," 227. The rubricism of past liturgical history is a good example of an uncritical, inert stance toward Christian ideology.

44. See Ricoeur, "Science and Ideology," 228. See also Ricoeur, "L'Herméneutique de la secularization: Foi, Ideologie, Utopie," 54.

45. See Ricoeur, "Science and Ideology," 228–29. See also Ricoeur, "Can There Be a Scientific Concept of Ideology?" 48–50.

46. Ricoeur, "Science and Ideology," 230. It is this distorted stage to which we usually refer when speaking about ideology.

47. See Ricoeur, "Can There Be a Scientific Concept of Ideology?" 59.

48. This is what is at stake and the reason for my adamant opposition to the Roman Catholic Church's promulgation of an official rite for Communion Services. If this practice is allowed to become widespread, we run a serious risk of losing our identity as a eucharistic church and, therefore, of destroying the one guarantee—liturgical (eucharistic) celebration—that the Paschal Mystery still characterizes Christian self-understanding.

49. P. Ricoeur, "Le 'Lieu' de la dialectique" in *Dialectics/Dialectiques,* International Institute of Philosophy, ed. Ch. Perelman (the Hague: Nijhoff, 1973), 95.

50. On freedom, and especially Ricoeur's "freedom in the second person," see Ricoeur, "The Problem of the Foundation of Moral Philosophy," 176–82.

51. Ricoeur sees law as the culminating step in the constitution of the meaning of value, norm, imperative, and law (see Ricoeur, "The Problem of the Foundation of Moral Philosophy," 187–89).

Chapter 4. The Paschal Mystery: *A Lucan Structure*

1. And all too often we do just that. Witness how often liturgy "planning" parallels that for a party: concern for decorations, music, innovation, coffee. While there is certainly nothing wrong with these preparatory aspects, we sometimes forget they are secondary to something far more important. When we lose sight of what is central to liturgy—celebration of the Paschal Mystery—we run the risk of no longer having authentic liturgy.

2. For some helpful comments on celebration as festivity see H. Rahner, *Man at Play* (New York: Herder and Herder, 1967); J. Pieper, *In Tune with the World: A Theory of Festivity,* trans. Richard and Clara Winston (New York: Harcourt and Brace, 1965); and H. Cox, *The Feast of Fools*: A Theological Essay on Festivity and Fantasy (New York: Harper and Row, 1969). Play and celebration were popular themes during the 1960s; Moltmann and Keen are two more names that come to mind.

3. An exegete might put such questions to the text as these: What kind of a meal was it? Is there a relation between this meal account and Acts? Does the disunity of table fellowship in Acts shed light on the disunity evidenced in the Lord's Supper table talk? Is there any influence of Pauline eucharistic theology in Luke? How does one define the various literary units and subunits? Do vv. 19b and 20 belong to the Supper account? What were Luke's sources? Was Luke a gentile or a Jewish Christian? For what community was he writing? Is the table talk simply evidence that Luke is not a very careful writer? Is Luke pursuing a contrast between fasting and banquet? Does the Lord's Supper in Luke have any apocalyptic overtones?

4. We point out that the Lord's Supper account in Luke is generally considered to be a single literary unit and has already been approached from other perspectives employing critical methodologies. See, for example, J. Neyrey's analysis of the unit as

a farewell speech (chapter 1 in *The Passion According to Luke: A Redaction Study of Luke's Soteriology* [New York: Paulist Press, 1985]). Also, R. I. Karris, O. F. M., "The Gospel According to Luke" in *The New Jerome Biblical Commentary*, R. E. Brown, J. A. Fitzmyer, and R. E. Murphy, eds. (Englewood Cliffs, N.J.: Prentice-Hall, 1990), 714f. See also P. S. Minear's analysis in terms of table companionship ("Some Glimpses of Luke's Sacramental Theology," *Worship* 44 [1970] 322-31). I am not suggestins that my perspective replace these or other analyses. I propose it complements them but carries the discussion into a different direction.

5. L. Bouyer, *Eucharist: Theology and Spirituality of the Eucharistic Prayer,* trans. Charles Underhill Quinn (Notre Dame: University of Notre Dame Press,1968), 79.

6. An interesting implication here is that the *haggadah* may be the Jewish answer to meaning and the historical question.

7. Some authors (for example, D. Hedegard *[Seder R. Amram Gaon, Part I,* Hebrew Text with Critical Apparatus, Translation with Notes and Introduction {Lund: A. B. Ph. Lindstedts, 1951}] 139 and 149 and L. Finkelstein, "The Birkat Ha-Mazon," *Jewish Quarterly Review* 19-20 [1928–1930] 212) claim there were four thanksgiving cup blessings, but Finkelstein indicates (p. 219) that prior to the Christian era there were probably only three. This discussion does not really affect our inquiry.

8. Bouyer, 84 and Finkelstein, 235.

9. This structure rests on accepting vv. 19b and 20 as belonging to the Lucan Lord's Supper account. Most scholars agree that the manuscript evidence is weighted in favor of accepting these verses as authentic. See J. A. Fitzmyer, *The Gospel According to Luke*, 2 volumes, The Anchor Bible (Garden City, N.Y.: Doubleday & Company, Inc., 1981 and 1985), 1387–89 for an analysis of the textual problem with these verses and 1405–6 for a bibliography. Textual evidence supporting a festal meal interpretation for Luke's Supper includes mention of the unleavened bread and Passover lamb (v. 7), eating of the passover meal (vv. 8 and 15), careful preparations (vv. 8–13), reclining at table (v. 14), two cups (vv. 17 and 20; see Fitzmyer, 1389). We are not arguing that the Lord's Supper was necessarily a Passover meal, only that the evidence points either that way or to another festal meal. Fitzmyer argues that at least it has a Passover character that ought to be recognized (ibid. 1389). On these verses from Luke and the Passover meal structure, see Karris, 715.

10. Hedegard, 144.

11. Both interpretations are possible; see Fitzmyer, 1390.

12. Fulfillment is a theme that threads its way throughout Luke's Gospel. Therefore, it is not surprising to find a contrast between "what was" and "a more perfect fulfillment." Moreover, other places in Luke where the conjunction *plēn* is found contrasts a new possibility with the old reality. See, for example, Lk 6:35, "but love your enemies"; Lk 10:20, "but rejoice . . . your names are written in heaven"; Lk 11:41, "and see, everything will be clean for you."

13. E. Barbotin, *The Humanity of God*, trans. Matthew J. O'Connell (Maryknoll, New York: Orbis Books, 1976), 285. Cf. Mt. 8:11-12.

14. There are differing opinions among exegetes for the number of meals. C. Stuhlmueller ("The Gospel of Saint Luke," in *Jerome Biblical Commentary,* R. E. Brown, J. A. Fitzmyer, R. E. Murphy, eds. [Englewood Cliffs, N.J.: Prentice-Hall, 1968], 138) notes six meals in which Jesus shares, all of them before the Lord's Supper account. E. E. Ellis *(The Gospel of Luke* [London/New York: Thomas Nelson Sons, 1966], 33) remarks that there are eight meal scenes, in keeping with what he presents as symbolic elements (he leaves out 10:38). J. Navone *(Themes of St. Luke* [Rome: Grego-

rian University Press, 1970], 16) comments that there are seven banquet scenes, the first five (5:29-32; 7:34-50; 11:37-54; 14:1-24; 15:1-32) depict the essential nature of Jesus' prophetic mission and the last two (22:1-32 and 24:13-35) deal with the problems of the New Israel.

15. Only for the first and seventh Lucan meal pericopes does the meal context appear in the synoptic parallels. The meal accounts in Luke show dependence on Luke's special source or else extensive redaction on the part of the third evangelist.

16. Note that this parable has no parallel in the other two synoptics.

17. Navone, 29-30 and Ellis, 191–92.

18. See Navone, 14.

19. P. S. Minear, *Commands of Christ* (Nashville, Tenn.: Abingdon Press, 1972), 180.

20. Minear, *Commands of Christ,* 181.

21. See Minear, *Commands of Christ,* 179-80.

22. This, of course, does not deny that there are subunits. See, for example, J. Fitzmyer, who divides the Passion Narrative into two major subsections, The Preliminary Events and The Passion, Death, and Burial of Jesus. The Preliminary Events subsection is further divided into eight subunits, the last four of which are the four dialogues (we discuss below the reasons for our position that there are five). We find it particularly interesting that each conversation is treated as a subunit at the same structural level as the Lord's Supper itself.

23. Nonetheless we suggest the parable is implicit. The Passion itself might be a kind of "parable" in the light of the parables told by Jesus, drawing on his very life to invite our appropriation of these events as a living parable of the contrast between the two kingdoms.

24. See, for example, Fitzmyer who titles this section "Jesus' Remarks on the Disciples and their Places in the Kingdom" (1411; see also 1407). Minear also lists four dialogues; he does not account for vv. 28–30 (*Commands of Christ,* 183–87). See Neyrey (23–24) for an exegete who divides this section into five dialogues as I have done.

25. See B. H. Throckmorton, Jr., ed. *Gospel Parallels: A Synopsis of the First Three Gospels* (Toronto, Camden, N.J., London: Thomas Nelson & Sons, 1967), 165–69. See also Fitzmyer, 1408.

26. Matthew and Mark both place the prediction of Judas's betrayal before the Institution Narrative. The dispute over who is the greatest occurs before Jesus enters Jerusalem in Matthew (20:25-28) and Mark (10:42-45); it is not the disciples who inquire but the mother of James and John who asks for a place of honor for her sons in the Kingdom. Matthew (19:28)—before the discourse on greatness—records Jesus' promise that the apostles will sit on the twelve thrones; there is no parallel in Mark for Lk 22:28-30. Peter's denial happens during the conversation on the way to the Mount of Olives in Matthew (26:33-35) and Mark (14:29-31).

27. See J. Jeremias, *The Eucharistic Words of Jesus* (London: SCM Press, Ltd., 1974), 97; also, W. Harrington, *The Gospel According to Luke* (Westminster, Md.: Newman Press, 1966), 247. J. M. Green (*The Gospel According to St. Luke* [New York: St. Martin's Press, 1969], 261) remarks that the Lucan account is dependent on the Marcan account but differs from it in several respects. He further adds that "the Lucan picture of the Supper represents a natural tendency to group together especially characteristic teachings of Jesus in the account of his last meal with his disciples" (262-63).

28. See Stuhlmueller, 158-59.

29. See C. H. Talbert, *Literary Patterns, Theological Themes, and the Genre of Luke-Acts*, Society of Biblical Literature Monograph Series 20 (Missoula, Mont.: Society of Biblical Literature and Scholars Press, 1974), 17.

30. Cf. Talbert, 26.

31. Two scholars who accept this position are J. Neyrey, chapter 1, "Jesus' Farewell Speech (Lk 22:14-38)" and X. Léon-Dufour, *Sharing the Eucharistic Bread: The Witness of the New Testament*, trans. Matthew J. O'Connell (New York: Paulist Press, 1987), 90-91.

32. See Neyrey, 7, for one description of the elements of a farewell speech.

33. See Fitzmyer, 1407. R. E. Brown (*The Gospel According to John* (xiii-xxi), The Anchor Bible [Garden City, N.Y.: Doubleday & Company, Inc., 1970], 598-600) lists thirteen features of a farewell speech. A number of them are noticeably lacking in the Lucan account: reassurance following sorrow at leaving; recital of past life; directive to keep commandments; injunction to unity and to love one another; calling down of peace on the disciples; concern for the endurance of one's name; closing the address with a prayer. My purpose here is not to argue definitively whether Luke's account has the literary genre of a farewell speech. I am only pointing out that there is enough doubt about the use of this genre that we do not have to conclude definitively that it was a farewell speech. The table talk, therefore, could stand as a unit.

34. I am indebted to L. Gregory Bloomquist, professor of New Testament at St. Paul University, Ottawa, Ontario, for this insight.

35. A concentric structure may be operative in these various groups of five elements, and is especially evident in the Infancy Narratives and the Our Father. When concentric, the center term (Magnificat, daily bread) is eschatological in tone. Concentric structure and eschatological theme are developed below when we examine the structure of the five dialogues.

36. Jeremias, 205.

37. Stuhlmueller, 158.

38. Ibid.

39. Ibid.

40. Stuhlmueller (159) comments that "practically all commentators take . . . [it] figuratively. The disciples must be ready for any and every circumstance." E. Franklin (*Christ the Lord: Study in the Purpose and Theology of Luke-Acts* [Philadelphia: The Westminster Press, 1975], 167) thinks that "the Lord's saying about the taking of a sword (22:35-38) contrasts the later times with that of the initial journey." Minear (*Commands of Christ*, 186) believes that since the apostles had swords already present with them that they had already prepared for combat and "like Ananias and Sapphira (Acts 5:1-11), they had violated their communal vows by an action compounded of deceit, greed, and fear."

41. Cf. Harrington, 252-53.

42. We are using elements of rhetorical analysis, especially in our remarks on concentric structure; this properly belongs to the critical methods. Our own method, however, remains postcritical in that we are more concerned with structure than with literary figures.

43. Minear, "Luke and Sacramental Theology," 326-27.

44. Actually, this is the only one of the five dialogues that is not a "dialogue" in the true sense of having both address and response. I believe this serves to underscore the singularity of this third "dialogue."

45. Neyrey, 24. The NRSV has "confer" but "appoint" is a more literal translation of the Greek.

46. See Minear, "Luke and Sacramental Theology," 328.

47. Our evidence for a concentric structure is based on a recurring pattern of themes and phrases. We already noted above the possible concentric structure of the Infancy Narrative and the Our Father. On concentric structure, see R. Meynet, *L'Évangile selon Saint Luc. Analyse rhétorique commentaire* (Paris: Les Éditions du Cerf, 1988), 13. Meynet's commentary on Lk 22:15–38 (see pp. 211f) includes a number of examples of concentric structure, but since he does not delineate subunits for this text and does not treat the five dialogues as a subunit, his use of this rhetorical figure is not very helpful for our purposes.

48. J. Breck comments that "the uniqueness of the chiastic structure lies in its focus upon a *pivotal theme*, about which the other propositions of the literary unit are developed" ("Biblical Chiasmus: Exploring Structure for Meaning," *Biblical Theology Bulletin* 17 [1987] 71). Here, Breck is using the chiastic figure as Meynet uses the concentric figure. Our point is not to argue definitions of literary figures but that the concentric structure (or chiastic, for some scholars) has a middle term that shapes the meaning of the subunit.

49. "Soteriology" and "eschatology" are technical theological terms, each with a long history of interpretation and variety of meanings. We might do well to pause and lend some concrete substance to the particular way in which we are using these two terms. Our springboard will be the rich source of material in Paul, though our conclusions about these two terms will be shaped to our own purposes.

Soteriology, etymologically considered, comes from the Greek meaning a word about or science of salvation. Paul frames his explanation within his particular theology and emphasizes that the author of our salvific plan is not Christ but God the Father. Our starting point for understanding soteriology is a gratuitous initiation (Rm 1:16; 10:10; 11:11) or a "call" (Rm 8:30) by God to respond to this saving plan, which is one conceived before the formation of the world (Eph 1:14) and in which God manifests munificence and fidelity in forgiving and vindicating God's people.

This salvific activity finds its most concrete expression in all God's promises, ultimately finding their YES in Christ (2 Cor 1:20). All things would be reconciled to God by being subordinated to the utterly obedient fidelity of Christ (Eph 1:9–10; Col 1:13–20; Rom 8:28–30). For Paul, Christ's "sacrifice" is a positive expression of love and obedience rather than a negative expression of fear and propitiation.

Though Christ's life, suffering, death, Resurrection, Ascension, and promised return—the Paschal event—is a decisive moment in the divine plan of salvation, nevertheless there is nothing automatic about salvation. We do not get a "free ride," so to speak. Just as Christ's obedience is manifested in a unique filial relationship as Son so, too, must our obedience be manifested as daughters and sons. We recognize and admit our lack of fidelity and errant ways, but this in the face of the loving call of God through Christ to restore the weakened or broken relationship. Our life, then, is one in which we are ever striving for a more thorough alignment of our will with completely faithful obedience.

Justification is a gift dependent upon faith and a response to the proclamation of the Good News of salvation (cf. Rm 10:17). Hearing the proclamation is an event that awakens faith and, in turn, calls forth obedience from us, a personal entrusting of self to what the Gospel announces. Salvation is allowing ourselves to be possessed by the Lord. Thus giving ourselves over, the fruits of salvation that we already enjoy are reconciliation (peace) which is a return to God's favor and intimacy (2 Cor 5:18–20; Rm 5:10–11; Col 1:20–21; Eph 2:16), and redemptive liberation, which is that "glorious freedom of the children of God" (Rm 8:21).

Paul is very much a realist: our human weakness means that salvation is something still to be accomplished (1 Thes 5:9; 1 Cor 3:15; Rm 5:9–10). There is a "not yet" built into our human response to proffered salvation that very much characterizes our human condition. Indeed, one way to look at salvation is that salvation is the "not yet" of God's redemptive action on our behalf to make us God's own. This is how we use "soteriology" in these pages. It is *our* "unfinished business" in completely conforming ourselves to Christ.

Yet, we look forward to the fullness of time when all weakness will be overcome, and Christ will return all things to the Father (1 Cor 15:24–25, 28; 1 Cor 8:5). Only then will salvation be definitively won. Only then will eschatological times be ushered in.

Eschatology. Paul's understanding of eschatology derives from Jewish speculation about the end of this worldly eon and the beginning of the next, but it is distinguished from all forms of Jewish speculation by the fact that Paul considers the eschaton to have already begun as a consequence of Jesus' Resurrection from the dead. There is an overlapping of redemptive time, in that the new age has begun before the old age has passed away. Eschatology is the "already" of redemption. This mingling of the two ages—living in the "not yet" (soteriology) as well as the "already" (eschatology)—constitutes the distinctive perspective of Pauline eschatology.

As "already," eschatology (2 Cor 6:2) reminds us that the time of God's salvific plan is already fulfilled (Gal 4:5); the "new creation" is already a present reality in Christ (2 Cor 5:17); "the end of the ages" has already come upon believers (1 Cor 10:11). Thus, for Paul, the death and Resurrection of Christ is the decisive turning point in the ages. We are living a time of faith between Christ's Resurrection and the future glory that is promised to faithful daughters and sons of God. Faith is the condition of salvation to which the crucified and risen Christ gave meaning and content.

For our specific purposes, the "not yet" is an expression of soteriology and reminds us of our human need. The "already" is an expression of eschatology and reminds us that we already participate in the fullness of the Kingdom.

For an introductory bibliography and a sound overview of Pauline soteriology, see S. Lyonnet, "Pauline Soteriology" in *Introduction to the New Testament*, ed. A. Robert and A. Feuillet, trans. P. W. Skehan et al. (New York: Desclée Company, 1965), 820–65. For Paul's view of eschatology, see E. Käsemann, "An Apologia for Primitive Christian Eschatology" in *Essays on New Testament Themes, Studies in Biblical Theology*, First Series, 41 (London: SCM Press, Ltd., 1971), 169–95.

50. See vv. 7, 15–16, 18, 20.

Chapter 5. Christian Self-Understanding

1. Relating Ricoeur's methodic textual hermeneutics and his theory of meaningful human action in this way is my own. Ricoeur himself sees action as text (see his "The Model of the Text: Meaningful Action Considered as a Text" in *Hermeneutics and the Human Sciences: Essays on Language, Action and Interpretation*, ed., trans., and intro. by John B. Thompson [Cambridge: Cambridge University Press, 1981] 197–221). Ricoeur's text studies are part of his hermeneutical theory; his analysis of human action is part of his philosophy of the human sciences. I believe that to bring these two differ-

ing inquiries together is fruitful for liturgical studies since liturgy concerns both interpretation and human living and, at the same time, remains faithful to Ricoeur's thought.

2. Here, I am identifying "cultus" with liturgy. We use cultus in its etymological sense, derived from the Latin word "to cultivate" which means to prepare the soil for the seed and nurture it to fruition. There is nothing automatic about producing an abundance of fruit. It takes work and care. This is true of liturgy as well. See note 15 of chapter 1.

3. Recall chapter 4 above for the analysis that counsels this dynamic/dialectic; see chapters 6–8 below for its usefulness for interpreting liturgy.

4. We have tended to express the baptismal YES largely in terms of ethical decisions and morality. My claim is that the most profound articulation of our YES is the celebration of Eucharist. See chapter 7.

5. See note 5, chapter 2 above.

6. On Christ as high priest, see Hebrews, *passim*. On the priesthood in which we all share, see for example 1 Pet 2:9–10: "But you are a chosen race, a royal priesthood, a holy nation, God's own people, in order that you may proclaim the mighty acts of him who called you out of darkness into his marvelous light."

7. See J. A. Zimmerman, "Priesthood Through the Eyes of a Non-Ordained Priest," *Eglise et Théologie* 19 (1988) 223–40. In the same issue, see P. J. Drilling, "The Priest, Prophet and King Trilogy: Elements of Its Meaning in *Lumen Gentium* and for Today," 179–206.

8. §§ 92, 104, 112.

9. §10 and §2, respectively.

10. A very good introduction to the Gifts of the Spirit can be found in J. Koenig, Charismata: *God's Gifts for God's People* (Philadelphia: The Westminster Press, 1978).

11. It is interesting to note the number of small Christian communities that have sprung up here and there, usually to last only a few short months or years and then disband. Though the ideal was strongly enough present to give birth to these communities, I believe many of them die rather quickly because they are not sufficiently grounded in a sound theological rationale for sustaining the community: a common identity in Christ.

12. I tend to avoid language such as "re-enactment," which gives the impression of repetition as if the Paschal Mystery is more than one event.

13. It is not our intention in these brief sections to give exhaustive treatments of these very complex issues. Rather, we presume a certain familiarity with these topics on the part of the reader, and we make only enough comments about each to shape our particular context.

14. On the other hand, to practice false humility (and a degenerate form of Christian anthropology) by denying that God's love overcomes the distance between Creator and creature is, in effect, to endorse a most radical kind of dualism.

15. See chapter 3 above.

Chapter 6. Liturgy of the Hours

1. We are not, however, giving a detailed commentary on each component of the respective liturgical rite. Our purpose here is to look at the structure (and whatever of

the components is helpful) in order to identify the depth meaning or integrating dynamic that makes the rite an authentic objectification of the Paschal Mystery.

2. In some other traditions, Liturgy of the Hours (in practice, usually Morning Prayer) has been retained in a parochial setting, but it often replaces Sunday Eucharist as a regular form of Sunday worship. See, for example, *The Book of Common Prayer* or *The Book of Alternative Services of the Anglican Church of Canada.*

3. I remind the reader that I am relying on Ricoeur's *text and action theories* as the framework guiding my analysis. The language of history, time, and emplotment comes out of Ricoeur's later work and though this has some important consequences for liturgical analysis, I am limiting myself in the present work strictly to his text and action theories.

4. Our purpose is not a historical one, so we do not develop this aspect of the study at length. For some basic historical information, see P. Batiffol, *History of the Roman Breviary* (London: Longmans, Green & Co., 1912); C. W. Dugmore, *The Influence of the Synagogue Upon the Divine Office*, Alcuin Club Collections 45 (London: Faith Press, 1964); J. Jungmann, *Christian Prayer Through the Centuries*, trans. John Coyne, S. J. (New York: Paulist Press, 1978); J. Mateos, "The Morning and Evening Office," *Worship* 42 (1968) 31–47; J. Mateos, "The Origins of the Divine Office," *Worship* 41 (1967) 477–85; P. Salmon, *The Breviary Through the Centuries*, trans. Sr. D. Mary (Collegeville, Minn.: The Liturgical Press, 1962).

5. For a good introduction to the synagogue service, see L. A. Hoffman, *The Canonization of the Synagogue Service* (Notre Dame: University of Notre Dame Press, 1979). As to whether or not synagogue prayer was the actual forerunner of the Liturgy of the Hours, scholarly opinion is divided. It is not necessary for us to address this problem here. For more reading, see P. F. Bradshaw, *Daily Prayer in the Early Church: A Study of the Origin and Early Development of the Divine Office* (New York: Oxford University Press, 1982); C. W. Dugmore, *The Influence of the Synagogue Upon the Divine Office*; D. F. Scotto, T.O.R., *The Liturgy of the Hours: Its History and Its Importance As the Communal Prayer of the Church After the Liturgical Reform of Vatican II* (Petersham, Mass.: St. Bede's Publications, 1987); R. Taft, S.J., *The Liturgy of the Hours in East and West: The Origins of the Divine Office and Its Meaning for Today* (Collegeville, Minn.: The Liturgical Press, 1986).

6. "Bishop" in the early history of the church meant something quite different from what it means today.

7. Our Scripture references are from the NRSV; accordingly, the Psalms are given by the Hebrew numbering.

8. So called because it was prayed with the bishop presiding from his chair (Latin: *cathedra* = chair).

9. Strictly speaking, cathedral office was not a Word service. Except on special occasions and in particular communities (the two communities that indicate a reading from Scripture were the Egyptian and Cappadocian churches), there is no textual evidence indicating that the Word was regularly proclaimed.

10. We have no text that indicates exactly what liturgical gestures were used, but certainly there was at least use of processions, candles, and incense. We can also probably assume that the typical prayer posture of uplifted hands was adopted.

11. I would argue that this kind of monastic prayer is more private than liturgical, a bind in which we are still caught today with our revised rite.

12. I am speaking to the early difference between cathedral and monastic offices here. This is not a commentary on contemporary monastic practice.

13. All Christians are obliged to pray the liturgical "office" daily because of their participation in the priesthood of Christ through their baptismal commitment; so we have a contradiction here between theory and practice.

14. Psalms customarily associated with morning prayer (Ps 63, 148–50) and evening prayer (Ps 141) are positioned in their respective hours as are other psalms that specifically mention morning or evening. But in the main, the psalter of the revised rite is sequential. On the distribution of psalms in the revised rite, see J. Gibert-Tarruell, "La Nouvelle distribution du psautier dans la 'Liturgia horarum,'" *Ephemerides Liturgicae* 87 (1973) 325–82.

15. *Sacrosanctum Concilium* §100 suggests that the Liturgy of the Hours be restored in parishes at least on Sundays and more solemn feasts, but the language of this paragraph remains limiting and simply highlights the office as the prayer of ordained ministers. Our position is that Liturgy of the Hours is the daily liturgical prayer of the church and that merely suggestive or conditional language calling for its parochial celebration is inappropriate in face of the liturgical reality.

16. There is a constant tension in the pastoral practice of the Roman tradition: We have introduced so many devotional elements into liturgical prayer that the liturgical character is sometimes lost in lieu of characteristics that more properly belong to private prayer. This is true not only with the Liturgy of the Hours but also of our Eucharistic Prayer. We lose the whole structural dynamic when we do this. Our liturgical rites must be *liturgical*, that is, a faithful objectification of the Paschal Mystery as a moment of distanciation (and, therefore, a critique of Christian living).

17. In the main, this analysis would be valid for Morning and Evening Prayer according to other traditions.

18. Indeed, *The General Instruction on the Liturgy of the Hours* makes no mention of these important structural elements.

19. Cf. *The General Instruction on the Liturgy of the Hours*, §§173–78.

20. We are selective in our material here in order to treat the psalms within the liturgical/methodological framework of this study. For the customary interpretation of the use of psalms in the Liturgy of the Hours, see *The General Instruction on the Liturgy of the Hours*, §§100–35. For a treatment of the psalms and their liturgical use, see W. Brueggemann, *Praying the Psalms* (Winona: Saint Mary's Press, 1984); D. Cox, *The Psalms in the Life of God's People* (Middlegreen, Eng.: Slough, 1984); K. McDonnell, "Prayer in Ancient Western Tradition," *Worship* 55 (1980) 34–61. For a general introduction to the psalms, see C. Stuhlmueller, *Psalms*, 2 volumes, Old Testament Message 21–22 (Wilmington, Del.: Michael Glazier, Inc., 1983, 1985).

21. Ricoeur refers to this as a "split" reference.

22. Cf. chapter 1.

23. "Performance" is used here in the technical sense of performative theory. For a summary, see J. A. Zimmerman, *Liturgy as Language of Faith: A Liturgical Methodology in the Mode of Paul Ricoeur's Textual Hermeneutics* (Lanham and New York: University Press of America, 1988), 52–54 and 102–3.

24. Semiotics characterizes this movement as *begin state, transformation,* and *end state.* For a good but not overly technical introduction to semiotic analysis in a religious context, see W. Vogels, *Reading & Preaching the Bible: A New Semiotic Approach* (Wilmington, Del.: Michael Glazier, 1986), 15–75. Especially helpful is his description of narrative and discursive analyses.

25. The short quotation (often from Scripture) that precedes each of the psalms in the revised rite is an example of this propensity to see the psalms in a Christological

light. This allegorical approach is a very ancient practice, dating back at least to the late second century. For a list of these Christological references, see B. Fischer, "Le Christ dans les Psaumes," *La Maison Dieu* 27 (1951), 86–109. See also D. F. Vanderbroucke, "Le Psautier, prophétie ou prière du Christ?" *Les Questions liturgiques et paroissiales* 5 (1952) 149–61.

26. It has long been practice to include a creation theme in liturgy. This is especially evident in the psalter and in the Preface of the Eucharistic Prayer.

27. There are some psalms that probably were composed by an individual, but nonetheless the psalms have come down to us as the cultic prayer of a people.

28. We make a distinction in these remarks between the origin of the psalms, which is not our concern, and their actual cultic usage through the centuries.

29. See J. A. Zimmerman, "The General Intercessions: Yet Another Visit," *Worship* 65 (1991) 306–19. Also, see the Winter 1993 (vol. 2) issue of *liturgical ministry,* the theme of which is the general intercessions.

30. The fundamental structure of liturgy is always address to God through Christ. In our context we are talking about one specific component of liturgical prayer that does not define the whole prayer. See *The General Instruction on the Liturgy of the Hours*, §§179, 181–82.

31.. See *The General Instruction on the Liturgy of the Hours*, §§180, 186.

32. The solemn prayers of the Good Friday liturgy are the only example of this ancient structure still preserved with a full complement of structural elements in a western liturgy today.

33. See *The General Instruction on the Liturgy of the Hours*, §§179, 185.

Chapter 7. Eucharist

1. Augustine, Sermon 272 (Migne, PL, vol. 38) 1247; my translation.

2. Vatican II suggested one relationship of liturgy and life by stating that Eucharist is the summit and fountain of our whole Christian life (*Sacrosanctum Concilium* §10).

3. As we saw in the last chapter, these four major structural divisions have their parallels in other liturgical rites as well. It is also important to recall that *Sacrosanctum Concilium* (§24) reiterated the importance of God's Word, and each revised sacramental rite includes a Liturgy of the Word.

4. Sometimes this is called the "apostolic greeting" because the three options given in the *Roman Missal* can be traced to apostolic times and are given in Sacred Scripture: "The grace of our Lord Jesus Christ and the love of God and the fellowship of the Holy Spirit be with you all" (cf. 2 Cor 13:14); "The grace and peace of God our Father and the Lord Jesus Christ be with you" (cf. Gal 1:3); and "The Lord be with you" (cf. Ruth 2:4; Jdg 6:12), "And also with you" (cf. Gal 6:18).

5. The fitting ordained minister for proclaiming the Gospel is the deacon, not the presider (see the *General Instruction of the Roman Missal*, §34). When this is respected, it is a clear sign of the connection between the proclamation of the Gospel and right living, since historically it has also been the role of the deacon to take care of those in the community who are needy and that precisely from the eucharistic table (see chapter 2). These two activities—proclaiming the Gospel and gospel living—are really two sides of one and the same liturgical activity.

6. The Preparation of the Altar and Presentation of the Gifts precedes the Preface

but this is a minor rite, a necessary "housekeeping" task preparatory to the Preface, which, properly speaking, opens the Liturgy of the Eucharist.

7. Some proclaimers have initiated a rubric of their own: at the conclusion of the evangelical proclamation, they hold up the *book*. This draws attention to the gospel book, which is an appropriate symbol during the gospel procession. But once the proclamation has been made the focus is no longer on the book for the book comes "alive," so to speak, in the very proclamation. That is, Christ is present in the meaningful human action of *proclamation*. The very proclamation is a Presence and so there is a shift in symbol from book to assembly. For a performative analysis of "proclamation," see my "Homily as Proclamation," *liturgical ministry* 1 (1992) 10–16.

8. During Ordinary Time, the *Common Lectionary* presents a semicontinuous reading of the Old Testament, different from the *Roman Lectionary* in which the first reading relates to the Gospel.

9. Efforts to tie it in by homilists stretch the point as well as presume a structural integrity that simply is not there. The Second Reading is an optional reading inserted so the faithful hear the practical points about Christian themes and living that are the subject of those letters. An exception is during festal seasons when the Second Reading does have thematic congruence. Its inclusion in the Liturgy of the Word was left to the discretion of conferences of bishops.

10. For this reason it would perhaps be better to abandon our use of early creeds with their doctrinal overtones and return to the simple trinitarian formula of the baptismal profession.

11. Note that the name "Offertory" of the Tridentine Rite has been dropped from the 1970 *Roman Missal*. This is because offering takes place during the Eucharistic Prayer. Nonetheless, vestiges of theological undercurrents remain in the post-Vatican II rite that were consistent with the theology of the Tridentine Rite but are no longer consonant with the theology of the post-Vatican II rite. For example, the Preparation of the Altar and Presentation of the Gifts of the revised rite includes two very beautiful *berakoth* (see chapter 4) prayers ("Blessed are you, Lord God King of the Universe") that express the beneficence of God and at the same time includes prayers that express the negative aspects of sacrifice and unworthiness. These conflicting theologies tend to disrupt the dynamic flow.

12. Although a hymn is frequently sung at this time, instrumental music can create a receptive ambience quite effectively.

13. One way to linguistically define prayer is by use of first and second person pronouns coupled with performative verbs. See my *Liturgy as Language of Faith: A Liturgical Methodology in the Mode of Paul Ricoeur's Textual Hermeneutics* (Lanham and New York: University Press of America, 1988), 137. On narrative genre, see especially pp. 125–26 and 155–58. See chapter 5 for a detailed analysis of the eucharistic rite.

14. Although the child can enter into the events of a story when s/he is old enough to read, this "entering in" is most compelling when the story is read aloud by someone else.

15. During the proclamation of the Eucharistic Prayer, we encounter the Christian story. Change in what is familiar breaks us out of the story's time and space and brings us back to chronological time and physical space. Perhaps the multiplication of eucharistic prayers in the wake of Vatican II's liturgical renewal is not necessarily a good thing in itself, especially when the purpose is to help the assembly to "pay more attention." This is exactly what is undesirable. It would be far better if each eucharistic assembly had its own "favorite story"—proclamation of the mighty deeds of salvation

that is faithful to the depth dynamic of the Christian tradition—to proclaim invariably. We want to do everything we can to facilitate the assembly's entry into the story (and give themselves over to the action).

16. The prayer immediately preceding the invitation to share some sign of peace draws on a postresurrection scriptural context.

17. This is another reason (see note 48 of chapter 3) why communion services, separated from the full eucharistic dynamic, are such a sacramental and theological disaster. They are a return to a medieval theology with its emphasis on adoration and real presence "out there." The eucharistic dynamic we have been unfolding begins with the community recognizing its common identity as Body; communion is a sign of acceptance. When receiving communion is separated from this dynamic, we have ritually obscured our identity as Body of Christ. For two analyses of the theological difficulties with communion services, see W. Marrevee, "'Priestless Masses'—At What Cost?" *Eglise et Théologie* 19 (1988) 207–22 and G. Austin, "Communion Services: A Break with Tradition?" in *Fountain of Life. In Memory of Niels K. Rasmussen, O.P.*, ed. G. Austin (Washington, D.C.: The Pastoral Press, 1991), 199–215. Eucharistic ministers who take communion to the sick or homebound do so as bearers who enable absent members to nonetheless participate as members of the assembly. The rite reinforces the connection of communion to the celebration itself for absent members. This link is clearly established especially with a Liturgy of the Word (simplified though it may be) and praying the Our Father and exchanging the Sign of Peace.

18. This particular dismissal rather than the other two options given in the *Roman Missal* best captures the imperative of praxis that is the import of the Concluding Rite.

19. Properly speaking, the appropriate day for Eucharist is Sunday. Daily celebrations are a late innovation. See R. Taft, "The Frequency of the Eucharist Throughout History," *Concilium* 152 (1982) 13–24.

Chapter 8. Liturgical Year

1. "Ordinary Time" is the name for this season as printed in the *Roman Lectionary*. The *Roman Missal* calls this time the "Sundays of the Lord." Since we are examining the *Lectionary,* we will consistently use "Ordinary Time" even though "Sundays of the Lord" better characterizes the meaning of this liturgical season.

2. We will see below how this actually shapes the meaning of Ordinary Time.

3. Except, perhaps, in certain of the proper Prefaces and the Presidential Prayers.

4. See *General Norms for the Liturgical Year and the Calendar*, §50a.

5. This is a significant and rather radical departure from the history of the development of the Roman Calendar where, because of a certain kind of piety, the focus was on the saints frequently to the detriment of the meaning of the Liturgical Year itself.

6. It may not be stretching our application of Ricoeur's methodic textual hermeneutics too far to see Advent as a moment of participation, Christmas as distanciation, and Epiphany as a moment of appropriation. We will see a similar tripartite pattern emerge for the Lent/Triduum/Easter cycle.

7. Historically, of course, this has not always been so; at one time Easter was the beginning of the Liturgical Year. For two good presentations on the historical development of the Liturgical Year, see A. Adam, *The Liturgical Year: Its History and Its Meaning after the Reform of the Liturgy*, trans. Matthew J. O'Connell (New York:

Pueblo Publishing Company, 1981) and T. J. Talley, *The Origins of the Liturgical Year* (New York: Pueblo Publishing Company, 1986).

8. The Baptism of the Lord is both the first Sunday of Ordinary Time and the conclusion of the Advent/Christmas/Epiphany cycle.

9. Obviously, different exegetical approaches to a text will emphasize different themes or content in the readings. Our purpose here is limited to showing a thematic dynamic that connects the Sundays. By so doing we are addressing the pastoral tendency to approach the Sundays disconnectedly, week by week, rather than to consider them as forming a thematic whole over a season. This fragmentation must be redressed if liturgy is to be experienced in dialectical relationship to our daily living. The Liturgical Year is holistic; a story is unfolding. It is vital that this be made clear. A good pastoral practice would be to connect the Sundays and bring out the thematic movement as part of the Introductory Rites or in the context of the homily. For one detailed commentary on these seasons, including the weekdays, see K. W. Irwin's *The Liturgical Seasons: A Guide to the Eucharist and Hours, Advent+Christmas, Lent, and Easter* (New York: Pueblo, 1985–1990). For a detailed discussion of the actual composition of the *Lectionary* and the reason why readings were chosen, see E. Nübold, *Entstehung und Bewertung der neuen Perikopenordnung des Römischen Ritus für die Messfeier an Sonn- und Festtagen* (Paderborn: Verlag Beonifatius-Druckerei, 1986).

10. In many parishes the Rite of Christian Initiation of Adults (RCIA) has been implemented, so with increasing frequency there are baptisms at the Easter Vigil.

11. This is the reason why Year A is used during Masses for the Scrutinies on the Third, Fourth, and Fifth Sundays of Lent; see *Rite of Christian Initiation of Adults*, §159. The Year A Gospels may also be used during Years B and C, even if there are no candidates for Baptism (see *Lectionary for Mass*, §13.1) because Lent is so closely associated with baptismal preparation.

12. The adoration of the cross could be part of devotional services celebrated at another time of the day and perhaps joined to the Stations of the Cross, especially if these latter were given scriptural content. Communion apart from celebration of the eucharistic rite is really an anomaly. See note 17 of chapter 7.

13. The structure of the revised Easter Vigil in the Roman Rite begins with the proclamation of the Light of Christ and then proceeds to salvation history. This seems like a structural way of putting the cart before the horse. It has the unfortunate pastoral effect of beginning with *the* high point. The salvation history that follows seems quite anticlimactic, and it is no wonder pastoral practice often pares the readings down to the minimum requirement. Rather, we suggest salvation history recital *leads to* Baptism and the high point of proclaiming the Light of Christ that is then sustained not only through the rest of the Easter liturgy but throughout the Easter season. The prominence of the Easter candle and its light from the Vigil until Pentecost support this suggestion.

14. The notion of "God's Kingdom" is a complex one. Our use here is along the lines of "allowing the Kingdom to come about in our lives." The Kingdom is established by God's Presence; our task is to open ourselves to it. See D. M. Schlitt, "Toward a New Christian Understanding of Faith, Hope and Love," *Eglise et Théologie* 20 (1989) 385–406.

15. In the development of the Liturgical Year, Christmas came later than the yearly celebration of the paschal events at Easter.

16. This approach helps us avoid a historical mentality that obscures the timelessness as well as the timeliness of the celebrations.

Chapter 9. Liturgical Spirituality

1. It might be well to recall that a dialectic—in our sense—is not that which is resolved but that which is held in dynamic tension. One pole sometimes is the stronger and sometimes the other is. Consequently, it is not a matter of overcoming one pole or the other but of learning how to live out of both of them.

2. We are following here a Jewish time reckoning, whereby the day begins at sundown. Our religious lives, contrary to our civil lives, begin at what seems to us to be the "end" of a day.

3. Neither dialectic, however, can by itself be the integrating principle because neither dialectic completely diminishes the other; both dialectics remain operative. We will see below that "presence" is this integrating factor.

4. Ricoeur explores the conflict of sameness and difference as critical for opening up the meaning of metaphor. See P. Ricoeur, "Metaphor and Philosophical Discourse" in *The Rule of Metaphor: Multi-disciplinary Studies of the Creation of Meaning in Language*, trans. R. Czerny with K. McLaughlin and J. Costello, S.J. (Toronto: University of Toronto Press, 1977), 257–313, esp. 301–8.

5. See *Sacrosanctum Concilium* §10.

6. "Private" masses are a contradiction, as is a "Jesus and me" attitude. They are foreign to authentic liturgical spirituality.

7. This, of course, does not preclude our refusing God's Presence.

Bibliography

Adam, Adolf. *The Liturgical Year: Its History and Its Meaning after the Reform of the Liturgy.* Translated by Matthew J. O'Connell. New York: Pueblo Publishing Company, 1981.

Austin, Gerard A. "Communion Services: A Break with Tradition?" In *Fountain of Life. In Memory of Niels K. Rasmussen, O.P.,* edited by Gerard Austin, 199–215. Washington, D.C.: The Pastoral Press, 1991.

Barbotin, Edmond. *The Humanity of God.* Translated by Matthew J. O'Connell. Maryknoll, N.Y.: Orbis Books, 1976.

Batiffol, Pierre. *History of the Roman Breviary.* London: Longmans, Green & Co., 1912.

Bernstein, Eleanor., C.S.J., ed. *Liturgy and Spirituality in Context: Perspectives on Prayer and Culture.* Collegeville, Minn.: The Liturgical Press, 1991.

Blair, Edward P. "An Appeal to Remembrance. The Memory Motif in Deuteronomy," *Interpretation* 15 (1961): 41–47.

Boff, Leonardo. *Sacraments of Life, Life of the Sacraments.* Translated by J. Drury. Washington, D.C.: The Pastoral Press, 1987.

Bouyer, Louis. *Eucharist: Theology and Spirituality of the Eucharistic Prayer.* Translated by Charles Underhill Quinn. Notre Dame: University of Notre Dame Press, 1968.

_____. *Life and Liturgy.* London: Sheed and Ward, 1965.

_____. *Liturgical Piety.* Notre Dame: University of Notre Dame Press, 1955/1983.

Bradshaw, Paul F. *Daily Prayer in the Church: A Study of the Origin and Early Development of the Divine Office.* New York: Oxford University Press, 1982.

Breck, John. "Biblical Chiasmus: Exploring Structure for Meaning." *Biblical Theology Bulletin* 17 (1987): 70–74.

Brown, Raymond E. *The Gospel According to John* (xiii-xxi). The Anchor Bible. Garden City, N.Y.: Doubleday & Company, Inc., 1970.

Brueggemann, Walter. *Praying the Psalms.* Winona, Minn.: Saint Mary's Press, 1984.

Buis, Pierre, and Jacques Leclercq. *Le Deutéronome.* Paris: J. Gabalda, 1963.

Carpenter, J. Eastlin. *Phases of Early Christianity: Six Lectures.* New York and London: G. P. Putnam's Sons, 1916.

Childs, Brevard S. *Introduction to the Old Testament As Scripture.* Philadelphia: Fortress Press, 1979.

_____. *Memory and Tradition in Israel.* London: SCM Press, Ltd., 1962.

Clements, Ronald E. "Deuteronomy and the Jerusalem Cult Tradition." *Vetus Testamentum* 15 (1965): 300–312.

Cogswell, James. "Lest We Forget: A Sermon." *Interpretation* 15 (1961): 32–40.

Conzelmann, Hans. *History of Primitive Christianity.* Translated by E. Steely. Nashville, Tenn.: Abingdon Press, 1973.

Cox, D. *The Psalms in the Life of God's People.* Middlegreen, Eng.: Slough, 1984.

Cox, Harvey. *The Feast of Fools: A Theological Essay on Festivity and Fantasy.* New York: Harper and Row, 1969.

Dahl, Nils A. "Anamnesis. Mémoire et commémoration dans le christianisme primitif." *Studia Theologica* 1 (1947): 69–95.

Dallen, James. "Liturgy and Justice for All." *Worship* 65 (1991): 290–306.

De Vaux, Roland. *Ancient Israel: Its Life and Institutions.* Translated by John McHugh. London: Darton, Longman & Todd, 1961.

_____. *The Early History of Israel.* Translated by David Smith. Philadelphia: Westminster Press, 1978.

Drilling, Peter J. "The Priest, Prophet and King Trilogy: Elements of Its Meaning in *Lumen Gentium* and for Today." *Eglise et Théologie* 19 (1988): 179–206.

Dugmore, Clifford William. *The Influence of the Synagogue Upon the Divine Office.* Alcuin Club Collections 45. London: Faith Press, 1964.

Dunn, James D. G. *Jesus and the Spirit.* Philadelphia: The Westminster Press, 1975.

Eichrodt, Walther. *Theology of the Old Testament.* 2 volumes. Translated by J. A. Baker. London: SCM Press, 1961–1967.

Eising, H. "*zkr.*" In *Theological Dictionary of the Old Testament*, eds. G. Botterweck and H. Ringgren, volume 4. Translated by David E. Green. Grand Rapids, Mich.: William B. Eerdmans Publishing Co., 1980: 64–82.

Ellis, E. Earle. *The Gospel of Luke.* London and New York: Thomas Nelson Sons, 1966.

Empereur, James L., S.J., and Christopher Kiesling, O.P. *The Liturgy That Does Justice.* Collegeville, Minn.: The Liturgical Press/A Michael Glazier Book, 1990.

Falls, Thomas B. *Writings of Saint Justin Martyr.* Fathers of the Church Series. New York: Christian Heritage, 1948.

Finkelstein, Louis. "The Birkat Ha-mazon." *Jewish Quarterly Review* 19–20 (1928–1930): 211–263.

Fischer, B. "Le Christ dans les Psaumes." *La Maison Dieu* 27 (1951): 86–109.

Fitzmyer, Joseph A. *The Gospel According to Luke.* 2 volumes. The Anchor Bible. Garden City, N.Y.: Doubleday & Company, Inc., 1981 and 1985.

Franklin, Eric. *Christ the Lord: A Study in the Purpose and Theology of Luke-Acts.* Philadelphia: The Westminster Press, 1975.

Gemser, Berend. "The Importance of the Motive Clause in Old Testament Law." *Supplements to Vetus Testamentum.* Volume 1. Leiden: E. J. Brill, 1953: 50–66.

Gibert-Tarruell, J. "La Nouvelle distribution du psautier dans la 'Liturgia horarum.'" *Ephemerides Liturgicae* 87 (1973): 325–382.

Gibson, Paul. "Liturgy and Justice." *Toronto Journal of Theology* 3 (1987): 3–13.

Grant, Robert. *Early Christianity and Society: Seven Studies.* San Francisco: Harper & Row Publishers, 1977.

Green, John Martin. *The Gospel According to St. Luke.* New York: St. Martin's Press, 1969.

Harrington, Wilfrid. *The Gospel According to Luke.* Westminster, Md.: Newman Press, 1966.

Harris, R. Laird, et al. *Theological Wordbook of the Old Testament.* Chicago, Ill.: Moody Press, 1981.

Hater, Robert J. *The Ministry Explosion: A New Awareness of Every Christian's Call to Minister.* Dubuque, Ia.: William C. Brown Company Publishers, 1979.

Hellwig, Monika. *The Eucharist and the Hunger of the World.* New York: Paulist Press/Deus Book, 1976.

Henderson, J. Frank, Kathleen Quinn, and Stephen Larson. *Liturgy, Justice and the Reign of God: Integrating Vision and Practice.* New York: Paulist Press, 1989.

Herbert, Arthur S. *Worship in Ancient Israel.* Ecumenical Studies in Worship 5. Richmond, Va.: John Knox Press, 1959.

Hiedegard, D. *Seder R. Amram Gaon, Part I.* Hebrew Text with Critical Apparatus, Translation with Notes and Introduction. Lund: A.-B. Lindstedts, 1951.

Himes, Kenneth R. "Eucharist and Justice: Assessing the Legacy of Virgil Michel," *Worship* 62 (1988): 201–24.

Hoffman, Lawrence A. *The Canonization of the Synagogue Service.* Notre Dame: University of Notre Dame Press, 1979.

Hughes, Kathleen and Mark R. Francis, eds. *Living No Longer for Ourselves.* Collegeville, Minn.: The Liturgical Press, 1991.

Irwin, Kevin W. *Advent+Christmas. Lent. Easter. The Liturgical Seasons: A Guide to the Eucharist and Hours.* New York: Pueblo, 1985–1990.

_____. *Liturgy, Prayer and Spirituality.* New York: Paulist Press, 1984.

Jasper, R. C. D., and G. J. Cuming, trans. and ed. *Prayers of the Eucharist: Early and Reformed.* 3d Revised Edition. New York: Pueblo Publishing Company, 1987.

Jeremias, Joachim. *The Eucharistic Words of Jesus.* London: SCM Press, Ltd., 1974.

Jungmann, Josef. *Christian Prayer Through the Centuries.* Translated by John Coyne, S.J. New York: Paulist Press, 1978.

Karris, Robert J., O.F.M. "The Gospel According to Luke." In *The New Jerome Biblical Commentary*, edited by Raymond E. Brown, Joseph A. Fitzmyer, and Roland E. Murphy, 675–721. Englewood Cliffs, N.J.: Prentice-Hall, 1990.

Käsemann, Ernst. "An Apologia for Primitive Christian Eschatology." In *Essays on New Testament Themes*, 169–95. Studies in Biblical Theology, First Series, 41. London: SCM Press, 1971.

Keating, Thomas. *The Mystery of Christ: The Liturgy as Spiritual Experience.* Amity, N.Y.: Amity House, 1987.

Kiesling, Christopher. "Liturgy and Social Justice." *Worship* 51 (1977): 351–61.

Klostermann, August. *Der Pentateuch: Beitrräge zu seinem Verständnis und seiner Entstehungsgeschichte.* Leipzig: Al Derchert, 1907.

Koenig, John. *Charismata: God's Gifts for God's People.* Philadelphia: The Westminster Press, 1978.

Lambdin, Thomas O. *Introduction to Biblical Hebrew*. New York: Charles Scribner's Sons, 1971.

Lampe, G.W.H. "Diakonia in the Early Church." In *Service in Christ*, edited by James I. McCord and T.H.L. Parker, 49–64. Grand Rapids, Mich.: William B. Eerdmans Publishing Company, 1966.

————. "The Eucharist in the Thought of the Early Church." In *Eucharistic Theology Then and Now*. Theological Collections #9, 34–58. London: SPCK, 1968.

Leenhardt, Franz J. *Le Sacrement de la sainte cène*. Neuchatel: Delachaux & Niestle, 1948.

Léon-Dufour, Xavier. *Sharing the Eucharistic Bread: The Witness of the New Testament*. Translated by Matthew J. O'Connell. New York: Paulist Press, 1987.

Lyonnet, Stanislas. "Pauline Soteriology." In *Introduction to the New Testament*, edited by A. Robert and A. Feuillet, 820–65. Translated by P. W. Skehan et al. New York: Desclee Company, 1965.

Madigan, Shawn. *Spirituality Rooted in Liturgy*. Washington, D.C.: The Pastoral Press, 1988.

Marrevee, William. "'Priestless Masses'—At What Cost?" *Eglise et Théologie* 19 (1988): 207–22.

Mateos, Juan. "The Morning and Evening Office." *Worship* 42 (1968): 31–47.

————. "The Origins of the Divine Office." *Worship* 41 (1967): 477–85.

McDonnell, K. "Prayer in Ancient Western Tradition." *Worship* 55 (1980): 34–61.

Meynet, Roland. *L'Évangile selon Saint Luc. Analyse rhétorique commentaire*. Paris: Les Éditions du Cerf, 1988.

Minear, Paul S. *Commands of Christ*. Nashville, Tenn.: Abingdon Press, 1972.

————. "Some Glimpses of Luke's Sacramental Theology." *Worship* 44 (1970): 322–31.

Mowinckel, Sigmund. *Le Décalogue*. Paris: F. Alcan, 1927.

————. *The Psalms in Israel's Worship*. Translated by D. R. AP-Thomas. Oxford: Basil Blackwell, 1962.

Muilenburg, James. "The Biblical View of Time." *Harvard Theological Review* 54 (1961): 225–52.

————. "A Study in Hebrew Rhetoric: Repetition and Style." In *Supplements to Vetus Testamentum*, 97–111. Volume 1. Leiden: E. J. Brill, 1953.

Navone, John. *Themes of St. Luke*. Rome: Gregorian University Press, 1970.

Neyrey, Jerome. *The Passion According to Luke: A Redaction Study of Luke's Soteriology*. New York: Paulist Press, 1985.

Nicholson, Ernest W. *Deuteronomy and Tradition*. Oxford: Basil Blackwell, 1967.

Nübold, Elmar. *Entstehung und Bewertung der neuen Perikopenordnung des Römischen Ritus für die Messfeier an Sonn- und Festtagen*. Pederborn: Verlag Beonifatius-Druckerei, 1986.

Oesterley, W.O.E. *The Wisdom of Egypt and the Old Testament in the Light of the Newly Discovered 'Teaching of Amen-em-ope.'* London: SPCK, 1927.

Pedersen, Johannes. *Israel: Its Life and Culture*. Volumes I-II. London: Oxford University Press, 1926.

Pelikan, Jaroslav. *The Emergence of the Catholic Tradition (100–600)*. The Christian

Tradition: A History of the Development of Doctrine. Volume 1. Chicago and London: The University of Chicago Press, 1971.

Pieper, Josef. *In Tune with the World: A Theory of Festivity*. Translated by Richard and Clara Winston. New York: Harcourt and Brace, 1965.

Pittenger, Norman. *Life as Eucharist*. Grand Rapids, Mich.: William B. Eerdmans Publishing Company, 1973.

Rahner, Hugo. *Man at Play*. New York: Herder and Herder, 1967.

Rankin, Oliver Shaw. *Israel's Wisdom Literature: Its Bearing on Theology and the History of Religion*. Edinburgh: T. & T. Clark, 1936.

Reventlow, H. Graf. "*Das Amt des Mazkir.*" *Theologische Zeitschrift* 15 (1959): 161–75.

Richardson, Cyril C., ed. *Early Christian Fathers*. New York: Macmillan Publishing Company, Inc., 1978.

Ricoeur, Paul. "Can There Be a Scientific Concept of Ideology?" In *Phenomenology and the Social Sciences: A Dialogue*, edited by Joseph Bien, 44–59. The Hague: M. Nijhoff, 1978.

_____. *Hermeneutics and the Human Sciences: Essays on Language, Action and Interpretation*. Edited, translated, and introduction by John B. Thompson. Cambridge: Cambridge University Press, 1981.

_____. "Le 'Lieu' de la dialectique." In *Dialectics/Dialectiques*, edited by Ch. Perelman, 92–108. International Institute of Philosophy. The Hague: Nijhoff, 1973.

_____. "*L'Herméneutique de la secularization: Foi, Ideologie, Utopie.*" *Archivo di folosofia* (1976): 56–68.

_____. "Nature and Freedom." In *Political and Social Essays*, edited by David Steward and Joseph Bien, 23–45. Translated by David Steward. Athens, Ohio: Ohio University Press, 1975.

_____. "Phenomenology of Freedom." In *Phenomenology and Philosophical Understanding*, edited by E. Pivcevic, 173–94. London: Cambridge University Press, 1975.

_____. "The Problem of the Foundation of Moral Philosophy." Translated by David Pellauer. *Philosophy Today* 22 (1978): 175–92.

_____. "The Problem of the Will and Philosophical Discourse." In *Patterns of the Life-World. Essays in Honor of John Wild*, edited by J. Edie, F. Parker, and C. O. Schray, 273–89. Evanston: Northwestern University Press, 1970.

_____. *The Rule of Metaphor: Multi-disciplinary Studies of the Creation of Meaning in Language*. Translated by R. Czerny with K. McLaughlin and J. Costello, S.J. Toronto: University of Toronto Press, 1977.

_____. *Sémantique de l'action*. Louvain: Université Catholique de Louvain—Cercle de Philosophie, 1971. Polycopy.

Rordorf, Willy et al. *The Eucharist of the Early Christians*. Translated by Matthew J. O'Connell. New York: Pueblo Publishing Company, 1978.

Saliers, Don E. "Liturgy and Ethics: Some New Beginnings." *The Journal of Religious Ethics* 7 (1979): 173–89.

Salmon, Pierre. *The Breviary Through the Centuries*. Translated by Sr. D. Mary. Collegeville, Minn.: The Liturgical Press, 1962.

Schlitt, Dale M. "Toward a New Christian Understanding of Faith, Hope and Love." *Eglise et Théologie* 20 (1989): 385–406.

Schmemann, Alexander. *Liturgy and Life: Lectures and Essays on Christian Development Through Liturgical Experience.* New York: Department of Religious Education, Orthodox Church in America, 1974.

———. *The World as Sacrament.* London: Darton, Longman & Todd, 1966.

Schmidt, Johanne Michael. "Vergegenwärtigung und Überlieferung." *Evangelische Theologie* 30 (1970): 169–200.

Schopp, Ludwig, gen. ed. *The Apostolic Fathers.* The Fathers of the Church. Volume 1. Washington, D.C.: The Catholic University of America Press, 1962.

Schrottroff, Willy. *'Gedenken' im Alten Orient und im Alten Testament, die Wurzel Zakar im semitischen Sprachkreis.* Neukirchen: Neukirchener Verlag, 1964.

Scotto, Dominic F., T.O.R. *The Liturgy of the Hours: Its History and Its Importance as the Communal Prayer of the Church after the Liturgical Reform of Vatican II.* Petersham, Mass.: St. Bede's Publications, 1987.

Searle, Mark. *Liturgy and Social Justice.* Collegeville, Minn.: The Liturgical Press, 1980.

Stuhlmueller, Carroll. "The Gospel of Saint Luke." In *The Jerome Biblical Commentary,* edited by Raymond E. Brown, Joseph A. Fitzmyer, and Roland E. Murphy, 115–64. Englewood Cliffs, N.J.: Prentice-Hall, 1968.

———. *Psalms.* 2 volumes. Old Testament Message 21–22. Wilmington, Del.: Michael Glazier, Inc., 1983, 1985.

Taft, Robert. "The Frequency of Eucharist Throughout History." *Concilium* 152 (1982): 13–24.

———. *The Liturgy of the Hours in East and West: The Origins of the Divine Office and Its Meaning for Today.* Collegeville, Minn.: The Liturgical Press, 1986.

Talbert, Charles H. *Literary Patterns, Theological Themes, and the Genre of Luke-Acts.* Society of Biblical Literature Monograph Series 20. Missoula, Mont.: Society of Biblical Literature and Scholars Press, 1974.

Talley, Thomas J. *The Origins of the Liturgical Year.* New York: Pueblo Publishing Company, 1986.

Throckmorton, Burton H., Jr., ed. *Gospel Parallels: A Synopsis of the First Three Gospels.* Toronto, Camden, N.J., and London: Thomas Nelson & Sons, 1967.

Thurian, Max. The *Eucharistic Memorial.* Part 1: The Old Testament. Translated by J. G. Davies. London: Lutterwworth Press, 1960.

Van Den Hengel, John W. *The Home of Meaning: The Hermeneutics of the Subject of Paul Ricoeur.* Washington, D.C.: University Press of America, 1982.

Vanderbroucke, D.F. "Le Psautier, prophétie ou prière du Christ?" *Les Questions liturgiques et paroissiales* 5 (1952): 149–161.

Vogels, Walter. *Reading & Preaching the Bible: A New Semiotic Approach.* Wilmington, Del.: Michael Glazier, 1986.

Von Rad, Gerhard. *Problems of the Hexateuch and Other Essays.* Translated by E. W. Trueman Dicken. Introduction by Norman W. Porteos. Edinburg: Oliver & Boyd, 1966.

Weinfeld, Moshe. *Deuteronomy and the Deuteronomic School.* Oxford: At the Clarendon Press, 1972.

———. "The Origin of the Humanism in Deuteronomy." *Journal of Biblical Literature* 80 (1961): 241–49.

Weingreen, Jacob. *A Practical Grammar for Classical Hebrew.* 2d ed. Oxford: At the Clarendon Press, 1959.

Weisner, Artur. *Introduction to the Old Testament*. London: Darton, Longman & Todd, 1961.

Willimon, William H. *The Service of God: How Worship and Ethics Are Related*. Nashville, Tenn.: Abingdon Press, 1983.

Wright, George Ernest. "Cult and History: A Study of a Current Problem in Old Testament Interpretation." *Interpretation* 16 (1962): 3–20.

Zimmerman, Joyce Ann. "The General Intercessions: Yet Another Visit." *Worship* 65 (1991): 306–19.

————. "Homily as Proclamation." *liturgical ministry* 1 (1992): 10–16.

————. *Liturgy as Language of Faith: A Liturgical Methodology in the Mode of Paul Ricoeur's Textual Hermeneutics*. Lanham, New York, London: University Press of America, 1988.

————. "Priesthood Through the Eyes of a Non-Ordained Priest." *Eglise et Théologie* 19 (1988): 223–40.

Zirker, Hans. *Die kultische Vergegenwärtigung der Vergangenheit in den Psalmen*. Bonner Biblische Beiträge 20. Bonn: Peter Hanstein Verlag, 1964.

Index